THE LITTORAL ZONE
AUSTRALIAN CONTEXTS
AND THEIR WRITERS

Nature, Culture and Literature
04

THE LITTORAL ZONE
AUSTRALIAN CONTEXTS AND THEIR WRITERS

Introduced and edited by
CA. Cranston and Robert Zeller

Amsterdam - New York, NY 2007

Cover Design: Erick de Jong

Cover image: Hannah Guenzel

The paper on which this book is printed meets the requirements of "ISO 9706:1994, Information and documentation - Paper for documents - Requirements for permanence".

ISBN-13: 978-90-420-2218-8
©Editions Rodopi B.V., Amsterdam - New York, NY 2007
Printed in the Netherlands

Contents

Acknowledgements

Thanks to two scholarly Associations, the Association for the Study of Australian Literature (ASAL), and the Association for the Study of Literature and the Environment (ASLE), which provided the opportunity and continuity necessary to develop the initial debate concerning the existence, or otherwise, of nature writing in Australian Literature. And of course, thanks to those scholars — members of the above Associations — whose various interests and knowledge contributed to furthering the various discussions. In addition, thanks go to our home institutions, The University of Tasmania (Australia), and Southeast Missouri State University (USA), for technical support, and for the financial support required to attend the conferences of the above Associations. And to Dr Susan Swartwout, and Miranda J. Henley, of Southeast Missouri State University Press for assistance in proofreading and indexing.

Acknowledgements for illustrations and copyright clearance on text:

Chapter 2, Figure 2: *An Open Swimmer*, by Tim Winton, first published Sydney: George Allen and Unwin Australia Pty Ltd, 1982. Cover photograph by Jeremy Prince. Chapter 3, Figure 4: 'The clearing line'. Satellite photo courtesy of the Australian Government Bureau of Meteorology; Figure 3: 'Instant Death to the Rabbits', from Laurie Anderson, *Windows on the Wheatbelt*, Bassendean, WA: Access Press, 1999, p. 197. Figure 6, facing p. 71: map of Australian deserts courtesy of the Australian Government Department of the Environment and Water Resources. Chapter 6: thanks to Robert Gray for permission to reprint 'A Poem of Not More Than Forty Lines on the Subject of Nature' from *Afterimages*, Sydney: Duffy and Snellgrove, 2002. Chapter 9, thanks to HarperCollins Publishers for permission to reprint 'Looking Down on Canberra' by David Campbell from *Collected Poems*, North Ryde, NSW: Angus and Robertson, 1989; and to The Estate of Michael Thwaites for permission to reprint lines from 'Psalm for an Artificial City' from the cycle of poems 'A Place of Meeting', published in *The Honey Man and other Poems*, Canberra: Trendsetting, 1993. Chapter 11, Figure 8: 'Planning work for soldier settlement blocks at Pegarah, courtesy of the King Island Museum, PO Box 71, Currie, King Island, Tasmania; Figure 9 'Heavy machinery at Reekara, brought to the island to clear the land, 1962', permission granted by Judith Payne, King Island, Tasmania. Chapter 12, thanks to the University of Queensland Press, St Lucia, for permission to reprint 'Antarctica' from John Blight's collection *Hart*, originally published Melbourne: Thomas Nelson, 1975, p. 6; thanks also to Fremantle Arts Centre Press for permission to reprint Alan Alexander's 'Antarctica' from *Principia Gondwana*, South Fremantle, WA: Fremantle Arts Centre Press, 1992, p. 65; and Caroline Caddy's 'Antarctica' from *Antarctica*, South Fremantle, WA: Fremantle Arts Centre Press, 1996, pp. 54-55.

Setting the Scene: Littoral and Critical Contexts

Robert Zeller and CA. Cranston

Several years ago, a series of ads promoting Australia as a tourist destination aired on North American television. In them, Paul Hogan came wading out of the surf to remind viewers that Australia is surrounded by water — that when they visit Australia they will be entering a littoral zone. It was in the littoral zone that the first contact between white and indigenous people occurred and where the white explorers or invaders had to begin to come to terms with an almost totally alien environment. Ever since then, Australian texts have been produced out of and in response to particular places.

Bruce Bennett has argued in *An Australian Compass* that "the study of actual places and regions, writers' relations with them, and depictions of them, should be inserted into our national consciousness" (Bennett 1991: 16-17). While Bennett was interested in correcting what he saw as an oversimplified emphasis on a Sydney-or-the-bush dichotomy, we believe that an investigation of place has broader implications for the study of Australian writing — clarifying, for one thing, its distinctive Australian orientations, but also deepening and enriching our appreciation of it as literature. We believe that the recent development in literary studies labelled ecocriticsm could be very productive in generating new insights.

To begin, we should define what we mean by *ecocriticism*. Broadly speaking, ecocriticism engages with texts as if actual places matter (thereby setting itself at odds with poststructuralism, whose practitioners might characterize it as being 'too literal'.) In Cheryll Glotfelty's oft-quoted definition, ecocriticism is "the study of the relationship between literature and the physical environment" (1996: xviii).[1] While other types of criticism have drawn on disciplines such as philosophy and psychology in their analysis of texts, ecocriticism has drawn on the sciences, in particular that of ecology, with its emphasis on the connectedness of natural systems. And as the etymological connection with *ecology* suggests, rather than privileging the human, ecocriticism acknowledges that humans are themselves part of natural systems, affected by them and affecting them in turn — unfortunately not always in mutually beneficial ways. In fact, it was in part the growing sense of environmental crisis that fuelled the turn to ecologically informed readings of texts. It was also in part the recognition that place-based writing (sometimes dismissively called 'nature writing', though it can encompass many genres) had for too long been ignored by literary critics. (As we note below, its neglect in Australia is one of the factors leading to this collection.)

Almost a decade after Bennett, Patrick Murphy, in *Farther Afield in the Study of Nature-Oriented Literature*, stated that ecocriticism

> has been limited by a focus on American and British literatures. In order to widen the understanding of readers and critics, it is necessary to reconsider the privileging of [...] certain national literatures and certain ethnicities within those national literatures. Such reconsideration will enable a greater inclusiveness of literatures from around the world within the conception of nature-oriented literature. It will also enable critics and readers [...] who focus primarily on American literature to place that literature in an internationally relative and comparative framework. I see such reconsideration as one of the ways by which we can refine our awareness and expand the field of ecocriticism. (Murphy 2000: 58)

Thus can the introduction of Australian literature as a body of works available for ecocritical approaches also deepen and enrich the practice of such literary criticism.

In the past several years, things have changed somewhat from the situation Bennett was responding to; work by Australians such as George Seddon, Peter Hay, Libby Robin, Tom Griffiths, Tim Bonyhady, Val Plumwood, and Tim Flannery has broadened our understanding of the concept of place in Australia. These and other scholars have prepared the ground for more ecocritical study of Australian writing, though, notably, none is a literary critic. Also, in recent years there have been several articles, both in journals and in collections, investigating particular authors from an ecocritical perspective. And recently *The Australian Humanities Review* added a section, 'Ecological Humanities', containing articles that engage with ecological and eco-philosophical concerns from writers as diverse as Deborah Rose and Kate Rigby.

Though the groundswell of ecocriticism originated in North America, there has also been a growing interest in internationalising the ecocritical enterprise, which has manifested itself in the founding of affiliates of ASLE in the UK, Japan, Korea, India, and Australia-New Zealand, as well as the more broadly based European Association for the Study of Literature, Culture, and Environment. More and more, sessions and presentations with an ecocritical bent are showing up on conference programs, and not just at conferences in the field of literature.

These preliminaries are by way of explaining why we believe that Australian literary studies and the enterprise of ecocriticism would both benefit by increased ecocritical study of Australian writing — hence this volume, which is a collaboration of scholars in Australia (some with USA connections) and North American colleagues (with strong Australian connections). The involvement of both groups of scholars is essential: North American scholars need to be wary of thinking they can merely step across the Pacific, as it were, and colonise the environmental branch of Australian literary criticism, a temptation given that both national literatures are almost entirely in English and that the majority of scholars using ecocritical approaches are based in North America. Being aware of this problem is especially important in a place-based scholarship like ecocriticism.

1. The Importance of Australian Literature for Ecocriticism

1. It is a means of extending the range of texts to which we apply ecocriticism.
2. Although Australian literature is written in English, it grows out of different physical and cultural landscapes from that of North America; and different historical and social circumstances, including different, though comparable, relations between European and indigenous peoples (whose culture has been comparably appropriated in environmentalist discourse).
3. Environmentalism has developed in similar ways in Australia and North America.

4. Thus, ecocritical studies of Australian literature not only can serve as a means of comparison to the critical practices of North American and European literary scholars, but also, and perhaps more importantly, could foster a mutually beneficial transnational exchange.

The first reason why Australian literary studies can benefit ecocritical practice has to do with the oft-made assertion (assumed by Murphy) that ecocriticism has tended to focus on North American writing, in particular writing of the United States, and more particularly on a fairly limited range of texts produced in the last century and a half. American scholars have tended to go in for writing (mainly celebratory) about wilderness, about excursions to wild places, about reflections on the relationships between humans and the natural world, and about efforts to right wrongs done to the natural environment. As part of the more general project of opening up the canon of literature studied in universities, we believe we need to expand the canon of literature available to ecocriticism. If ecocriticism is a generalisable critical approach, stressing inclusivity and interconnectivity, then it needs to be more generally applied.

This leads to the second reason. There are enough apparent similarities between North American and Australian cultures that it is easy for Americans to get the impression that Americans and Australians are, after all, pretty much alike. Queenslander Herb Wharton, a Murri, a writer, and an ex-stockman, warns against unthinking substitution of like experiences. For instance, in the cattle industry, "One thing for sure, it was an insult to call a drover or stockman a cowboy"; furthermore most stockmen "believed they could learn little or nothing from the American cowboy in the handling of stock, droving or riding bucking horses" (1996: 60). As we will see, the pastoral industry itself has specific resonances within the Australian context.

Two things that make Australia distinctive are its history and, perhaps more obviously, its very different natural environments (including, for those from the northern half of the globe, inverted seasons). Both of these things have influenced Australian writing, and to that extent such writing becomes amenable to study using ecocritical approaches. Because the British colonised Australia as a penal colony and because upon their arrival they found an almost totally unfamiliar

natural environment, the early arrivals were not likely to take a positive view of the land. Indeed, white Australians are still to some
degree trying to figure out how to live sustainably on a continent
characterised to a large extent by poor soils and cycles of drought and
flood (see Flannery 1995).

The early history of convictism, the development of a pastoral
economy, and the gold rushes of the mid nineteenth century (and late
nineteenth century in Western Australia) also helped to create different sorts of cultural landscapes, both in terms of human-created environments and in terms of the ways writers might view the natural
world. In *His Natural Life* (1872), Marcus Clarke depicts the landscape of Van Diemen's Land as imbued with imminent threats and
unspeakable horror. In *The Recollections of Geoffry Hamlyn* (1859),
Henry Kingsley's upper-class characters discover in Australia "a new
heaven and a new earth", where they are able to redeem their fortunes.
In Katharine Susannah Prichard's goldfields trilogy — *The Roaring
Nineties* (1946), *Golden Miles* (1948), and *Winged Seeds* (1950) —
the natural world intersects with the worlds of politics, economics, and
engineering.

To take an iconographic figure as illustration, Henry Lawson's
writing, as Brian Matthews has argued, was influenced, for both better
and worse, by how he experienced the bush on his trip to Bourke in
1892. And that writing (and its construction of the Australian landscape in response to directives from A.G. Stephens of the *Bulletin*)
demonstrates a historically traceable reciprocity between constructions
of landscape and literature which may have, in turn, shaped generations of readers' perceptions of the country he was writing about
(perceptions that are only now being corrected and expanded, as Tom
Lynch's chapter in this volume suggests).

Also, white settlers similarly dispossessed the indigenous inhabitants, only to turn around later and celebrate them simplistically as
having a more 'authentic' connection to the land than the conquering
group. In doing so, they have appropriated the Native Americans on
the one hand and the Aboriginal peoples on the other as environmental
exemplars (see Rolls in this volume). While it is true that both native
peoples had been living on their respective continents for many millennia, it is also true that those peoples had also shaped the environment the Europeans encountered when they arrived (again, see

Flannery 1995). This is not the place for an extended discussion of either or both histories, but suffice it to say that both groups have become a part of the discourse of sustainability advanced by environmentalists in North America and Australia.

The third reason has to do with the question of 'why Australia?' While Australia's political and social histories are markedly different from those of the United States, the histories of their environmental movements are rather similar, as Peter Hay of the Environmental Studies program at the University of Tasmania has observed in *Main Currents in Western Environmental Thought*. Contrasting environmental movements in Western countries, he states,

> It was in North America and Australia that a concern for wilderness returned to centre stage, for in Europe (with the exception of the northern reaches of Scandinavia) tracts of land no longer existed upon which the transforming hand of humankind was little in evidence. (Hay 2002: 17)

Hay (who is also a poet and essayist) goes on to list several philosophers in North America and Australia whose "in-principle defence of wildness" (p. 17) has helped to shape environmental thinking. And it would be easy to point out other parallels. The United States had the world's first national park (Yellowstone, 1872); Australia had the second very soon after (Royal National Park, 1879). The U.S. had its battles over Hetch Hetchy, Dinosaur National Monument, and Glen Canyon; Australia its battles over Lake Pedder, the Franklin River, and Fraser Island, to give just a few examples. In each case, environmentalists deployed similar sorts of tactics, including media campaigns and direct action.

Fourth, although the writing of environmental history is well established in Australia, ecocriticism of Australian writing has, for whatever reasons, been scarce. To some extent, North American and European ecocriticism can serve as a model, but because of the unique features of the culture, Australian ecocriticism will develop in its own direction and, in so doing, may broaden the range of ecocritical practices. We hope that this collection will be an early step along that path.

2. The Importance of Ecocriticism in Australian Literary Studies

1. Place has always figured prominently in Australian literature.
2. There is a long tradition of Australian nature poetry that can be studied in ecocritical terms.
3. Environmental issues are becoming more prominent in Australian literary texts.
4. There is a body of nature writing in Australia that has gone virtually unstudied because it has traditionally not been considered part of the canon of Australian literature.
5. Thus, an ecologically informed literary criticism can supplement and expand the study of Australian literature by engaging with work done in other disciplines.

On the one hand, Australian literature and its readers stand to gain from the wider engagement with text and context that the new critical practices would bring, more especially because the reading of literature through the frameworks currently available is likely to stimulate a degree of anxiety concerning its relevance in a time of environmental crisis. And Australian contexts might well benefit from an increased awareness among scholars of how literature shapes, for better or worse, environmental thinking. On the other hand, the ecocritical framework might engender anxiety in theoretically oriented scholars because it requires some partnership, or at least familiarity, with the natural sciences, in which one must test one's theories against physical reality.

One aspect of ecocriticism involves the practice of reading-in-place. According to Lawrence Buell, "to connect the literature of place with the actual place that gave rise to the literature can deepen not only one's sense of the book itself but one's sense of what it means to be in communion with place" (1995: 337). This can mean, if possible, actually reading the text in proximity to the place that informs it. The practice can provide an experience of lacunae and ecological change that might remain text-bound otherwise. But obviously this sort of reading is not always possible. It can also mean investigating the place in its natural and historical complexity as a precursor and adjunct to the study of text. In addition to this immersion approach of actually being on the ground (or in the water or air), such study entails consulting the variety of texts from which one can learn about a place — including histories, field guides, archaeological remains, and maps — as well as talking with local inhabitants. Contexts can thus become contested spaces, and our readings can be both complicated and enriched as we study place as something other than mere 'setting'.

The first of the reasons why scholars of Australian literature could benefit from ecocritical approaches lies behind Bruce Bennett's observation quoted above. Much Australian prose fiction is clearly and strongly situated in particular places. We have already mentioned Marcus Clarke and Henry Lawson; but place is also an essential element in such nineteenth-century texts as Alexander Harris's *Settlers and Convicts* (1847), where he describes the decimation of the cedar forests in New South Wales, and Louisa Meredith's writings about Tasmania, where she was an early voice for conservation. Think also of Joseph Furphy's Riverina, Eve Langley's Gippsland, Xavier Herbert's Northern Territory, Thea Astley's North Queensland, and Tim Winton's coastal Western Australia, to give but a few obvious twentieth-century examples. We are not referring merely to the authors' choice of setting; in each case an understanding of place is essential to a sensitive and informed reading of the text — to reading the characters' actions and coming to grips with the authors' social and/or moral concerns. By moving the study of place from the periphery to the centre of critical consideration, by moving what is sometimes still considered mere background to the *foreground* in its influencing of character action, ecocritical approaches could radically shift the reading positions of Australian literary scholars.

In 'The Land Itself', Philip Hodgins writes,

> Beyond all arguments is the land itself,
> drying out and cracking at the end of summer
> like a vast badly-made ceramic, uneven and powdery,
> losing its topsoil and its insect-bodied grass seeds
> to the wind's dusty perfumes, that sense of the land,
> then soaking up soil-darkening rains and filling out
> with the force of renewal at the savoured winter break. (1995: 9)

This poem grows out of a specific agrarian landscape in Victoria, and out of arguments about that place. Ecocritics can study how that place and those arguments inform this poem. But of course this kind of poetry is nothing new. There is a long tradition of Australian poetry about the natural world (conceding the trickiness of the term 'natural world'), from Charles Harpur and Henry Kendall in the nineteenth century to poets as diverse as John Shaw Neilson, David Campbell, Judith Wright, and Oodgeroo Noonuccal in the twentieth and Les Murray, and John Kinsella in the twenty-first. Not that Australian critics have ignored the importance of the natural world, either as a source of poetic inspiration or as a source of imagery. For instance, in *The Landscape of Australian Poetry*, Brian Elliott criticises Harpur for his inaccurate entomology in 'A Midsummer Noon in the Australian Forest' (1967: 67-68).

Elliott's book, in fact, could be called the first Australian work of ecocriticism even though it was published in 1967, well before the term *ecocriticism* was coined. In his first chapter, Elliott makes the case for an ecologically informed criticism of Australian poetry:

> The first need in a new country or colony must obviously be in one way or another to comprehend the physical environment. In poetry we find this need reflected, in colonial times, in an obsessive preoccupation with landscape and description. At first the urge is merely topographical, to answer the question, what does the place look like? The next is detailed and ecological: how does life arrange itself there? What plants, what animals, what activity, how does man fit in? The next may be moral: how does such a place influence people? And how, in their turn, do the people make their mark upon the place? How have they developed it? Next come subtler inquiries: what spiritual and emotional qualities does such a people develop in such an environment? In what way do the forces of nature impinge upon the imagination? How do aesthetic evaluations grow? How may poetry come to life in such a place as Australia? (p. 4)

This passage is certainly ecocritical in approach, though a reading of the whole book shows that Elliott does not follow through on that approach, nor answer all of the questions he poses. One can see here the usual organic metaphor that informs the writing of much literary history — the inevitable growth and evolution of the literature as the nation matures. Also, the approach suggests a rather simplistic environmental determinism — the idea that the physical environment inevitably shapes the imagination of its writers. Even if one were to accept this concept, the sheer variety of the Australian natural environment (not to mention the vicissitudes of human psychology) would make it hard to apply. Dorothea Mackellar's 'My Country' is a case in

point in terms of its imagistic (in)applicability to tropical North
Queensland and temperate Tasmania. In addition, writers move from
place to place throughout their lives, sometimes leaving Australia for
long periods — writers such as Henry Handel Richardson, Christina
Stead, Patrick White, Russell Braddon, and more recently, Peter
Porter, Peter Conrad, and Peter Carey. It may well be that, as with
James Joyce leaving Ireland, they had to leave Australia in order to
write about it, or, to put it another way, that being elsewhere enabled
them to sift through Australian images and experiences.

Finally, though, Elliott's approach presupposes that the critic him-
or herself is familiar with the natural environments that inform the
works under consideration. It suggests further that critics should
practice place-based criticism, as, for instance, Ian Marshall does in
Story Line (1998), where he walks through the Appalachian landscapes of the works he discusses, and John Elder does in *Reading the
Mountains of Home* (1998), where he writes about Robert Frost's
'Directive' and uses it as a kind of field guide to the mountains near
his Vermont home. Our writing about the works we discuss here,
however, will as much as possible be informed by our experiences of
the places — experiences both literary and physical, theoretical and
phenomenological, cultural and ecological, as noted above.

To move on to the third point, a number of Australian literary texts
deal with environmental issues. To take an obvious example, consider
Judith Wright, whose early environmentalism comes through in poems such as 'Lament for Passenger Pigeons' and 'Australia 1970',
which begins,

> Die, wild country, like the eaglehawk,
> Dangerous till the last breath's gone,
> Clawing and striking. Die
> Cursing your captor through a raging eye. (1971: 292)

Wright exults that the natural world seems to be paying humans back
for their mistreatment of it. Perhaps *exult* is the wrong verb, since the
poem is also a cry of dismay at what people have done to the Australian environment; if we must suffer in return, because of drought or
erosion or fire, then it is no more than we deserve. And with that
suffering might well come the realisation that what we do to the Earth
we do to ourselves. Also published in 1970 was Geoffrey Lehmann's

'Pear Days in Queensland', the title referring to the introduced invasive prickly pear (Lehmann 1972: 449-51). Another example of ecological colonisation and warfare can be found in James McQueen's novel *Hook's Mountain* (1982), which takes on the issue of clearfelling Tasmania's forests; and some of Tim Winton's concerns about what is happening along the coast of Western Australia come out in *Dirt Music* (2001).

To move to our fourth point, in discussing the first *Oxford History of Australian Literature* (1981), Les Murray (1997: 148-49) notes that a major omission in it was a discussion of non-fiction prose, and offhand he lists a number of writers meriting inclusion. Among these are three — E. J. Banfield, Francis Ratcliffe, and Eric Rolls — who should also be mentioned among Australian nature writers (or, in the case of the British biologist Ratcliffe, writers about Australian nature). One could argue, and it is an observation that Pete Hay once made, that the genre of the belletristic nature essay did not develop in Australia as it did in North America. There are, however, many examples of Australian nature writing that have for one reason or another not made their way into literary critical consciousness. One such example is the work of Tasmanian J.R. Skemp, whose nature essays were collected as *My Birds* (1970), published posthumously and brought again to public attention in *Along These Lines* (Cranston 2000). Similarly, one would not think ordinarily to look to social realist writer John Morrison for an example of the belletristic form, but there it is in his essay 'The Moving Waters' (1987). So it seems possible that once scholars become acquainted with the ecocritical approach and the importance of nature writing, the belletristic nature essay's lack of development in Australia might be found to be greatly exaggerated.[2]

In fact, Australia does have a long tradition of natural history writing, much of it in newspapers (such as the contributions of E.J. Banfield and Henry G. Lamond to the *North Queensland Register*), but quite a lot in book form. A recent example is Graham Pizzey's *Journey of a Lifetime* (2000), a collection of essays published in Melbourne newspapers over a period of thirty years. In addition, other genres, such as journals of exploration and travel narratives, include passages of natural description. The major Australian literary histories have not paid much mention to prose writing about the natural world. This is an area wide open for further exploration — one ecocriticism ought to tackle. (A step in this direction is *Hearts and Minds* [2000], where Michael Pollak and Margaret MacNabb survey environmentally oriented Australian literature and film, including interviews with writers, visual artists, and directors.)

The progenitor of the modern genre of nature writing is usually assumed to be Gilbert White's *Natural History of Selborne*, which was published in 1789 (a year after the arrival of the First Fleet). As E.D.H. Johnson has noted, "The treatment of natural history as a branch of literature is a long-standing tradition among the English. The golden age of this genre of writing, however, lasted for little more than a century between, roughly, 1770 and 1880" (1966: vii). This was the very period in which American literature achieved a distinctive status and Australian literature began to develop.

While the development of American nature writing in the nineteenth century has been widely studied, much less critical attention has been paid to the development of Australian writing about the natural world. While there might well be some similarities between the two traditions, it is likely that such study would find significant differences as well, rooted in divergent mythologies.

For example, in the United States, the idea of a boundless nature was tied up with the idea of American exceptionalism, that America was a land specially blessed and destined for greatness; it was a key part of a national myth and encouraged nature writing. In the words of Leo Marx,

> The myth affirms that Europeans experience a regeneration in the New World. They become new, better, happier men — they are reborn. In most versions [of the myth] the regenerative power is located in the natural terrain: access to undefiled, bountiful, sublime Nature is what accounts for the virtue and special good fortune of Americans. [...] The landscape thus becomes the symbolic repository of value of all kinds — economic, political, aesthetic, religious. (1964: 228)

In Australia (another 'New World'), the bush myth that eventually developed, whatever one's view of its power or validity, usually depicted nature as something to be endured or battled against rather than celebrated, its value being mainly of the economic variety. Not for very many was Australian nature evidence of the colonies' boundless possibilities. The comic adventures of Dad and Dave in *On Our Selection* (1899) and its successors, and the films of Charles Chauvel, such as *Heritage* (1935) and *Sons of Matthew* (1949), are populist constructions of this perspective. They depict not possibilities but penury and contribute to the notion of the 'battler' on the land.

In both the United States and Australia, the increasing popularity of amateur nature study also helped foster writing about the natural world and create an audience for it. Michael Branch points out the American "vogue for 'scenic tours,' and [...] amateur naturalism such as the casual bird-watching which was so popular during the period" (Branch 1996: 284). The amateur naturalist could be someone like the Harvard-educated Henry David Thoreau, or it could be someone like Susan Fenimore Cooper, whose *Rural Hours* (1850) has received ecocritical attention in recent years. In Australia, as Tom Griffiths (1996) has shown, some of those in the middle class pursued antiquarian interests. And nineteenth-century Quaker education could require of its students that they compose essays about nature; the writings of Quakers such as William Wells (Gardam 1987) and James Backhouse (1843) provide yet another possible source for future ecocritical literary studies.

In both countries, by the end of the nineteenth century, natural history had become a vocation rather than an avocation, and amateur natural history writing was a branch of journalism. Thus, the study of Australian nature writing must to some extent devote itself to periodicals and to collections of pieces from such publications. We should mention here Alec Chisholm's 1964 collection *Land of Wonder: The Best Australian Nature Writing*, which until recently was one of the few sources available to someone interested in the genre of Australian nature writing, unless he or she wanted to hunt through libraries and newspaper indexes. For those interested in fiction, *A Treasury of Australian Wildlife Stories*, edited by Bill Wannan, appeared only a year earlier. More recently, Suzanne Falkiner's *The Writers' Landscape — Wilderness* (1992) incorporates commentary alongside two centuries of place-based literature.

A final point. We mentioned above the names of several people, none of them literary critics by trade, whose work could inform ecocritical studies of Australian literature. As examples, consider two works, George Seddon's *Landprints* (1997) and Tim Bonyhady's *The Colonial Earth* (2000). Seddon's book ranges widely over Australian history, geography, and writing, exploring how Australians have developed a sense of place, how they have shaped their environments, and what that sense and that shaping imply for Australia's future. Bonyhady draws on his research into Australian history — art history in particular — to argue for "the richness of Australia's history of environmental concern" (Bonyhady 2000: 11). Neither book is mainly concerned with literary writing, but both discuss the shaping influence of place on humans in Australia, down to the very language they speak, whether that language is expressed in words, in architecture, or in the visual arts. For that matter, such expression need not be either verbal or visual. In Peter Sculthorpe's String Quartet no. 11, 'Jabiru Dreaming', the very use of traditional Western instruments was transformed by the composer's visit to Kakadu and his study of indigenous music.

In his environmental history of the Monaro, W.K. Hancock states, "the discovery of Australia, or of any Australian region, is not a once-and-for-all achievement, but rather a continuing effort, whose end — if ever there is an end — still lies far from sight" (1972: 12). This study is a start into the exploration of how the Australian land has been discovered by its writers.

3. The Plan of the Book

Gilbert White believed that those who "undertake only one district are much more likely to advance natural knowledge than those that grasp at more than they can possibly be acquainted with: every kingdom, every province, should have its own monographer" (1997: 125). Likewise, in planning this collection, we wanted contributors to focus on a place or type of place in order to advance our knowledge about the writing it has engendered. Rather than choosing to organise the collection historically or to focus on particular authors, we asked scholars in Australia and the United States to choose an Australian region and then discuss how it informs Australian writing. (Unfortunately, as can happen with any such project, two of the invited scholars had to withdraw due to other commitments.) Literally, pride of place goes to the regions these authors discuss rather than to the literary canon. If place-based criticism is to be meaningful, it must be practiced by scholars who not only have specialised knowledge of Australian literature and its traditions but also know a place well —

admitting that such knowledge can be gained in various ways: by inhabitation, by actually walking the ground, through the study of historical and scientific texts, or some combination of these. Places change over time, and people's perceptions of them can depend on where they come from and the frames they use to view it.

This collection begins on a beach and ends in the Antarctic, two quite different landscapes which could be said to figure in Australia's national imaginary. Both Bruce Bennett and Elizabeth Leane engage with a variety of texts and the impacts that place has had on their authors and on Australian culture more generally. In between, our contributors discuss a variety of places and authors whose writing those places have influenced. Obviously a collection such as this cannot be all-inclusive, given the size and variety of the two fields we are bringing into conjunction: Australian landscapes and Australian literature. As a result, many places, and types of place, go undiscussed, and some major Australian literary figures receive little or no mention. We hope that future ecocritics will take umbrage at these omissions and thereby be prompted to produce the work that is here unfortunately omitted.

In fulfilling their mandate to engage in place-based criticism of Australian writing, our contributors have chosen to take a variety of approaches: from the personal to the scholarly, from broad to narrow in focus, from historical to contemporary. They range from the breadth of Tom Lynch's discussion of deserts to Mark Tredinnick's focus on the North Coast of New South Wales and the pastoral in the poetry of Robert Gray. Even there, however, there are broader implications for the study of what the traditional mode of pastoral might mean in Australia, where there is a well-developed 'pastoral industry', with all of its economic importance and environmental impact; and his discussion of the pastoral resonates with other chapters in the collection.

Several authors (Tony Hughes-d'Aeth, Kate Rigby, Robert Zeller) trace the 'development' of their places as it is reflected in writing about it. Development can mean such things as exploration and settlement, land clearing, agriculture, mining, urbanisation, the creation of national parks, and tourism. And there can also be a development, as all three suggest, in people's ways of seeing a place and of their attitudes toward it.

Because of the importance of Judith Wright as both a poet concerned with the natural world and a committed activist for Aboriginal rights and environmental protection, we asked Wright's biographer Veronica Brady to contribute an overview of the relationship between poetry and place in Wright's writing. The chapters by Kate Rigby and Ruth Blair discuss particular places that figure in Wright's work. Likewise, the issue of indigeneity is important in ecocriticism, and a number of chapters touch on the issue of Australia's indigenous peoples, of white constructions (Australian and American) of Aboriginal peoples, and how they figure in place-based writing. We asked Mitchell Rolls from Tasmania's Aboriginal Studies centre, Riawunna, to contribute a chapter on that subject.

The reader may wonder about the book's title, since only a few of the contributors deal, literally, with littorals. Given Australia's status as the world's only island-continent, one of its defining characteristics is its extensive littoral. Since that littoral encircles the continent, the word *zone* is an apt companion, deriving as it does from the Greek word for *girdle*. Further, the vast majority of Australia's population inhabits its littoral zone; this is where Australians make most of their contact with the natural environment and where, if we are to believe Robert Drewe, the most significant events in their lives occur (see Bruce Bennett's chapter in this volume). Australians are, literally, littoral people.[3]

Nowhere is the littoral zone more evident than when one is on an island, and CA. Cranston's chapter examines three islands and the work of writers who have chosen to dwell there. The chapter provides an example of an ecocritical praxis that engages with place, the people who live there, and the texts that emerge from the conjunction of the two. Perhaps not coincidentally, all the writers are women; the literature under discussion demonstrates a wish to recover for their children (and, in the case of Oodgeroo, for her children's children), a future in the place they choose to live.

While Australia is not all littoral and comprises many zones, from the tropical to the Antarctic, the chapters here all deal with a littoral of another sort — that where place meets language. For hundreds of years, Europeans 'knew' that the Great South Land, otherwise known as Terra Australis Incognita, must exist. Hence in European imaginations the place existed in words, literally, before it took on a physical shape when explorers landed on its shore, littorally. Later, some nineteenth-century Australian explorers sought an inland sea that they 'knew' must exist. They literally wrote the places they traversed into Western consciousness (see Carter 1987). As noted above, the term *zone* derives from Greek; *littoral* derives from Latin. This should serve as a reminder that among the many changes the European invaders brought with them was the linguistic and cultural heritage with which, for better or (often) for worse, they attempted to possess and inhabit Australia and which its writers, such as Les Murray and Peter Porter, would use to write about Australians' sense of place.

4. The Boeotian vs. the Athenian: A Few Words about Les Murray

At the start of this Introduction we mentioned Bruce Bennett's interest in correcting a simplified city-or-the-bush dichotomy in his publication *An Australian Compass*. This work was part of a discourse arising out of an early public debate between Australian expatriate Peter Porter and Australian Republican Nationalist Les Murray. In 'On First Looking into Chapman's Hesiod', Porter declares, "Some of us feel at home nowhere, / Others in one generation fuse with the land" (1975; rpt. 1989: 72). Les Murray set himself in 'Boeotian' opposition to Porter's 'Athenian' view, arguing that Australian poetry, and indeed poetry in general, partakes of what he calls the Boeotian — traditional, local, rural:

> What is at issue are two contrasting models of civilization between which Western man has vacillated; he has now drawn the rest of mankind into the quarrel, and resolving this tension may be the most urgent task facing mankind in modern times. In the past, Athens, the urbanizing, fashion-conscious principle removed from and usually insensitive to natural, cyclic views of the world, has won out time and again, though the successes of Boeotia have been far from negligible. Now, I think, there are senses in which we may say that the old perennial struggle is coming to a head, with Australia finding herself, very much to her surprise, to be one of the places in which some sort of synthesis might at last be achieved. (1978: 173)

He observes that the Boeotian tradition is common in Australian poetry, citing as examples some of the works of David Campbell and

Geoffrey Lehmann. (See Kate Rigby's chapter for a discussion of Campbell's poetry.)

There are a couple of reasons the struggle might be "coming to a head" — one being the increasing pace of globalisation, with its preference for the cosmopolitan over the provincial and the imported over the local; another perhaps being, as noted above, the increasing awareness of ecological crisis. That is, if we are to "think globally and act locally", we need the synthesis of the Athenian and the Boeotian Murray describes — and which in its celebration of farming and self-sufficiency could be seen as increasingly relevant, a blueprint for twenty-first-century 'peakniks', the intellectual class turned sustainability farmers responding to 'peak-oil' theory. On the other hand Murray's views, predominantly masculine and anthropocentric, could also be seen as problematic by ecofeminists and deep ecologists. So a brief look at place in Murray's writing will serve as the open-ended conclusion of this introduction and a springboard to the chapters that follow.

A number of Murray's poems figure the landscape of the North Coast of New South Wales, an area also inhabited by settler Australians Judith Wright and Robert Gray, two other poets discussed in this collection. In 1986, Murray took up property near Bunyah, returning to the landscape of his childhood he had left in 1957 to attend the University of Sydney ('Murray' 2006); and this place is reflected in a number of his important poems as well as in essays such as 'A Working Forest' (a title that stresses the relationship between economy and ecology). In 'Laconics: The Forty Acres' (a title that stresses the relationship between an Australian-identified speech pattern and the cow cocky) he says,

> We have bought the Forty Acres,
> prime bush land.
>
> If Bunyah is a fillet
> this paddock is the eye. (2002: 128)

Here, place is domesticated landscape, its potential grazing stock linguistically prefigured in economic terms of the butcher's cut. Dead timber will be burnt; immigrant grass will be planted, and land will be passed down through the male line:

Where we burn the heaps
we'll plant kikuyu grass.

Ecology? Sure.
But also husbandry. (p. 129)

In his Boeotian view of the land, Murray juxtaposes a term of Germanic origin (from the Old English *hus*, 'house') to one derived from Greek (*oikos*, 'house'). In its original sense, *husbandry* had a meaning similar to that of *economy* and *ecology*: 'household management'. Thus, in this pair of lines, Murray achieves at least a sort of linguistic synthesis between Athens and Boeotia, between Europe and Australia.

Speaking of his home place as "Our croft, our Downs" (p. 129), he depicts it both as part of the old-world bucolic tradition and as a very specific local place entwined with his family's history. For Murray, ecology emphatically includes human society, as husbandry always has. Tom Griffiths has coined the term 'sustainable habitation' to characterise the kind of relationship with nature that Murray tries to get at in some of his poems: "What are the landscape's other values, other than for production, and how can we help people talk about them and take them seriously?" (Griffiths 2002: 241).

Although this bucolic sensibility can be found in many of Murray's poems, we would refer specifically to 'The Buladelah-Taree Holiday Song Cycle' (2002: 137-46; first published in 1976) and 'The Idyll Wheel: Cycle of a Year at Bunyah, New South Wales, April 1986-April 1987' (2002: 281-301; first published in 1989). In the former, he reworks the Aboriginal song cycle form (in particular, the 'Wonguri-Mandjigai Song: Song Cycle of the Moon-Bone') in terms of the white inhabitants of his home area. In the latter, he stakes out his Boeotian position in a cyclical work of another type, though again one that harkens back to an old poetic tradition.

Reworking the Aboriginal song cycle can be seen as an engagement with the literary politics of land ownership under dispute (and now negotiation) since the continent was declared terra nullius. The High Court Mabo decision which declared terra nullius invalid, and opened the way for ongoing Native Title claims, provides a framework for Andrew McGahan's Queensland novel, *The White Earth* (2004). The title engages in naming as claiming (referring to '[t]he actual owners of the land [...] the White family' [p. 23]); it also refers bluntly to ownership anxieties arising out of Native Title claims. As the character John McIvor states while attempting to mobilise other white landowners against legislation that he fears might see the 'Pure Merinos' dispossessed, "Australia — every square inch of it — is *our* sacred site." (p. 209). Murray, more sensitive to a confluence of indigenous and settler cultures, nevertheless similarly affirms a belonging to the land (that in addition belongs to his family) based on the Murray 'tribe's' continued presence on that land.

'The Buladelah-Taree Holiday Song Cycle' opens with residents of the North Coast of New South Wales at dinner, awaiting the return of people from Sydney for the Christmas holiday. This establishes the link between place and family that is strong in Murray's work:

> for this is the season when children return with their children
> to the place of Bingham's Ghost, of the Old Timber Wharf, of the Big Flood That Time,
> the country of the rationalized farms, of the day-and-night farm, and of the Pitt Street farms,
> of the Shire Engineer and many other rumours, of the tractor crankcase filled with chaff,
> the places of sitting down near ferns, the snake-fear places, the cattle-crossing-long-ago places. (2002: 137-38)

The place thus named (or renamed) is peopled and has its legends and is not static.[4] Those who return to it by way of the "Long Narrow City" are anxious to get out "and walk on bare grass"; as they walk, they are "relearning that country" (p. 138). The poem proceeds to catalogue the midsummer activities of humans on the landscape (barbecues, cricket) as well as the creatures that animate that landscape, from mosquitoes to ibis. Nature as depicted in the poem is cyclical. Also at home there, birds come and go, migrating like the seasonal visitors. And in the final section the Southern Cross "hangs head-downward, out there over Markwell; / it turns upon the Still Place, the pivot of the seasons, with one shoulder rising" (p. 145).

As its title suggests, 'The Idyll Wheel' is also cyclical, in this case the cycle being that of the year from April to April:

> *As forefather Hesiod may have learned too, by this time,*
> *things don't recur precisely, on the sacred earth: they rhyme.*

To illuminate one year on that known ground
would also draw light from the many gone underground

with steel wedges and glass and the forty thousand days lost or
worked, daylight to dark, there between Forster and Gloucester. (2002: 281)

As with the song cycle, the poems that make up the series deal with the natural world and with the people (the white 'autochthonous' tribes) who now inhabit the place — their work, their yarns, their losses. ("Why does so much of our culture work through yarns [...]?" Murray asks in 'Aspects of Language and War on the Gloucester Road' [2002: 279].) These are hardly idylls in the traditional sense, but to Murray the local traditions, the generations of being on the land, and being buried in it, have helped to sacralise the earth.

Murray's Boeotian vision, his attention to the land and those who live there, can be a starting point into this exploration of Australian ecocriticism. In the often-'Athenian' world of literary studies, it is a reminder (sometimes uneasy) of the issues accompanying attempts to ground our consciousness in the local.

Notes

[1] For further definitions as well as links to a number of articles dealing with the theory and practice of ecocriticism, visit the ASLE Web site at http://www.asle.umn.edu/archive/intro/intro.html.

[2] This issue of whether there is a tradition of belletristic nature writing in Australia was discussed in CA. Cranston's response to Robert Zeller in a paper at the 2000 conference of the Association for the Study of Australian Literature, later published in the collection *Australian Literature in the 21st Century* (Cranston 2001).

[3] In fact, they were so conceived of long before the place was even 'discovered' by Europeans. Marco Polo referred to a place called Beach that was supposed to be south of Java ('Great' 2002).

[4] In another of Murray's bucolic poems, 'The Boeotian Count' (in the sequence 'Walking to the Cattle Place'), where cattle are named rather than numbered, it is possible to see the synthesis of two ancient cultures, Greek and Aboriginal. For instance, see Herb Wharton's account of illiterate stockmen: "They could always tell if there were a few horses missing, but not by counting. They would just say, "Old Bay horse and his mate, little pony fella and another mare, one that bucks and bolts sometimes, the one that threw you against the tree last year" (1996: 55). Counting is naming, is history: Wharton counts humans in just such a way.

Bibliography

Backhouse, James. 1843. *A Narrative of a Visit to the Australian Colonies*. London: Hamilton, Adams.

Bennett, Bruce. 1991. *An Australian Compass: Essays on Place and Direction in Australian Literature*. South Fremantle: Fremantle Arts Centre Press.

Bonyhady, Tim. 2000. *The Colonial Earth*. Melbourne: Melbourne University Press.

Branch, Michael. 1996. 'Indexing American Possibilities: The Natural History Writing of Bartram, Wilson, and Audubon' in Glotfelty, Cheryll, and Harold Fromm (eds) *The Ecocriticism Reader: Landmarks in Literary Ecology*. Athens: University of Georgia Press: 282-302.

Buell, Lawrence. 1995. *The Environmental Imagination: Thoreau, Nature Writing, and the Formation of American Culture*. Cambridge, MA: Harvard University Press.

Carter, Paul. 1987. *The Road to Botany Bay: An Exploration of Landscape and History*. New York: Knopf.

Chisholm, Alec H. (ed.). 1964. *Land of Wonder: The Best Australian Nature Writing*. Sydney: Angus and Robertson.

Cranston, CA. 2000. *Along These Lines: from Trowenna to Tasmania*. Launceston, Tas.: Cornford Press.

——. 2001. 'Tasmanian Nature Writing and Ecocriticism' in Mead, Philip (ed.) *Australian Literary Studies in the 21st Century*. n.p.: Association for the Study of Australian Literature.

Elder, John. 1998. *Reading the Mountains of Home*. Cambridge, MA: Harvard University Press.

Elliott, Brian. 1967. *The Landscape of Australian Poetry*. Melbourne: F.W. Cheshire.

Falkiner, Suzanne. 1992. *The Writers' Landscape — Wilderness*. East Roseville, NSW: Simon and Schuster.

Flannery, Timothy Fridtjof. 1995. *The Future Eaters: An Ecological History of the Australasian Lands and People*. New York: George Braziller.

Gardam, Faye (ed.). 1987. *Immense Enjoyment: The Illustrated Journals and Letters of William L. Wells, 1884-1888: The Life of an Early Quaker Family in Tasmania*. Devonport, Tas.: Devon Historical Society.

Glotfelty, Cheryll. 1996. 'Introduction: Literary Studies in an Age of Environmental Crisis' in Glotfelty, Cheryll, and Harold Fromm (eds) *The Ecocriticism Reader: Landmarks in Literary Ecology*. Athens: University of Georgia Press: xv-xxxvii.

'The Great South Land *Terra Australia Incognita*'. On line at http://www.arts.usyd. edu.au/departs/religion/Mythoz/The%20Great%20South%20Land.pdf (consulted 31.01.07).

Griffiths, Tom. 1996. *Hunters and Collectors: The Antiquarian Imagination in Australia*. Cambridge: Cambridge University Press.

——. 2002. 'The Outside Country' in Bonyhady, Tim, and Tom Griffiths (eds) *Words for Country: Landscape and Language in Australia*. Sydney: University of New South Wales Press: 223-44.

Hancock, W.K. 1972. *Discovering Monaro: A Study of Man's Impact on His Environment*. Cambridge: Cambridge University Press.

Hay, Peter. 2002. *Main Currents in Western Environmental Thought*. Bloomington, IN: Indiana University Press.

Hodgins, Philip. 1995. 'The Land Itself' in *Things Happen*. Pymble: Angus and Robertson: 9.

Johnson, E.D.H. (ed.) 1966. *The Poetry of Earth: A Collection of English Nature Writing*. New York: Atheneum.

Leer, Martin. 1994. '"Contour-line by Contour": Landscape Change as an Index of History in the Poetry of Les Murray' in *Australian Literary Studies* 16: 249-61.

Lehmann, Geoffrey. 1972. 'Pear Days in Queensland' in Heseltine, Harry (ed.) *The Penguin Book of Australian Verse*. Ringwood, Vic.: Penguin: 449-51.

Marshall, Ian. 1998. *Story Line: Exploring the Literature of the Appalachian Trail*. Charlottesville: University Press of Virginia.

Marx, Leo. 1964. *The Machine in the Garden: Technology and the Pastoral Ideal in America*. New York: Oxford University Press.

Matthews, Brian. 1972. *The Receding Wave: Henry Lawson's Prose*. Carlton: University of Melbourne Press.

McGahan, Andrew. 2004. *The White Earth*. Crows Nest, NSW: Allen and Unwin.

Murphy, Patrick D. 2000. *Farther Afield in the Study of Nature-Oriented Literature*. Charlottesville: University Press of Virginia.

Murray, Les. 2002. *Collected Poems 1961-2002*. Potts Point, NSW: Duffy and Snellgrove.

——. 1978. *The Peasant Mandarin: Prose Pieces*. St. Lucia, Qld.: University of Queensland Press.

'Murray, Les'. 2006. On line at http://www.austlit.edu.au (consulted 13.02.2007).

Pizzey, Graham. 2000. *Journey of a Lifetime: Selected Pieces by Australia's Foremost Birdwatcher and Nature Writer*. Sydney: Angus and Robertson.

Pollak, Michael, and Margaret MacNabb. 2000. *Hearts and Minds: Creative Australians and the Environment*. Alexandria, NSW: Hale and Iremonger.

Porter, Peter. 1989. 'On First Looking into Chapman's Hesiod' in *A Porter Selected: Poems 1959-1989*. Oxford: Oxford University Press: 71-72.

Seddon, George. 1997. *Landprints*. Cambridge: Cambridge University Press.

Wannan, Bill (ed.). 1963. *A Treasury of Australian Wildlife Stories*. Melbourne: Lansdowne.

Wharton, Herb. 1996. *Unbranded*. St. Lucia, Qld.: University of Queensland Press.

White, Gilbert. 1997. *The Natural History of Selborne* (ed. Richard Mabey). New York: Penguin.

Wright, Judith. 1971. 'Australia 1970' in *Collected Poems 1942-1970*. Sydney: Angus and Robertson: 292.

Figure 1

A Beach Somewhere:
The Australian Littoral Imagination at Play

Bruce Bennett

Abstract: A remarkable array of late twentieth and early twenty-first century Australian novelists and short story writers have presented images of West Australian
beaches and coastlines. These authors include Robert Drewe, Jack Davis, Randolph
Stow, Peter Cowan, Dorothy Hewett, and Tim Winton. Their human dramas have a
peculiar poignancy when played out against the natural elements of these Western
coasts. Sexual, emotional, or spiritual crises occur in maritime settings that both
enhance their memorability and reveal humanity's fragile hold on the continent.

1. A Personal Response

We all have a beach somewhere. Mine is called City Beach. It is
located some fifteen kilometres from the city of Perth and eight kilometres from my home in suburban Wembley. It is the late 1950s. As
you pedal steadily up the last of the sand dunes transformed into
asphalt road, you catch your first glimpse of the ocean. Although it is
early afternoon, the sea breeze is already in, and beyond the gleaming
white beach, the blue sea is flecked with white. Out on the horizon is
your island of distant desire which the Dutch named Rottnest. The
beach is now very close, as you rest on the pedals for the last downhill
run, then park your bike, grab your towel, and race for the water.

I am distant now in time and place from that first beach of childhood and adolescence and its images have been overlaid by others.
Hitchhiking around the British Isles with an Australian friend in the
mid-1960s, I recall an Australian horror at the brown sand, pebbles,
and deckchairs on what was called a beach. Clearly, this was no 'real'
beach, but it fulfilled the powerful need to reinforce the superior place
of belonging 'back home'. We had something to be proud of back
there! A beach on vacation in Biarritz was better, its sand whiter, but

it was spoilt by the encroachment of high-rise hotels. The ultimate beach of early middle-age was at Penang where, with two young children, we stayed right on the beach in an unpretentious hotel and dined at white-clothed tables under the stars. I was stung in the murky waters by an unidentified sea creature and treated with Chinese herbal medicines. My luck was greater than that of some others. The hotel and other buildings were swept away by the sea in the Boxing Day tsunami of 2004.

2. Lure and Threat: Robert Drewe

The simultaneous lure and threat of oceans and beaches has been captured for many Australians in Robert Drewe's work. His collection of stories *The Bodysurfers*, his edited volume *The Picador Book of the Beach*, and parts of his memoir *The Shark Net* together compose a fresh exploration of beach culture in Australia and internationally since the 1950s. Drewe's beaches begin on the same strip of coastline west of Perth as mine, just a few kilometres further south. *The Shark Net* brilliantly recreates the younger Drewe's apprehensions of threat and danger in the sea to which he is drawn by fascination and need. The danger is principally represented in the image of sharks which grew in the young man's imagination. That he *needs* to imagine sharks, and to research them, is a sign of his own uncertain sense of self, exacerbated by the recent loss of his mother and his marriage to a girl he has "got pregnant". Murder, violence, and the dark places of the heart are part of his experience, urban Perth which was never far from the river:

> I'd grown up on the ocean and river shores. In younger days my friends and I had crabbed and prawned and fished, patrolled the rock pools and reefs with our *gidgies* and *kylies*, our versions of Aboriginal fish-spears and boomerangs. We knew the tides and reefs, the hot easterlies and blustering westerlies of our coast. (Drewe 2000: 298)

Drewe also sees the coast and sea more generally in national and even mythological, Jungian terms:

> In Jungian terms, there is no doubt that water does add a mythological femaleness and sensuality to art. [...] I have a theory that the five most important stages in a

contemporary Australian's life — sexual and otherwise — occur on or near the beach. (Falkiner 1992: 210)

Drewe's five "stages" of a life-cycle by the sea are enumerated as follows:

> The first sexual act usually occurs on or near the beach, then any given couple usually goes to the beach on their honeymoon; after the honeymoon the family's Christmas holidays take place at the beach, even for country people — and here there is almost a reversal of roles, in that the children are allowed to stay up late and operate adult machinery like outboard motors and eat junk food, while the parents are allowed to act the goat and become children. Then later the couple retires to somewhere like the central coast or the Gold Coast — the east coast from Woy Woy up is one long retirement home, and it's the same in the west. And finally, they are sent to old people's homes on the coast, to die in the fresh air. (Falkiner 1992: 210)

Drewe's contribution to understanding the role of coastlines in the Australian imagination is enormous. In his story 'The Last Explorer' in *The Bodysurfers* (1983: 147-55), he symbolically turns the old explorer's last gaze from Australia's inland deserts, which have for so long dominated Australian writers' perception of the mysteries, to the coast and sea. Drewe's proposal of a Jungian mythology and psychology of water in the Australian context develops further in his novel *The Drowner*, whose protagonist is based on C.Y. O'Connor, the West Australian engineer who oversaw the construction of a water pipeline from the Darling Ranges near Perth to the Eastern Goldfields, then shot himself in the surf at Robbs Jetty south of Fremantle when this project was almost complete. Tragedy, as well as comedy and farce, have been and continue to be enacted on these coasts.

3. "Almost sacramental": Jack Davis, Randolph Stow

Aboriginal poet and playwright, Jack Davis, has given a religious dimension to the Swan River and the sea into which it flows in the opening phase of his play *Kullark (Home)*, in which the doomed warrior hero, Yagan, chants and dances a creation story:

Woolah!

You came, Warrgul […]

You made a home for me
On Kargattup and Karta Koomba,
Kargattup and Karta Koomba.
You made the *beeyol beeyol*,
The wide clear river,
As you travelled onward to the sea […]

Then, oh *wirilo, wirilo*,
The jungara came across the deep blue waters
To rend my soul, to decimate and kill. (Davis 1984: 12)

Although white Australian writers have generally avoided such bold claims on a myth of creation, there is a strong tendency in some of their writing towards what Tim Winton has called "an almost sacramental view of the physical world" (Rossiter 2004: 33). As John Gatta has shown in his book *Making Nature Sacred*, literature, religion, and the environment are deeply entwined in American literature from the Puritans to present times. With the exception of some major works such as *Moby-Dick* and *The Old Man and the Sea*, however, this literature relates largely to the land, including gardens or ponds in the North and swamps in the South.[1] Overarching many representations of the environment in American literature is what Glen Love has described as a renewal of the 'pastoral' impulse:

> The lasting appeal of pastoral is, I think, a testament to our instinctive or mythic sense of ourselves as creatures of natural origins, those who must return periodically to the earth for the rootholds of sanity somehow denied us by civilization. (Love 1996: 231)

Sense impressions as well as the mythology of the West Australian coasts have nowhere been better evoked than by Randolph Stow in his novel *The Merry-go-round in the Sea*. Through the boy Rob Coram's point of view, Stow recalls a mythology of the West Australian coast north and south of Geraldton:

> Costa Branca, Rob thought, catching his breath. Aunt Kay had taught him that. The first name of his country, the Portuguese name. The White Coast.

> The Portuguese had named the Abrolhos too: the keep-your-eyes-open is-
> lands. The Dutch had not changed their name. But Costa Branca had been
> forgotten, had become just a part of New Holland. Yet it had been the first, the
> oldest named land in Australia. (Stow 1968: 113)

The wreck of the *Batavia* on treacherous rocks off these shores and
the massacre that followed on shore are also part of the boy's imagination: "Hundreds of men had died on that night [...] the Graveyard of
Ships, the graveyard of bones and treasure" (p. 113).

If the coast and sea represent Last Things, they also bring the
senses alive. Rob swims in the sea and has the sense of a precarious
paradise of childhood. In the distance, across white sand and water,
mysterious mirages appear. Through everything, the wind blows: "The
town was a town of wind, horizons of windmills, a sky for kites, a
harbour white-petalled with sails" (p. 34).

4. "Between rhapsody and detachment": Peter Cowan, Dorothy Hewett

Commenting on American nature writers from Thoreau to the present,
Scott Slovic remarks that most of them vacillate "between rhapsody
and detachment, between aesthetic celebration and scientific explanation" (1996: 353). While rhapsody and detachment are also apparent
in Australian nature writing, literary writers of the West Australian
coasts seem to gravitate towards the romantic, if not always rhapsodic
end of this spectrum: they seem imbued with something of the energy
they perceive there, with hints of romantic dynamism in their connection with the great Indian Ocean.

In Peter Cowan's short stories from the 1940s to the 80s, he explores a range of reactions to the sea and coasts of Southwest
Australia. One of Cowan's stories, the lyrical prose piece called 'Requiem', which was first published in *Drift* in 1944, evokes the
thoughts and feelings of a man proposing to depart for war who has a
'last swim' with his girlfriend at the beach. Cowan was a great ad-
mirer of Sherwood Anderson, Dos Passos, and Hemingway. In this
story of the 1940s, Cowan adopts a Hemingwayesque stream of consciousness approach to the young man's observations and memories:

Well, we'll go, she said. They got up and took their towels from the bushes outside the small natural cavity the bushes formed. Then carefully they went down
the cliff face where they had cut the path, and reaching the sand he ran over it and
he wanted to cry out, and he felt the strength in him and the sea and the sand and
the timeless place about him so that when the water closed on him he felt, yes, I
have lived, if they smash me tomorrow I have lived in these things that are of
more reality and of more worth than us in our meanness and filth and proud
smallness. (Cowan 1998: 152)

The story's title 'Requiem' serves as a reminder of what endures for
this man in the face of his impending departure and possible death.
Cowan's continuing interest in the enduring reality of the physical
land and seascapes and the transitory nature of human occupation of
the earth was evident both in his stories and novels and in newspaper
articles from the point of view of an informed geographer and dedicated conservationist.

The restraint of Cowan's characters, presented in a realist-
impressionist mode, contrasts radically with Dorothy Hewett's characters in her autobiography, poems, novels, and plays as they interact
with the coasts and beaches of Western Australia. Cowan is reticent
about his childhood, and his characters are generally constrained by
circumstances. Hewett, on the other hand, vividly recalls her childhood on a farm near Wickepin in the Great Southern region of
Western Australia and her family's holidays on the South Coast:

After the harvest, we travel 250 miles to the South Coast and live for two to three
months in a tiny cottage of two rooms and a kitchen beside the sea. The landscape
is forbidding and melancholy, with black rocks and low dark scrub lit by the occasional gleam of sunlight on granite or wave or sand dune. (Hewett 1990: 9)

Hewett expresses here the beginning of a long love affair with "the
wild sea and historic past" (p. 10) where "at night, the lighthouse on
Breaksea flicks on and off across the Southern Ocean and steamers
with smoking funnels sail by on their way to the ends of the world" (p.
10).

Hewett's play *Song of the Seals* drew on her strong association of
the sea with childhood experiences. Set at Mystery Bay, "a lonely
beach between the sea and the spotted gum forest" (Hewett 1983: 66),
the play is a musical fantasia which revolves around the imaginings of
Willow Ogilvie, a fourteen year old girl who combines nature and art:

her mother was a selchie and her father a concert pianist. The opening scene of the play presents Willow, her voiced backed over by music and sounds of the sea:

> The summer I turned fourteen I came to my grandmother's house on Mystery Bay. The grandmother I'd never seen. [...] All around me the air was full of noise [...] the cries of seabirds, the sucking of the surf [...] and something else, a sighing and humming that seemed to come from the waves. (p. 67)

The sounds that seem to come from the waves draw Willow into the mysterious life of seals.

Hewett's late novel, *The Toucher*, published in her seventieth year, associates the south-west coasts of Australia with the memory and imagination of a character who is in the last phase of her life. The novel's protagonist, Esther La Farge, recalls the "only decent man [she] ever had" as a sailor from the sea:

> After thirteen years at sea he walked with a slight roll, balancing his body lightly on the balls of his feet. He came into the long room drained of light with the rain drumming against the plate-glass window and fell in love. (Hewett 1993: 163)

However, the romance of the sea for Hewett takes a somewhat different form as Esther reflects on the capacity of the ocean to both create and destroy:

> There was something elemental about it — the black salt-streaked granite, the foaming sea, the shrieking birds — something brutal and absolute, like death or murder. Out there past the gap, embedded in limestone, they'd found a 20,000 year old female skeleton preserved since the Ice Age. The force of the wind could tear you over the edge. There was a story about a honeymoon couple sucked to their deaths in the blowhole. Esther imagined them like Paolo and Francesca clasped together, whirling through the vast caverns. (pp. 228-29)

This part of nature, the wild sea, links childhood and age: "It had always seemed sinister to her, even as a child, and yet she belonged to it: the clarity, the patience, the isolation were part of her. She dissolved into it: sea, rocks and sky; the dark curve of a land splashed with light; a giddy sense of clinging to the edge of things" (p. 229). Hewett's romantic pantheism is almost religious in its intensity. Against this epiphanic vision of the elemental sea, the older Esther contrasts her middle years in the Communist Party when she felt "safe, cloistered, part of a unified vision, chaos held at bay, history made easy" (pp. 229-30). These observations, like many others in the novel, are strongly autobiographical.

Unlike the more quiescent poems of healing in *Peninsular*, Hewett's volume set mainly on the Mornington Peninsula in Victoria after a serious illness, Esther's encounter with the South-western ocean in *The Toucher* is more violent, the emotional scenery more volatile and chaotic. The contrast is akin to that between the temperate Grange and elemental Heights in Emily Brontë's *Wuthering Heights*, one of Hewett's favourite novels. In this state of heightened excitement, Esther reflects on the indigenous people and the whites who followed, finding shreds of comfort, perhaps, not in social ideologies but in notions of a 'chain of being' in an otherwise arbitrary universe:

> The thin, dark-skinned naked hunters and gatherers carrying their paperbark torches, the greedy white-skinned builders and sowers, all strangers on this continent; and yet we're here, part of the chain of being, with our own brutal history. Life or death, all arbitrary, even the planet itself, colliding, exploding in space, a vanishing atom. (Hewett 1993: 230)

5. Environmental Values and "dizzy moments": Tim Winton

Literary images of disorder, violence, and mortality are not the images that tourist authorities wish to promote. A three-page spread in the *New York Times* travel section in January 2006 observed that "today, for all its remoteness, Western Australia feels firmly tethered to the wider world" (Apple 2006: 8-9). "Perth reminds me of San Diego", the writer says; the city's "shimmering postmodern skyscrapers" are like Houston's; and "the America's Cup was raced in the waters off Fremantle". New seaside subdivisions are called "Florida, San Remo, Waikiki". In the Southwest, Margaret River "has avoided the fate of the Napa Valley and other arcadian winegrowing areas whose very beauty has proved their undoing". And the sea, which can be angry and disorienting, is presented in its pristine, arcadian form:

> From coastal Caves Road one morning, we turned onto a spur that led out of the forests and down off the plateau. Suddenly, we caught sight of a swath of sea. As we reached a broad, clean beach, backed by limestone cliffs, we were alone. We could see the surf leaping above offshore rocks in the distance, then calming it-

self. By the time they reached us, the waters were transparent green, turquoise and blue. (p. 9)

Like the other Australian writers mentioned, Tim Winton finds something deeper and more personally meaningful in the coasts of Western Australia than these touristic images.

Winton's novels and stories, from *An Open Swimmer* and *Shallows* to *Dirt Music* and the recent collection of stories *The Turning,* return repeatedly to the coasts on which the author has lived and their interaction with his characters' lives. Winton became a key figure in the environmentalist movement when he publicly opposed the construction of a marina and resort on the Ningaloo Reef off the north-west coast — and Winton has said that he entered this campaign reluctantly, preferring a quieter, less public role on marine-related issues:

Figure 2: *An Open Swimmer*

Having been a spearfisher and angler and surfer all my life, having lived in a whaling town, you know, seen stuff happen and come to see how fragile things are, I suppose it made some sense. The renewed proposal to build a marina and resort on the Ningaloo Reef kind of forced my hand, really. It was a nightmare on the horizon. All the major green groups formed an alliance to fight it. We had no money, no real lever. We couldn't come up with anything better than me, the public idea of me anyway, to get the issue some attention, put pressure on government, engage the public through the media. (Rossiter 2004: 33-34)

While environmental values clearly inform Winton's outlook, as they do the writings of Drewe, Cowan, Davis, and Hewett, his view of nature is not primarily political. Indeed, what principally characterises Winton's literary representations of sea and coasts is both his sense of at-oneness in these environments and his recognition of their numinous possibilities. In *An Open Swimmer*, for example, Jerra Nilsam and his old school friend Sean have different perspectives on their fishing trip off the West Australian coast. Jerra is the dreamer who searches for the fish that holds a pearl, while Sean is more practical. When Jerra catches a fish and hauls it aboard, his whole body and spirit seem united with that of his fellow creature as he holds it while it thrashes about in its death throes: "Bashing. It was bashing the gunwale. The fish buckled up, almost out of the boat. He fell on it, hugging the fin spikes in his chest. With a spastic twitch it deflated, mumbling" (1982: 7-8).

This is action writing with an extra dimension — with hints of a mystery in the sea and its creatures to which humans are linked though they have not yet discovered how. Much of Winton's fiction seems to ask what further pearls may be dreamed about and perhaps discovered on the coasts, coves, and beaches that surround the Australian land-mass.

Although Winton does not entirely fit Slovic's description mentioned earlier of nature writers who "vacillate between rhapsody and detachment, between aesthetic celebration and scientific explanation", his fiction does have affinities with both the naturalist and modern lyric novel traditions. His novel *Dirt Music* shows this unique mix in operation as it explores the interaction of humans with coastal land and seascapes. The major contrast in the novel is between the fishing settlement at White Point on the central West Coast (based on Lancelin where Winton lived for some years) and the relative wilderness of the tropical Northwest Coast and its islands. Reactions to these environments are traced principally through the character Luther Fox, an outsider from the south who escapes to the north, and Georgie Jutland, the woman who learns to love him and ultimately rediscovers him there.

Once a place for loners and dropouts, White Point has developed into a base for a successful fishing industry. Winton as realist/naturalist renders both the present and past of this piece of coastal Australia:

> The only safe anchorage for many miles, White Point was then just a bunch of tin sheds in the lee of the foredune. A sandy point, a series of fringing reefs and an island a mile offshore created a broad lagoon in which the original jetty stood. The settlement lay wedged between the sea and the majestic white sandhills of the

interior. [...] Nowadays rich fishermen built pink brick villas and concrete slab bunkers that made their fathers' hovels look pretty. (Winton 2001: 16-17)

No sentimentalist, Georgie wonders that "people could produce such a relentlessly ugly town in so gorgeous a setting" (p. 17). A more primitive but 'natural' struggle for existence is demonstrated when Luther Fox escapes the law and his past to deal with his inner demons alone in Australia's Northwest Kimberley region:

Fox makes a fine camp beneath an overhang at the base of the island's mesa bluff. [...] From this position he can see across the treetops down to the belt of boabs and then the beach. [...] His days are lived according to the tide. (pp. 351, 354)

Among the coastal mangroves he encounters crocodiles and turtles and learns to catch what he needs among the queenfish, trevally, Spanish mackerel, pikey bream, and other creatures of the sea. Winton's modern Crusoe camps, fishes, and forages in a profuse tropical island setting of figs, berries, and pandanus nuts, but the author's subtext is his character's search for emotional and spiritual redemption. This occurs in part through his adoption of Aboriginal modes of survival and through the faith in him of his lover from the south who searches for and finds him.

Tim Winton's part real, part fictional coastal settlements at Angelus (based on Albany) and White Point (Lancelin) recur in a number of stories in *The Turning*, which reveal characters in various states of emotional and spiritual need. In 'Cockleshell' (Winton 2004: 113-32), a boy's troubled feelings about a girl from a neighbouring house by the beach at Angelus are played out as the pair spear spiked cobbler together in the shallow waters. Broken relationships, alcohol, and family violence lurk in the background and erupt in an unexpected way. Apparent miracles occur along with betrayals and cover-ups. Nothing is as it seems in these temporary settlements by the sea.

The title story in *The Turning* (pp. 133-61) explicitly addresses the subtext of spiritual need and regeneration in the fishing settlement of White Point. A friendship between two young married women leads to revelations of alcoholism, marital violence and betrayal, and religious belief. Raelene begins to see a way beyond the endless round of alcohol, violence, and sexual abuse in her marriage through the Christian faith of her friend Sherry and Sherry's husband Dan. A 'turning' in Rae's life occurs as she walks alone on the beach at night:

> [T]here was a time on one of those walks along the stormy beach when there was no moon out and you could sense the heavy cloud but not see it racing inland and you only had the pale, vague strip of land to navigate by. Rae found herself walking with her hands outstretched, overcome by the apprehension that she was about to stumble into something on the smooth, empty beach. She became breathless, panicky, and just as she'd started muttering aloud, talking herself down from this queer spin she was getting herself into, a patch of stars opened up low in the sky ahead of her and stopped her in her tracks. (p. 149)

This "dizzy moment" is a prelude to a series of insights, or revelations, which enable Rae to transcend the physical brutality of her marriage, and perhaps to move on from it. Significantly, the epiphanic moment occurs on a beach at night, in a liminal space between land, sea, and stars where a single human consciousness can momentarily see beyond the habits and routines of everyday existence to her place in the universe.

6. Conclusion

The examples I have cited show coasts and beaches of Western Australia as vital elements in the literary consciousness. The relative remoteness of Western Australia from metropolitan centres may contribute to a sense of its inhabitants feeling 'on the edge'. But this can be a literary advantage. At any rate, a number of major writers have endorsed Robert Drewe's emphasis on beaches as sites of critical significance in the life-cycle of many Australians. Drewe himself, Jack Davis, Randolph Stow, Peter Cowan, Dorothy Hewett, and Tim Winton have presented human dramas played out against the sea, sand, wind, rocks, and vegetation of these Western coasts. They make human settlement seem unstable and temporary. Sexual, emotional, and spiritual crises occur in concert with or against the elements, and human lives assume a place in the universal dramas of destruction and renewal.

Notes

[1] Thoreau's pond at Walden has assumed a mythical significance in American literary history. The swamps of the African-American South have evoked exotic spirits. See Gatta (2004: 175-81).

Bibliography

Primary Sources

Cowan, Peter. 1994. 'Requiem' in Wilding, Michael (ed.) *The Oxford Book of Australian Short Stories*. Melbourne: Oxford University Press. 152-53.

Davis, Jack. 1984. *Kullark / The Dreamers*. Paddington: Currency Press.

Drewe, Robert. 1983. *The Bodysurfers*. Sydney: James Fraser.

——. 1996. *The Drowner*. Sydney: Pan Macmillan.

—— (ed.). 1993. *The Picador Book of the Beach*. Sydney: Pan Macmillan.

——. 2000. *The Shark Net*. Ringwood: Viking/Penguin.

Hewett, Dorothy. 1983. *Golden Valley and Song of the Seals*. Sydney: Currency Press.

——. 1994. *Peninsula*. South Fremantle, WA: Fremantle Arts Centre Press.

——. 1993. *The Toucher*. Ringwood, Vic: McPhee Gribble.

——. 1990. *Wild Card: An Autobiography, 1923-1958*. London: Virago.

Stow, Randolph. 1968. *The Merry-go-round in the Sea*. Harmondsworth: Penguin.

Winton, Tim. 2001. *Dirt Music*. Sydney: Pan Macmillan.

——. 1982. *An Open Swimmer*. Sydney: George Allen and Unwin.

——. 2004. *The Turning*. Sydney: Pan Macmillan.

Secondary Sources

Apple, R.W. 2006. 'Out West, Aussie Style' in *The New York Times* (1 January 2006).

Falkiner, Suzanne. 1992. *Wilderness*. Sydney: Simon and Schuster.

Gatta, John. 2004. *Making Nature Sacred: Literature, Religion and Environment in America from the Puritans to the Present*. Oxford and New York: Oxford University Press.

Love, Glen A. 1996. 'Revaluing Nature: Toward an Ecological Criticism' in Glotfelty, Cheryll, and Harold Fromm (eds) *The Ecocriticism Reader: Landmarks in Literary Ecology*. Athens and London: University of Georgia Press, 1996: 225-40.

Rossiter, Richard. 2004. 'The Writer and the Community: An Interview with Tim Winton' in *Westerly* 49: 29-38.

Slovic, Scott. 1996. 'Nature Writing and Environmental Psychology' in Glotfelty, Cheryll, and Harold Fromm (eds) *The Ecocriticism Reader: Landmarks in Literary Ecology.* Athens and London: University of Georgia Press: 351-70.

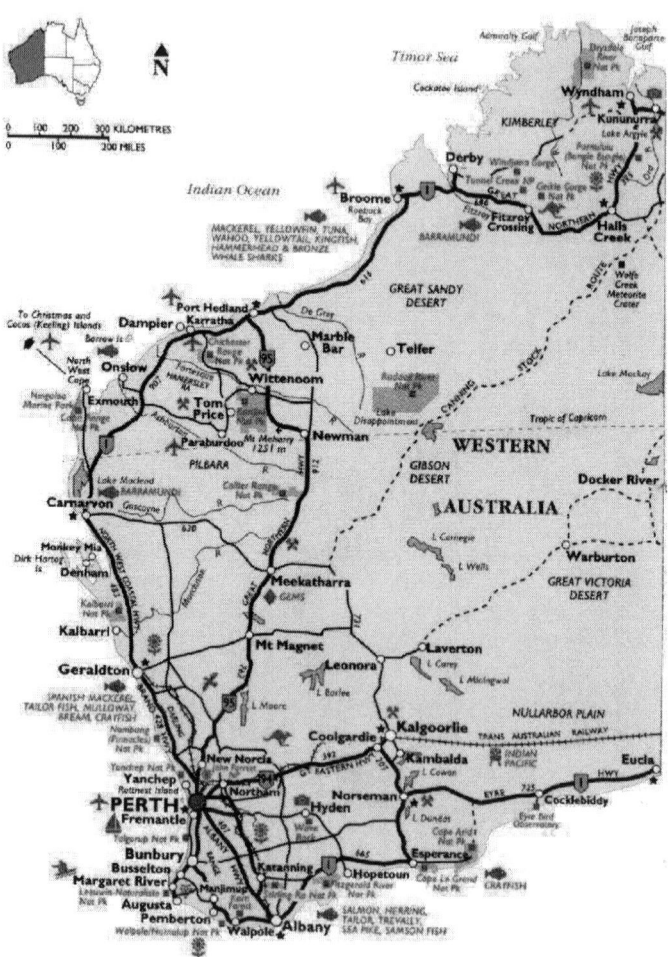

Figure 3

The Shadow on the Field:
Literature and Ecology in the Western Australian Wheatbelt

Tony Hughes-d'Aeth

Abstract: Satellite images show a sharp line marking the end (or beginning) of the country cleared for farming in south-western Australia. It is the most visible clearance line on the planet and demarcates an area the size of Scotland from which, in the space of two generations, the native vegetation was almost entirely stripped. This chapter attempts to trace this far-reaching ecological event in the creative literature of those generations, focussing on the inter-war years.

> "It seems — it seems unnatural," said Rose slowly.
> "Yes — yet they say Nature is never unnatural." (Pollard 1927: 69)

1. The Clearing Line

Most nights I watch the television news right until the end so I can see the weather report. The presenter stands in front of a virtualised image of Western Australia on which appear in harmony with his prompts the various data and signs that allow him and us to participate in the narrative of our state's weather. At some point, maybe five years ago, the solid colour map of the western half of the continent was replaced with a colourised satellite image which ranged in colour from fawn to forest green. To my naïve eye it seemed that the green portions of this map roughly matched the green parts of our state. I was most struck, and have been ever since, by the sharp line that ringed Perth to the north and east, stretching roughly from Geraldton to Esperance and marking out an area most West Australians know as the wheatbelt.

Inside the ring was a wheat-coloured yellow, outside the ring a muted eucalyptus green. The line that separates the two, known by analysts as the 'clearing line', is the most obvious visible sign from space of humans' effect on the planet. These pixels are abstractions, but they are not merely metaphoric. They bear a strict indexical relationship to the surface of the land they represent. The pixels are given a colour value based on the degree of 'reflectance' measured by the satellite camera.[1] The more light the brighter the pixel, the less the darker. The sharp line is created by the spectral contrast between native perennials (bush) and crop and pasture grasses. It is made sharper by the comparative flatness of the country. The clearing line follows the rabbit-proof fence which also marks the minimum rainfall threshold below which cropping is unsustainable.

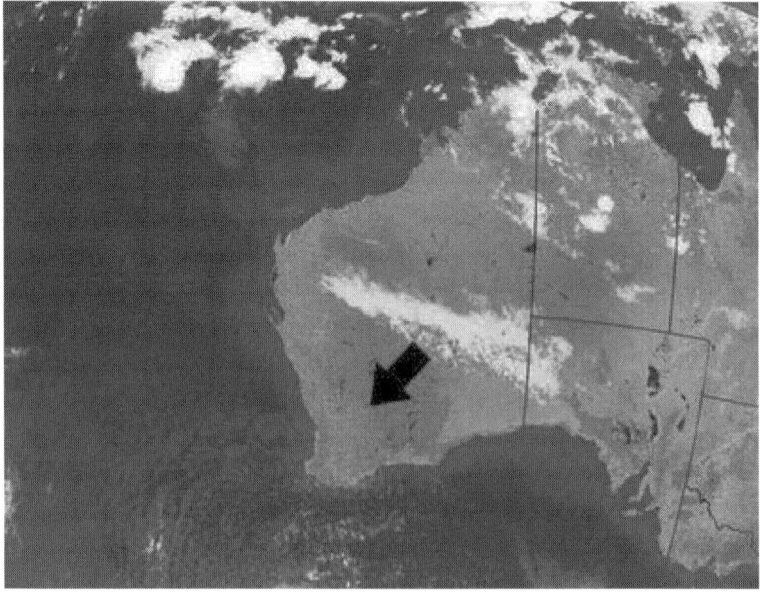

Figure 4: 'The clearing line'

Depending on how you look at this line, it is either natural or man-made. At first blush it seems overwhelmingly, disconcertingly artificial. Read ecologically the line can also be seen as a line of resistance, rather than a line of encroachment: the point at which the instrumental energy of agricultural colonisation was no longer able to extend itself. It draws to mind other imperial demarcations, like the vast walls that marked the limits of the Roman and Han Chinese empires, which despite the rumours *cannot* be seen from space. It is this picture, taken every day from well beyond the biosphere, that leads us to the central ecological problematic of the Western Australian wheatbelt, which is that of radical disappearance. In the space of less than one hundred years, an area the size of Scotland has been cleared of its native flora and fauna. Not completely, of course; there are state and national parks and other remnants, but the satellite tells the story in summary. It's gone.

It is difficult to replicate the sense of shock that such an absence might once have generated. To the acculturated the wheatbelt will often appear a pleasant blend of fields and trees, an undulating fertile country beneath bright blue skies. One has to imagine a person who did not know what a field was, or what wheat, or indeed crops were. Such a person was Ronald Gidgup Senior, a Noongar-Yamaji man who grew up on station country outside of Carnarvon before moving with his father to Bruce Rock in the wheatbelt in 1941.

> Coming from the station country down to the farming country was different. I never knew what a farming area was until I saw the land was cleared and there were these big haystacks. I thought they were people's homes but they weren't because they were made out of hay. I had never seen a cleared field before and I couldn't work out why all the bush was gone. When you live in station country that's all you see, the bush. I didn't know what wheat was, I had never seen wheat. (2000: 75)

Gidgup's memories retain in an undiminished way the estrangement that ensues when one realises for the first time that something one had thought belonged to the order of permanence has been simply and utterly erased.

Environmental historians like Andrea Gaynor have begun to trace the history of this dramatic ecological remapping. What they have found is that from a very early stage the land registered signs of disequilibrium, in particular salinity, erosion, and species loss, and that farmers and scientists recognised this but other imperatives prevailed. Governmental policies of land classification and release for settlement involved loan schemes which were conditional on clearing land. In 1930, with the financial crash, the cash-strapped Federal Government declared 'Grow More Wheat Year' in a desperate quest for export revenue (Barr and Cary 1992: 132). More typically the land was seen as being a dreary waste which was finally being put to good use. The process, though mediated by governmental practices and agricultural science, worked primarily at the level of individual aspiration. After all, the land was cleared not by the government but by thousands of families who had forfeited other opportunities so they could try to make a living from wheat. The wheatbelt grew, like the Great Wall of China in Kafka's parable, according to an inner logic that no single point within it could ever grasp. This essay is an attempt to discern the imaginative dimension that underwrites an enterprise of far-reaching ecological consequence by reference to the creative literature written about the Western Australian wheatbelt during the first half of the twentieth century.

2. Songs of Wheat

In his classic account of the rise and fall of the South Australian wheatbelt, *On the Margins of the Good Earth* (1962), D.W. Meinig situates the emergence of this farming region as part of a world-wide agricultural colonisation of "sub-humid, middle latitude, 'open' countries" to the cultivation of grain. It took place rapidly and almost simultaneously in the latter part of the nineteenth century: "in western Kansas and central Manitoba; in Manioba and Assiniboia; in the Walla Walla and the San Joaquin; in the eastern Ukraine and western Siberia; in the inner Pampa and on the High Veld" (Meinig 1962: 3). In Australia, wheat farming first emerged on a large scale in South Australia, which serviced the market created by the gold boom of the 1850s. By the 1870s, Australia switched from being a net importer to a net exporter of wheat. In the ensuing decades wheat spread throughout the colonies, in an intermittent arc from the Darling Downs in Queensland, through western New South Wales, across northern Victoria to South Australia, and into the south of Western Australia by the early twentieth century.

While the wheat industry advanced significantly during the latter part of the nineteenth century, it did not loom large in the colonial imaginary, and was distinctly subsidiary to the pastoral agriculture of cattle and sheep in the nationalist aesthetics typified by the *Bulletin* literature and Heidelberg paintings of the 1890s. Shearing and droving were characterised by a romantic nomadology that tapped a fantasy of masculine independence from homely duties and womanly demands. With Federation in 1901, there is a perceptible shift in the forms of imaginative investment in rural practices, with a greater emphasis on the productive feats of the grain farmer and the role this had in nation-building. At this time, wheat became a subject in literary production. In particular, wheat ballads started to appear in the midst of the traditional pastoral songs in the pages of the *Bulletin* and the *Lone Hand*. Two poems, by C.J. Dennis and Banjo Paterson, serve to capture the ideological and psychic comforts that wheat farming promised in this era. Both these poets were of course central agents in the creation of a nationalist idiom which mapped national ideologies onto rural vernacular mythologies. Dennis's poem, simply titled 'Wheat', appeared in his first volume *Backblock Ballads and Other Verses* published in 1913. The first verse and refrain contain the key elements of the song:

> Oh! The ways o' makin' money in this world o'
>   Many lands
> An' the means to eke a livin' out are countless
>   As the sands.
> There are thousands in the cities gettin' nothin' out
>   O' life
> But the day-to-day excitement of eternal business
>   Strife.
> Yet a life o' rush and bustle ain't the sort o' life
>   Fer me;
> You can keep yer sudden fortunes, for I'd much the
>   Sooner be
>
> A-growin' —
> Wheat, wheat, wheat. It's a game that's hard to beat —
> Sowin' it an' growin' it — it's what the nations eat.
> Tho' it ain't a life o' pleasure,
> An' there's little time for leisure,
> It's contentin', in a measure, is the game of growin'
>   Wheat. (Dennis 1913: 52)

For Dennis, wheat-farming is primarily a therapeutic alternative to modern life. The honest toil of the crop farmer is an antidote to the stresses of urban capitalism, with its ever-present threats of financial and psychological collapse ("You can court your nervous breakdowns, you can slave to make / your pile" [p. 54]). The "sowin'" and "growin'" place the farmer out of the dulling cycle of consumerism and into a habit of life that is closer to both the rhythms of nature and the potency of productive capitalism.

The violent character of the resumption of wooded land for use in the growth of cereals, not adverted to in Dennis's ballad, emerges in Paterson's 'Song of the Wheat', published initially in the *Lone Hand* in 1914 and republished as the opening poem in his volume *Saltbush Bill, J.P., and Other Verses* in 1917, whilst Paterson was serving in the Middle East. 'Song of the Wheat' articulates the transformation of the country west of the Dividing Range from pastoral to crop use. Here is the opening stanza:

> We have sung the song of the droving days,
>   Of the march of the travelling sheep—
> How by silent stages and lonely ways
>   Thin, white battalions creep.
> But the man who now by the soil would thrive
>   Must his spurs to a ploughshare beat;
> And the bush bard, changing his tune, may strive
>   To sing the song of the Wheat! (Paterson 1914: 403)

The martial tone could hardly be accidental, and what for Dennis had been a delicate kind of copping out, becomes for Paterson a call to arms. What is significant though is the manner in which the eruption of war allows, effectively in retrospect, a symbolic context for the agricultural colonisation of the rangelands of south-western New South Wales:

> Yarran and Myall and Box and Pine—
>   'Twas axe and fire for all;
> They scarce could tarry to blaze the line
>   Or wait for the trees to fall,

Ere the team was yoked, and the gates flung wide,
  And the dust of the horses' feet
Rose up like a pillar of smoke to guide
  The wonderful march of Wheat. (p. 403)

The shocking speed with which one agricultural moment was being eradicated, the pastoral age over whose last years Paterson had so distinctively presided, in the place of a new mode of exploitative, close-settlement, is given a meaning by a war that people would soon struggle to give meaning to. The interlinking of war and wheat is much denser than might first be thought. What becomes evident in the literature of wheat farming is that the metaphorics of war exist in all their ambivalence. The mechanised transformation of agriculture and war only make sense from a strategic position, beyond the blazing destruction that envelops its participants.

In the ensuing decades of the 1920s and 30s, the wheat poem remained a staple in the *Bulletin*, which featured numerous contributions from Australia's wheat-producing regions. Largely they fall into either the militaristic, imperial tradition of Paterson or the therapeutic tradition of Dennis, at times combining both. Charles Souter from South Australia published a series of light-hearted poems in the line of Dennis in 1926, which describe the various stages of wheat farming in metered couplets ('Harvestin'', 'W'eat-Cartin'!'). R.G. Henderson of New South Wales published an ode to 'The Wheat' in which the grain speaks nobly of itself in the first person, revealing how it has shaped human history since the time of the pharaohs. Despite its displacements, Henderson's poem, like Paterson's, shows a clear sense of the close relationship between the mass-production of grain and the reshaping of the world through the mechanisms of globalising capital: "For me they barter their brightest silks and / Forge their greatest guns" (Henderson 1926: 7). Such optimism is present but more tempered in subsequent years, often adopting a polite fatalism. Nevertheless, in the wheat song one discerns the formation of a national ideology of wheat-growing which still persists in many ways, encrypted into our imagery and iconography.

3. The End of the Grower of Golden Grain

The last of the wheatbelts, Western Australia's wheat country grew in
response to the gold mining boom of the 1890s and emerged first in
the corridor that linked Perth to the goldfields some 570 kilometres
almost due east. In this period, the colony's population quadrupled.
The rail link was completed in 1896, and C.Y. O'Connor's famous
water pipeline in 1903. Soon lines spurring south and north opened the
plateau east of the Darling Ranges to clearing and farming in a band
that would before long be known as the wheatbelt. The Great Southern
rail line ran inland and south to Albany, creating the wheatbelt towns
of Beverley, Pingelly, Narrogin, Wagin, and Katanning (Whitwell and
Sydenham 1991: 15). By the end of the 1920s, a vast crescent of land
from Geraldton in the north, east to Southern Cross and even far to the
south-east at Esperance was set into the production of wheat. In reality
this did not occur in a spatially uniform way but by a diffused process
of release and selection once land had been surveyed and categorised
in terms of soil and rainfall. It took several decades, arguably a century, but would eventually result in that discrete polygon etched on a
planetary scale in the weather report on the evening news.

High post-war prices saw a rapid expansion of the wheatbelt during
the 1920s. The expansion was fuelled by returning veterans, British
migrants, and refugees from the mining recession in the neighbouring
goldfields. In the north-eastern corner of the wheatbelt, where farming
gives way to mining, is the Yilgarn. Lyall Hunt, author of a history of
the Yilgarn, notes that only in Libya is wheat grown in drier conditions. One who tried his luck as a crop farmer in the early days of the
Yilgarn was the poet and short-story writer Cyril E. Goode, who
began clearing and farming land at Turkey Hill in 1923 before succumbing to "drought and depressions" in 1931. Goode wrote poems
for local newspapers and magazines that were collected in *The
Grower of Golden Grain* (1932). Goode's poems are jauntily bitter,
after the *Bulletin* style, and are divided into two sections. The poems
of the first section offer a sense of the animating dream in the wheatbelt enterprise with "pleasant ordered waving wheatfields [...] [o]n
rich clay slopes and flats". Those of the second section, 'Poems of the
Depression: The End of the Grower of Golden Grain', voice the
collapse of this dream. These latter poems pivot around this central

impossibility offered up by the Depression in which wheat was worth less than it cost to grow. The 'Song of the Bankrupt Wheatgrower' concludes that "it wasn't much sense, for I got eighteen pence, / Two shillings at least below zero". This economic crisis precipitates a broader crisis of faith in the promise of wheat. 'Whither Bound?' addresses the very enterprise of wheat farming itself, not as a financial adventure but in all its imaginative allure as a place and practice of fulfilment. The opening stanza is plain enough as a description of the material effects of the collapse of the wheat price:

> The harvest is over — the debts are unpaid;
> We're destitute, whereas we should have been made,
> Depression has taken firm hold of the land,
> Impotent we struggle beneath her strong hand. (p. 30)

But the poem slowly folds into a metaphysical lament:

> Are martial upheavals and chaotic schemes
> The nearest approach to idealists' dreams?
> Can never poor drowning humanity reach
> The firm golden sands of Utopia's beach? (p. 30)

Ecologically, what is notable in the poems is how this disillusionment is given form in the foundational acts of 'the grower', which is to clear the land of its bush. Often twinned in these ballads are the processes of clearing as difficult, arduous preparatory work — sometimes ugly and depressing and sometimes possessing a sort of dark or terrible beauty — and the economic failure of farmers. In other words there is not a causal connection between the violent character of the land's clearance and the subsequent collapse of the wheat price, but they nevertheless recur in the same poetic space, as if a relationship might yet somehow exist between them.

How was the land cleared? This varied over time and according to the vegetation. Laurie Anderson, a long time wheatbelt farmer, gives a good overview. The initial take-up of land in the wheatbelt tended to be in Gimlet and Salmon Gum country, which grew in the heavier soils favoured as more productive. These trees were ringbarked and left to die. When they had dried, the understorey was fired. In thinner mallee and York gum country a 'scrub roller' was used, which was a larger iron cylinder, typically from an old boiler, dragged across the scrub by a bullock team, and in later years, a tractor. After about 1950, the country was generally cleared by two bulldozers dragging between a length of heavy anchor chain. Once the scrub had been levelled, the burning would take place. Anderson tells how this was always a "big event":

> The 'burn' was usually done with neighbours joining forces all hoping for a good stiff wind to keep the stumps alight, this would save days of labour later in carrying, by hand, wood to stack around any stumps not burned to or below ground level.
>   I have very evocative memories going back to burns after tea with a shovel — taking coals from big ember heaps and placing them on the up wind side of stumps that had not caught alight. The thousand winking eyes of the coals and the sweet smell of the burning strawberry Jam tree wood remain forever imprinted in my mind. (Anderson 1999: 7)

A.B. Facey recalls a similar scene in *A Fortunate Life* (1981). He describes how a fire break was carefully cleared around the intended field and then set ablaze to burn inward. As a young boy it fell to Facey to move through the blackened remains on the following day and to heap unspent fuel on the stumps of the larger trees in the hope of burning them right out of the ground (Facey 1981: 68). Cyril Goode was also entranced by the vividness of "the burn" which he describes in his poem 'The Clearer':

> Like a carnival city viewed from a height
> (Whose lights are a changing medley),
> Will the burning timbers appear at night,
> With their embers glowing redly
>
> Then for weeks, on oppressive awful days,
> Ere the final stumps are level,
> The clearer will work in the smoky haze
> Like a mediaeval devil. (Goode 1932: 16)

Goode's 'clearer' was in this poem a kind of fugitive figure working alone on a contractual basis, distinct in character and purpose from the 'grower' of his other poems. This contrasts with the collectively organised labour of Anderson's memory, or the gritty plainness of Facey's, but in each case the event is charged with an unearthly and magical potency that gives expression to the profound transformation that was being effected.

Goode's later work often returns to his experiences on the Yilgarn. A feature of his later poems is the discord that exists between the bucolic images of golden fields and the realities of modern industrial farming. For instance, 'The Power Farmer's Soliloquy' evokes the moment "When the roar of an engine and clatter / Breaks into your dreams" and the "grind of the gearing [...] echoes afar" (Goode 1944: 16). These poems are an implicit rebuttal of the liberation from industrialised wage slavery that was promised in the poems of Paterson and Dennis. Indeed after the collapse of his farming venture in the Depression, Goode would find work in the war years in a Victorian munitions factory. In his poetry the elements of factory work have tragically followed the farmers, with clattering engines breaking into their dreams and the clearing of the land experienced as bodily shock and auditory assault.

In 1950, Goode published a collection of prose called *Yarns of the Yilgarn*, which were marketed as 'westerns' to capitalise on the post-War popularity of American stories in this vein. Goode's 'west' was this same memory-scape of his earlier farming venture at Turkey Creek. In stories like 'The Power Farmer', 'Making Adjustments', 'White Ants', and 'A Matter of Morrels', a Lawsonian world of wry failure predominates. They follow the basic trajectory established in *The Grower of Golden Grain*, satirising the enthusiasm of new settlers affected by "land fever" and their quixotic optimism in setting about the task of "carving a home out of the chaos" (Goode 1950: 65). Through the irony is seen a picture of the clearing of the wheatbelt, tackled with entrepreneurial zeal: "Followed four or five years of chopping down and burning up [...] and no holidays either!" (p. 38). Goode's vivid sketches of life on marginal crop land, "second class country" that attracted only "half loans" from the Agricultural Bank, are infused with retrospective futility. One of the striking features of his writing is the rapidity and certainty with which the farmer's dreams collapse, but not before vast tracts of arid woodland have been axed and burnt and then ploughed by loan-purchased tractors sold by avuncular company reps. The stories begin with the same hope — "visions of well stocked farms where a few years before gums, scrub and mallee had stretched to the horizon" — and end unremittingly in defeat.

These human stories of failed ambition and cruelled dreams inter-pose before a narrative of radical ecological change, a change that is both the driving force in the actions of the characters and the mocking reminder of their futility. In 'The Power Farmer', the protagonist of the title dies at the very moment he finally gets his ruinously expen-sive tractor to work. Before finding the deceased power farmer, the narrator and his friends set out across the open fields: "How the place had changed. One could see for miles in every direction. When we had first taken up our blocks there was no such thing as a 'skyline' — just the nearer dark green bush" (p. 33). The eradication of the "dark green bush" and its obdurate opacity is paralleled in these stories with a painful disillusionment, as if the stripping away of ambitions needed to be written violently into the found environment.

4. Denizens of the Bush

Whilst clearing was the moment of ecological annihilation, it should not be thought that the early farmers were insensible to the richness that existed in the wheatbelt bushland. Indeed their actions brought them into close proximity with the natural environment, which re-mained in fringing vestiges on land unsuitable for cropping or set aside for road reserves or other purposes. J.K. Ewers was a seminal figure in Western Australian writing, the inaugural president of the W.A. branch of the Fellowship of Australian Writers (FAW) and the subject of a minor sensation with his politically radical novel *Money Street* (1933), which painted a class-riven Perth in the early years of the Depression. Ewers worked as a school-teacher in the south-eastern wheatbelt near the town of Tammin between 1924 and 1926. An ambitious and observant young man, he cherished a desire to make a life as a writer and had already begun contributing poems, stories, and articles to newspapers and magazines, including 'The Wheat Men' published in the *Bulletin* in 1927. During this time the young Ewers pursued an amateur interest in the study of nature. He would send his work to the *West Australian* newspaper, which published a column called 'Denizens of the Bush'. The author of this column was James Pollard, who wrote under the pen name 'Mopoke' and often included observations by Ewers about birds and insects in the Tammin district (Ewers 1983: 102). Pollard, then living in Bruce Rock, not too far from Tammin, became a close friend of Ewers and would also become involved in the establishment of the FAW.

This popular genre of 'nature studies' had its origins in nineteenth-century natural history and linked amateur fieldwork with the discourses of classificatory science. Whilst distinct, it shared with what we now call ecology a heightened concern with the intricacy of natural processes. One gets a strong sense of this in Ewers' autobiography *Long Enough for a Joke* (1983), where his wheatbelt recollections are punctuated by vivid ornithological and entomological descriptions. These intimately evoked vignettes of birds and insects tap into Ewers' own experience as a young and lonely teacher in South Tammin. Ewers also corresponded with noted lepidopterist George Lyell, through whom he was able to obtain "killing bottles, setting boards, rustless entomological pins, an insect case and even a butterfly net" (Ewers 1983: 103). From his exploits Ewers sent many specimens to Lyell in Victoria. Beneath the polite good cheer of Ewers' memoir a poignant picture emerges of him as a kind of Nabokov of the wheatbelt, moving restlessly between catching butterflies and catching words adequate to his experience, sending butterflies to Lyell and poems to the *Bulletin*, the one evoking the fragile complexity of the found environment, the other invoking, as erotic object, the feminised singularity of the cultivated environment that was replacing it.

James Pollard's novels — *The Bushland Man* (1926), *Rose of the Bushlands* (1927), and *Bushland Vagabonds* (1928) — were set in or close to the wheatbelt, and are a sustained example of how the ecological awareness that was incipient in the discourse of natural history was incorporated at an imaginative level to help constitute the colonisation of the wheatbelt as a psychically viable enterprise. *The Bushland Man* is Peter Rodon, a ranger for the Western Stock Company. The novel is a fairly conventional romance with Rodon as its hero; he befriends Rene Neil, the daughter of a local family. Rodon's territory is the wooded country of the Darling Ranges which separate the undulating plateau of the wheatbelt from Perth and the coastal plain.[2] At various points in the novel one looks down from the Ranges on each of these vistas, for Pollard both dispiriting in their way, indicative of a monocultural tedium that the forested hills refute. In his spare time, Rodon, like Pollard and Ewers, devoted time to the study of 'bush life'. "I was always interested in natural history", he tells the avid Rene, "and roaming most of the west I have learned much about its bushland creatures" (Pollard 1926: 99). He tells her how he sends specimens to "scientists in the East". In his rough bush camp he keeps a small library of books on natural history and works by Kipling, Conrad, Ruskin, and Henry Kendall, whose bush poems most nearly answer his own sensibilities. Later, visiting his home in the Perth hills, Rene is shown a room lined like a museum with insects in cases and specimens in bottles. Like Ewers, he works for scientists who supply him with "collecting-boxes, killing-bottles, nets, cases, and other paraphernalia of the active entomologist" (p. 173).

The novel's rather thin plot concerns the theft of timber from Rodon's block and the developing romance between Rodon and Rene. The meeting of the two characters occasions a series of nature walks in which Rodon discourses on the plants, birds, and insects they find. Through this device Pollard details the ecology of the Range country and the remnant wheatbelt bush, reproducing in fictional form the columns he wrote for his newspaper readership. When the two are separated, the disquisition is continued by correspondence, Rodon signing each letter "Your Bushland Man".

> "I captured an interesting fellow this morning," he wrote once, "one of the 'wanderers,' a fine big fellow with golden-feathered wings, the veins forming a mazy black pattern. It had brushy feet and a downy body, and the most inquisitive eyes you could wish a butterfly to possess." (p. 227)

Late in the novel Rodon reflects upon this practice of specimen hunting and is troubled by the contribution it might be making to the dwindling numbers of native species whose study they furthered. He tells Rene about the necessity of preserving areas of the state for Nature: "They are needed because so many of our animals are restricted in their homing instincts to certain localities" (p. 296). He also voices a concern for the fate of the jarrah forests, which Rene had thought were inexhaustible. In a move anticipating many novels and films later in the century, Rodon is both a naturalist and a natural man, uniting in one figure the scientific endeavour with its object.

5. Nature's Man

Whilst wheat farming was the cause of the destruction of most of the ecological fabric of south-western Australia, the venture was conceived as being one which brought the farmer into proximity and, indeed, sympathy with nature. To see how this worked one need only look at the novels of Pollard and Ewers. In *The Bushland Man*, the progression of the romance between Rodon and Rene is conveyed precisely in these terms, as the emergence through the encrusted layers of civility of a natural sympathy between the two, natural in the fullest sense that this word had in the 1920s. In the novels of both Pollard and Ewers there is a constant shifting through and around an idea of nature that traverses human bonds and biological regimes. Wheat-farming is framed as a practice that marries competing imperatives. At one point Rene quizzes Rodon about him taking up work in wheat farming, but he is reluctant, citing the drudgery and monotony of the tasks, suggesting by his remarks that there is something unnatural or demeaning to the fullness of manhood in the kind of servitude it required:

> "You're a strange man, Pete. Thousands of men are wheat-farming and leading happy lives."
> "Yes. I've only mentioned the unattractive side, and only as I see it. The life is hard, clean, and healthy — a man's life."
> "And a woman's," said Rene gently.
> "Yes," he agreed quietly, adding after a slight pause, "together." (p. 249)

This exchange, in which Rodon concedes some ground, highlights the position of wheat-farming as a compromise between natural manhood and domestic union, as if the battle between the sexes and within the desiring structure of humans might find its best fit in the variegated wheatbelt landscape of fields and forests.

In *Rose of the Bushlands* (1927), Pollard moves down from the Ranges and into the wheatbelt proper. Joseph O'Meare returned from the war in 1918 and purchased "four thousand acres of mixed country". The land offered Joseph a convalescence from his injuries in the war where he had been badly gassed and despite treatment a "nervous wreck". Rose, Joseph's niece, comes to live with him when her father died. She was herself born in the wheatbelt but had left to finish her schooling in Perth and then university in Melbourne. The main drama of the novel revolves around uniting the two strands in Rose's character, the first being her "natural" affinity with the country she was born in, and the second her education into the principles and values of refined metropolitan life. Whilst she has an intuitive grasp of the land, she is naïve in the practicalities of working it, and this naivety is also that of the implied reader of this 'bushland' romance, allowing the novel to operate as an education into the workings of the modern wheat farm of the period following the Great War.

Rose falls in love with one of the farmhands, Steve. The complication for the social dynamics of the novel is that he is an orphan, father unknown, and former ward of the state. Once again, the resolution of this social drama is keyed into the rapprochement between nature and civility that is the impetus behind the imaginative investment in wheat farming. Like all of Pollard's heroes Steve embodies this integration of orders at the level of character. Also, typically, it is the heroine who recognises and articulates this synthesis:

> [Rose] had thought of him that way as a bushman, as a man of the bush. Now she saw him in the same light as a man of the land. Somehow that gave him an added value. He was not merely a quiet, serene man of the backwoods, of the aloof bush-lands. He was a son of the soil. She glimpsed something of what has been written. She knew how the man had lived and grown, alone with the wild. She felt that destiny had led him to this place of his in the life of the land. He was Nature's man yet, and always would be, but in the service of Nature. (Pollard 1927: 171)

In this way the wheat farm and the wheat farmer enmesh wildness with submission. A metaphysical distinction is opened between the bush and the land only for wheat to be strung across as its bridge. The climax of the novel involves Joseph, delirious with illness, imploring Rose to marry Steve in spite of his earlier objections. He hears a voice tell him, "PRAY TO NATURE, MY SON!" and with his own death hovering, realises that Rose, "the child of the bushlands", belonged with Steve, a "man of Nature's".

The overarching pressure to sign this natural treaty is unsettled by one of the novel's principal subplots which involves the battle to protect the crop from rabbits. Rose is initially upset by the relentless need to kill these animals, but is led towards its necessity by Steve. At the time rabbits were controlled by baiting, trapping, fencing, shooting, and 'fumigating'. This latter practice involved plugging all the entries to a warren and feeding poisonous gas, usually carbon monoxide, in through a pipe. Specialised machinery was built for this purpose,

Figure 5 : 'Instant Death to the Rabbits' (Anderson 1999: 197)

but often, as in the novel, a pipe was simply attached to the exhaust of a car. Steve and Joseph then insert carbon soaked rags into the warren as a "finishing touch":

"The fumes of the burnt petrol and air are poisonous," her uncle explained, "so much so, in fact, that men sometimes succumb to them. You can imagine the effect on rabbits."
Rose nodded, her face clearing. (p. 68)

No explicit link is made, but the fumigation of the rabbits by Joseph strongly echoes his own gassing on a different western front, one that in many ways persists as a determining emotional reality for all the characters of the novel. The permission for this truth to be uttered comes when Joseph falls ill, and the war which he had sought to escape by taking up wheat-farming re-intrudes with febrile lucidity:

"Twenty-eight hours of solid shelling, and men smashed to pieces all around me. [...] [T]hat blasted mule as it died wailed like a banshee. It was ripped clean through. [...] Gas! Gas-shells with the barrage, and the gas-alarms were all blown to glory — and a thousand demons were running loose in the night and lighting a thousand fires every minute! My God! Gas." (p. 286)

Here a second entanglement occurs between the ecological and the social, not this time at the level of romantic synthesis but in the spill of traumatic decompression. The repressed scene of war — no one in the novel ever mentions the war — is replayed in the obsessive gassing of endlessly encroaching rabbits. The phrase "a thousand fires" points obliquely to the repeated burnings needed to clear the land for farming, while even the duration of the bombardment, 28 hours, echoes literally the informal name of the wheat-belt's ring-neck parrot called 28s for the way their call resembles the sound of this number. In this way the novel imbricates the industrialised carnage of the trenches with the ecological violence that underwrote the settlement of the wheatbelt.

6. Men Against the Earth

In November of 1938, J.K. Ewers commenced writing a book he called 'Avea Lea', which drew on his experience in the wheatbelt a decade earlier. The manuscript ran to five hundred pages when it was completed during the war years. Failing to find a publisher at the time, he broke it in two and it appeared as *Men Against the Earth* (1946) and *For Heroes to Live In* (1948). Ewers had plans of extending the

Avea Lea novels into a tetralogy, writing a third volume with a grant from the Commonwealth Literary Fund. However, when his third volume failed to find a publisher, he abandoned this vision without writing a fourth volume. The first two volumes encompassed the period from the founding of the wheatbelt in the early 1900s to the onset of the Depression. The third volume took the story forward to the outbreak of World War II. Ewers would come to regard these novels as his most important work and hoped they would one day be republished in unified form under the title *The World of Avea Lea*, after the novel's heroine. The novel was ambitious in its conception and, more self-consciously than any other literary work, sought to tell the history of the wheatbelt. M.V. Peacock's *The Mildmays of the Wheatbelt* (1940) was a more modest account of life in the wheatbelt during the Depression years. For Peacock, the wheatbelt was an achieved locality, but Ewers wanted to historicise it through a generational saga. This was a human history but was also at some level an 'environmental' history. The word is not yet what it would become, but was beginning its semantic migration. The title *Men Against the Earth* was taken from M. Barnard Eldershaw's *My Australia* (1939) in a passage that neatly encapsulates the agonistic proto-environmentalism of the late 1930s: "Man against the soil, the soil against man, the adjustment of one rhythm of life to the other, the going on together, which is the only final victory" (Eldershaw 1939: 227). It was in the wheatbelt, writes Ewers, that he learned "the real rhythm of Australia", which was one based on a dry static summer and a wet frenetic winter, a theme that would subsequently form the basis of Barbara York Main's Thoreauvian natural history of the wheatbelt, *Between Wodjil and Tor* (1967). Interestingly these seasons, the inverse of European notions, were for Ewers "epitomised" by the wheat, which was in sympathy with the natural cycle by living in winter and dying in summer.

Men Against the Earth begins in the early 1900s at a time when there was great enthusiasm for the growth in world demand for wheat by "all the bread-eatin' countries of the world". The heroine's father, Tommy Lea, has taken up land back along the newly built rail line connecting Kalgoorlie to Perth, and is full of the optimism of the time: "I tell you, you'll be glad to grow wheat on any bit o' land where it'll grow. I'm startin' on sandplain this year. I scrub-rolled a hundred

acres in September" (Ewers 1946: 4). The novel depicts a stripped
back landscape in which wheat was a heroic venture, grown out of
masculine defiance, or indeed, echoing the early wheat songs, as
testament to a paradoxical and troubled masculine *fertility*. This is
constantly undermined by a countervailing and at times overbearing
sense of barrenness in the radically emptied country. Tommy's father,
visiting the farm from his own in the dairy country of the southwest, is
troubled by the extensive clearing: "They cut it all down and never
thought of planting anything else for shade or ornament" (p. 64).

Avea is presented, much as Rose in Pollard's novel, as a child of
the land, unspoiled by the city, which she doesn't visit until she is ten
years old. 'South Yorallin' is a fictionalised version of South Tammin,
where Ewers was posted as a school teacher in 1924. Ewers' own
experience is echoed in that of the school-teacher Ross Daniels
('Danny') with whom Avea falls in love. Growing into womanhood
she takes over more of the duties of running the farm, particularly
with the onset of the Great War and the departure of so many men.
Avea becomes the locus and spiritual guarantor of the dream of wheat:
"[S]he let her mind think it was just an even sea of wheat stretching
for miles and miles. And all hers! It was a good feeling. She would
like to own paddocks full of wheat" (p. 203). Whilst the wheat paddocks and their vicissitudes articulate an embattled fertility constantly
threatened with desiccation, the key courtship in the novel, between
Avea and Danny, is as in Pollard's novels refracted through the living
elements of the remnant bushland, whose patterns they observe. The
intimacy of their observation is the sign of their own growing intimacy.

The sequel *For Heroes to Live In* (1948) is more expansively pastoral than the first volume and through the character of Danny gives
expression to the implicit ideology of wheat, which is that it makes
men into men. The formerly bookish school-teacher Danny returns
from the First World War with a strong desire to escape the sedentary
work of teaching and mix his labour with the earth. He sheds his
boyish nick-name and becomes Ross:

> Ross felt he wanted to be part of this richness, sharing with others the experience
> of growing with the crops the earth grew, becoming part of it. Avea was like that.
> She was at home in this environment in a way he could never be until he, too,
> shared the life with them. He had lived on the earth. But now he wanted to live

with it and by it, drawing sustenance for both body and soul from it. (Ewers 1948: 15)

As it had for Joseph O'Meare, in Pollard's *Rose of the Bushlands*, the land planted with wheat takes on a redemptive role for the war-ravaged Ross. Racked by coughing fits from being gassed and with his faith in human nature in tatters, Ross seeks convalescence in the farming of wheat. In this he enacts the mission of the returned servicemen land-schemes of the post-war years. This appears to work for a while. The district prospered with more and more soldier settlers, and the wheatbelt grew ever eastward pushing out towards Southern Cross on the edge of the now depopulated goldfields. Wheat prices remained high and even climbed following the war, and the ensuing wealth saw the spread of mechanisation in both the home and on the fields.

The turning point in the novel, as it was for Goode's *Grower of Golden Grain*, is the onset of the Depression and the collapse of wheat prices. This causes a profound crisis in belief and drives many off the land, unable to cover the costs of growing wheat. The novel concludes with the death of Ross in what may either be an accident or a suicide. He is overcome by a feeling that the terrible suffering of the War had been for nothing. He hallucinates, somewhat in the manner of a photographic negative, the inverse of the ideology of wheat. Instead of the fields of grain representing the fulfilment of the world's need and hunger and the affirmation of male fertility, he sees the fields as a pitiless and mocking enemy, a literalisation of the 'no man's land' in which he had fought and suffered:

> The thought stung him to a sudden passion. The stubble and the standing wheat became transformed into all the things he had ever fought or wanted to fight against [...] row upon serried row of Germans advancing grey-green over no-man's land [...] ignorance and prejudice standing in the way of understanding [...] privilege and vested interests holding up the world, starving millions, crushing others in an attempt to safeguard themselves, reducing labour to a pittance, killing dreams, smashing ambitions, stifling hope. (p. 240)

Out of Ross's despair erupts the repressed counter-narrative to the heroic story of wheat. The story of wheat based itself on feeding the world, on giving bread to the hungry. In doing so it imagined itself outside the capitalist machinery that was disfiguring the lives of those in the city. Of course the reality of the wheat industry was that it was entirely enabled by the rise of global capitalism and its concomitant mechanisation. The collapse of prices in the Depression brought this home and punctured the sustaining mythology that had kept Ross afloat in the midst of the incomprehensible carnage of the trenches.

7. The Uncertain Sacrament

The dismal conclusion to Ewers' *For Heroes to Live In* encapsulates the extreme ambivalence that marks the literature of the wheatbelt. Where for Ross the wheat lands had once produced a visual and 'natural' affirmation of life beyond the city, they came to hold only recriminations. In other parts of the wheatbelt Ross hears that blocks are being lost to salinity: "The more they cleared, the more the salt came up" (p. 218). He questions why the government settled it at all. Against this Avea is positioned as a source of optimism and simple faith in the future of wheat, whilst retaining a critical position in relation to the urge toward mastery that had fuelled the clearing and farming of the wheatbelt.

> But they slashed the earth, they made it their servant, they set their seal upon it — a seal of straight fences, a lattice of straight roads. They disturbed nature's laws of life and made things grow in straight lines because it pleased them to do this, because it was economical to do this. (p. 169)

The "they" in this passage are "the humans", and Avea's place outside of this pronoun is the lingering hope of us all. What Pollard and Ewers sought was an integration of human and non-human interests through an idea of 'Nature' as both biotic richness and motive centre for human behaviour. They found this in the utopian hopes of wheat farming which they linked to a romantic repudiation of social codes. They also posited it in the figure of the farmer-naturalist of their fiction and personal practice. Cyril Goode was less convinced. In his story, 'A Matter of Morrels' — Morrel being the name of a tree and 'Morrel country' indicative of more marginal soil — the protagonist is an amateur naturalist who submitted articles about insects and birds he found on his property to city magazines. In the pessimistic universe of Goode's stories, this farmer's curiosity about the denizens in his bush is inflected with a bleak absurdity. He is eventually killed by a particularly resistant Morrel tree he has dynamited out of desperation. Lying paralysed beneath the tree but conscious, the protagonist is visited by a praying mantis, the very species he had first noticed on setting up camp on his newly marked out property, and the subject of one of his articles: "there was his strange little friend with its fists held up in the attitude of prayer" (Goode 1950: 54). It is a haunting moment in which the eco-system looks back at the scientific gaze that sought to hold it.

The ambivalence of wheatbelt literature is the debris from the collision between the instrumental imperative of wheat as an industry that exploits the earth and the redemptive mission of wheat as a sacramental bonding with the earth. The dream of wheat was to salvage the social structure of capitalism by returning consumption from its alienated status to its most basic level, that of eating. The wheat, ingested as bread, brings the alienating practices of modern capital back to the earth and into the body. It was also to redeem modern man in a vitalist program of physical outdoor labour and mixing work with soil. Ironically it was not the Great War that upset this dream, indeed it fuelled it, but rather the Depression. The collapse of wheat prices was much worse than a drought. To understand this is to realise that whilst the narrative of wheat sought to ground itself in the 'reality' of the soil, it was in actuality grounded in the reality of the market system. A drought was a rebuke from this first 'notional' reality of the earth; a below-cost price was a rebuke from the deeper reality of the market.

The implications of this are tantalising. One can perceive a shift in emphasis in the creative arts of the late 30s, seen for instance in the founding of nativist journals like the *Meanjin Papers* (1940-) and the *Jindyworobak Anthology* (1938-53) — Goode, Pollard, and Ewers would appear in each — whose purpose it was to promote poets who were "in sympathetic understanding of their environment" (Ingamells 1938: n.p.). The word *environment* itself is at this point moving beyond the mere denotation of surroundings to underscore relationships of connectedness and suggest a kind of rightness of being, capturing the aura held previously by 'Nature'. Similar patterns can be seen emerging in the novels of Eleanor Dark and M. Barnard Eldershaw, the poetry of Judith Wright, and the paintings of Russell Drysdale. It may well be that the cataclysmic intrusion of the unimaginable — that commodity prices could drop to nothing — into the imaginative fields of the 1930s psyche helped catalyse a fundamental reconfiguration of the relation to land and the environment, one in which collapse was possible, the intimation for the first time of the deep fragility of ecosystems. On this argument, the birth of an ecological consciousness is the sign transcoded into nature of the contingency in the material basis of our social existence. It lends historical weight to Frederic Jameson's observation that "it seems easier for us today to imagine the thoroughgoing deterioration of the earth than the breakdown of late capitalism" (Jameson 1994: xii). In basing itself in the globalising aspirations of early twentieth-century productive capitalism, the wheat industry, recorded in the literature of its participant-observers, opens itself up for re-reading in terms of the later globalisation of ecological awareness, uncertain of how the pixels will look in years to come.

Notes

[1] I am indebted to Jeremy Wallace at the Commonwealth Scientific and Industrial Research Organisation in Western Australia for fielding my enquiries so fully.
[2] For a consideration of the Darling Ranges in literary terms see Bruce Bennett, 'The Hills are Alive' (1991: 97-112).

Bibliography

Primary Sources

Dennis, C.J. 1913. 'Wheat' in *Backblock Ballads and Later Verses*. Sydney: Angus and Robertson: 52-54.
Eldershaw, M. Barnard. 1939. *My Australia*. London: Jarrolds.
Ewers, John K. 1948. *For Heroes to Live in*. Melbourne: Georgian House.
——. 1983. *Long Enough for a Joke: An Autobiography*. Fremantle, WA: Fremantle Arts Centre Press.
——. 1946. *Men Against the Earth*. Melbourne: Georgian House.
——. 1933. *Money Street: A Novel*. London: Hodder and Stoughton.
——. 1927. 'The Wheat Men' in *Bulletin* (14 July 1927): 6.
Facey, A.B. 1981. *A Fortunate Life*. Fremantle, WA: Fremantle Arts Centre Press.
Goode, Cyril E. 1944. *The Bridge Party at Boyanup and other Verses*. Melbourne: J. Roy Stevens.
——. 1932. *The Grower of Golden Grain and Other Inland Ballads*. Melbourne: Southland Press.
——. 1950. *Yarns of the Yilgarn*. Melbourne: Oldfort Publications.
Henderson, R.G. 1926. 'The Wheat' in *Bulletin* (14 October 1926): 7.

Ingamells, Rex. 1938. *The Jindyworobak Anthology*. Adelaide, SA: F.W. Preece.
Main, Barbara York. 1967. *Between Wodjil and Tor*. Perth and Brisbane: Landfall Press and Jacaranda Press.
Paterson, A.B. 1917. *Saltbush Bill, J.P., and Other Verses*. Sydney: Angus and Robertson.
——. 1914. 'Song of the Wheat' in *Lone Hand* 15(91): 403.
Peacock, M.V. 1940. *The Mildmays of the Wheatbelt*. Perth, WA: Patersons.
Pollard, James. 1926. *The Bushland Man*. London: Hodder and Stoughton.
——. 1928. *Bushland Vagabonds*. London: Hodder and Stoughton.
——. 1927. *Rose of the Bushlands*. London: Hodder and Stoughton.
Souter, C.H. 1926. 'Havestin'' in *Bulletin* (23 December 1926): 22.
——. 1926. 'W'eat-Cartin'!' in *Bulletin* (18 March 1926): 22.

Secondary Sources

Anderson, Laurie. 1999. *Windows on the Wheatbelt*. Bassendean, WA: Access Press.
Barr, Neil, and John Cary. 1992. *Greening a Brown Land: The Australian Search for Sustainable Land Use*. South Melbourne, Vic.: Macmillan Education Australia.
Bennett, Bruce. 1991. 'The Hills are Alive' in *An Australian Compass: Essays on Place and Direction in Australian Literature*. Fremantle, WA: Fremantle Arts Centre Press.
Gaynor, Andrea. 2002. 'Looking Forward, Looking Back: Towards an Environmental History of Salinity and Erosion in the Eastern Wheatbelt of Australia' in Gaynor, Andrea, Matthew Trinca and Anna Haebich (eds) *Country: Visions of Land and People in Western Australia*. Perth: Western Australia Museum: 105-24.
Gidgup, Ronald Senior. 2000. *Ngulak Ngarnk Nidga Boodja (Our Mother, This Land)* (Tjalaminu Mia, Project Manager). Perth, WA: The Centre for Indigenous History and the Arts.
Hunt, Lyall. 1988. *Yilgarn: Good Country for Hardy People: The Landscape and People of the Yilgarn Shire, Western Australia*. Southern Cross, WA: Yilgarn Shire in association with the Western Australian College of Advanced Education.
Ingamells, Rex. 1938. 'Editor's Note' in *Jindyworobak Anthology*. Adelaide: F.W. Preece: n.p.
Jameson, Frederic. 1994. *The Seeds of Time*. New York: Columbia University Press.
Meinig, D.W. 1962. *On the Margins of the Good Earth: The South Australian Wheat Frontier 1869-1884*. Chicago: Rand McNally for the Association of American Geographers.
Whitwell, Greg, and Diane Sydenham. 1991. *A Shared Harvest: the Australian Wheat Industry, 1939-1989*. South Melbourne, Vic.: Macmillan Education Australia.

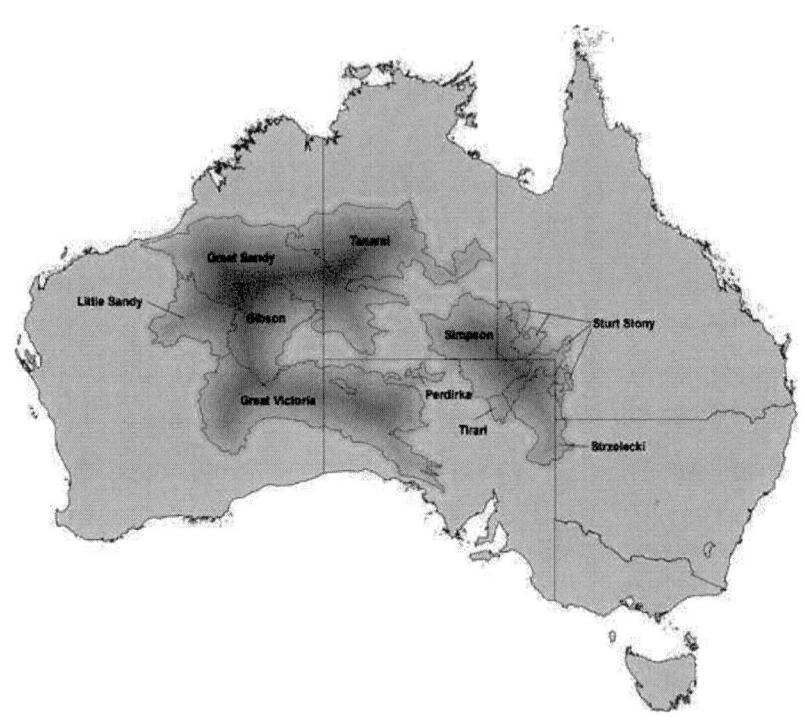

Figure 6: Australian Deserts

Literature in the Arid Zone

Tom Lynch

Abstract: This chapter surveys and assesses from an ecocentric perspective some representative literary portrayals of the Australian deserts. Generally, it contrasts works that portray the desert as an alien, hostile, and undifferentiated void with works that recognise and value the biological particularities of specific desert places. It explores the literature of three dominant cultural orientations to the deserts: pastoralism, mining, and traversal. It concludes with a consideration of several multi-voiced and/or multi-genred bioregionally informed works that suggest fruitful directions for more ecocentric literary approaches.

> [...] in European imaginations deserts =
> fear; in an Australian imagination it could
> be different.
> Susan Hawthorne (qtd. in Bartlett 1998:
> 119)

1. Desert Places

Australia is the world's driest inhabited continent, with regions defin-
able as deserts making up roughly 70% of the total landmass. Arid
Australia contains nine popularly recognised and distinct deserts: The
Nullarbor Plain, and the Great Victoria, Gibson, Great Sandy, Tanami,
Simpson, Sturt Stony, Tirari, and Strzelecki Deserts (Ellis 1998: 9-
15). However, in its 'Interim Biogeographic Regionalisation for
Australia', Environment Australia 2000 identifies roughly 30 distinct
bioregions within the arid zone (2000). Whichever divisions one
chooses to recognise, works of most interest from an ecocritical point
of view understand that deserts differ from one another in important
ways. Unfortunately, authors and scholars of desert writing have not
always found such distinctions important.

Much writing set in the deserts, especially fiction, portrays the desert as a more-or-less undifferentiated blankness, a threatening otherness that challenges all notions of normality. Gaile McGregor, for
instance, remarks that "In novel after novel, the aspect emphasised in
descriptions of the land, quite apart from any specific features that
might be invoked, is its alienness" (McGregor 1994: 13). Many descriptions of the Australian deserts continue to portray them in the
bleakest of terms. Numerous explanations can account for such a
phenomenon. Of particular interest to ecocritics, I think, because of its
wedding of language and landscape, is the lexical explanation formu-
lated by J.M. Arthur in which the English language itself is implicated
in the widespread Australian inability to see the deserts on their own
terms, and hence the subsequent disdain and fear that is frequently
expressed for desert places. As Arthur documents, the English language, which evolved on a small, wet, foggy island, is poorly suited
for rendering the landscapes of Australia, especially the large, dry,
clear landscapes of the desert (Arthur 2003: 26). When the English
language is used to describe Australia's landscapes, especially arid
landscapes, those lands will always seem to be flawed and deficient,
more notable for what is absent than for what is present. (Even the
word *desert* has this flaw.)

   In the discussion that follows I will focus on three particular orientations to the arid zone: pastoralism, mining, and the traversal. I
conclude with a consideration of several multi-voiced bioregional
projects.

2. Pastoralism

As they have done nearly everywhere they have gone, English-
speaking settlers to the Australian deserts introduced a pastoral culture
based on the herding of cattle and sheep. Quite a few novels exist
dealing with the transformation of wild desert landscapes into pastoral
settlements.[1] Because of the ambiguous legacy of pastoralism, its
undeniable drama and heroism mixed with its imperial heritage and
ecological destructiveness, the most astute novels evince ambiguity
and discontent about the pastoralising process. Olaf Ruhen's parable
of pastoralism, *Naked under Capricorn* (1957), is an especially rich
text in this regard. Most of the action takes place in the country of the

Eiluwarra people,[2] which (if we can assume this is a variant spelling of Iliaura or Alyawarre) allows us to locate the story in the Hart or Jervois Ranges northeast of Alice Springs, in the Tanami Desert and Burt Plain bioregions. The novel portrays the desert not as an undifferentiated void but as an ecologically rich area. In fact an important theme concerns the growing ability of the main character, Davis Marriner, to read and understand the landscape, and hence to sympathise with it and with its native inhabitants when the land is degraded as the tragedy of pastoralism unfolds. In this way Ruhen implies that ecological ignorance serves the imperial project as it enables one to ignore the degradation caused by one's endeavours.

By the end of *Naked under Capricorn*, Marriner has prospered, discarded his Aboriginal wife, and married a white woman from the coast who has brought her notions of domesticity and landscape aesthetics with her. Instead of his original shack, Marriner now lives in a "painted homestead, set in its burgeoning gardens". However this home, of which Marriner feels he ought to be proud, instead seems to him "unbelievably out of place" (Ruhen 1957: 191). "The house was a picture; its lawns green and forever cool from the sprinkled water, its boundaries marked with groves of flowering trees, its verandahs cool and restful" (p. 192). Rather than revelling in the triumph of his imperial project, however, Marriner perversely prefers "the scattered collection of native humpies" (p. 192).

A thriving genre of pastoral literature in the deserts is the station-wife or station-daughter memoir.[3] In works of this sort, the desert is portrayed as a decidedly ambiguous sort of home; indeed the desert is often not so much a home as it is what must be overcome in order to create a home. Myrtle Rose White published several accounts of life on the various stations that her husband, referred to always as 'the Boss', was hired to manage: *No Roads Go By* (1932), *Beyond the Western Rivers* (1955), and *From that day to This* (1961). These books are set in the Broken Hill Complex and the Simpson-Strzelecki Dunefields bioregions northwest of Broken Hill. While White attempts to make these various stations homey for the Boss, the properties do not belong to them, and their tenure there is in the control of others. White reveals great affection for these remote stations, but she does not remain on them. The desert is a place of sojourn, but

not a home. In White's work, people of the arid Outback are invaria-
bly friendly, resourceful folk always willing to help a neighbour, and
even a stranger, in trouble. For the most part, however, the desert itself
is portrayed as a bleak place judged almost entirely on the basis of its
suitability for pastoral success.

The American writer Wallace Stegner has famously argued that before Americans can live comfortably and responsibly in the American
West, they will need to "get over the color green" (Stegner 1992: 54).
As we have seen in Ruhen's *Naked under Capricorn*, a similar situation exists in Australia, where promoting the colour green in the desert
is part of the colonial process and is often perceived as a particularly
female response to the desert. Like the character of Marriner's wife in
Naked under Capricorn, White never gets over the colour green. She
has, she asserts, "a passionate love for green", and finds it difficult to
be "faced with unclothed red sandhills for months and years on end"
(White 1932: 87). In the process of 'beautifying' her homestead at
Noonameena she installs both vegetable and flower gardens, "two
large lawns", and a large variety of other imported shrubs and trees.
The first year these plantings prosper, but by the end of the third year
they have nearly all died and blown away (p. 70).

Another work in the station-wife genre is Marie Mahood's *Icing on
the Damper* (1995), which focuses mainly on her time at Mongrel
Downs in the Tanami Desert bioregion northwest of Alice Springs.
Like White's books, Mahood's is a tribute to her husband Joe, who is
portrayed throughout as the epitome of the competent Outback stockman, fully at home in the arid landscape. In contrast, Mahood, like
White, portrays herself as a willing but slightly unsettled resident of
the remote arid regions. For example, she describes her feelings during the family's move from Alice Springs to Mongrel Downs:

> Joe pointed out landmarks to us and it was easy to see that he was completely at
> home in that land of red sand, grey mulga scrub and huge anthills, where the hori-
> zon seemed to stretch to infinity. To me, its very vastness was awe-inspiring and a
> little frightening. (Mahood 1995: 78)

Joe Mahood is not only a competent Outback stockman but, contrary
to the stereotype of the ignorant Outback yokel, is also a talented
painter and an amateur naturalist. Because of these interests, he has a
keen eye for the aesthetics of the landscape, and he and his family

enjoy exploring the details of the natural world around them. After a spell of rain, Mahood writes,

> There were limitless carpets of wildflowers and such a variety of birds that the bird book was referred to almost daily. Joe always carried a framework for pressing plants in his vehicle and he discovered two Australian firsts, which had to be sent to Kew Gardens to be named, and three Territory firsts. [...] Nature was so prolific that each day brought a new magic to observe. (p. 99)

Rather than portraying the Tanami Desert as a barren wasteland, passages such as this show an evolving appreciation for its beauty and bounty. In general, Mahood does a much better job than White of getting over the colour green and assimilating to the aesthetics of the desert.

As time passes, the station-wife memoir is being replaced by a closely related genre, the station-daughter memoir. A number of recent books have appeared in this genre, in particular Kim Mahood's *Craft for a Dry Lake* (2000). Kim Mahood, the daughter of Marie and Joe, left the arid Outback for an urban life, becoming a successful artist who, at the book's beginning, is living in a coastal city. As both a native-born Outbacker and a university-educated artist, Mahood can triangulate her experiences in the desert from two very different perspectives. This parallax lends a depth of field to her perspective that few other writers can generate. *Craft for a Dry Lake* exhibits one of the most complex physical and psychological portrayals yet written of the arid zones of Australia. Mahood is very interested in the sensuous details of place and in recording how her body inhabits the places she encounters. In her narrative she's not just a recording eye, but an experiencing body engaged in a somatic and visceral relationship with the land. As she progresses on her journey from Queensland to the Northern Territory, approaching the Tanami Desert, she describes how the external world begins to interfuse with her body, producing a psycho-somatic integration of land, body, and mind:

> The colours begin to intensify, the light sharpens. I begin to feel something in my bones and nerves and viscera. I would not describe it as an emotion. It is more like a chemical reaction, as if a certain light and temperature and dryness triggers a series of physical and nervous realignments. I stop the car, get out and walk a little distance away from the road. My pulse rate is up, everything takes on a hallucinatory clarity. I sit first, breathing deeply, then stretch full length, inhaling

the smell of dry grass and earth, feeling the texture of grains of dirt along my bare arms. It is almost too much, this sense of belonging, of coming home. (Mahood 2000: 35)

Mahood works to break down the self/other distinction that has served to foster the sense of the desert as an alien place.

3. Mining

Gold and other mineral rushes in the Australian deserts brought hordes of miners, resulting in instant boom towns, most of which have now busted. Mining remains, however, an important source of livelihood. Nevertheless, mining is hard on the land, of necessity destructive, and the ethic of destruction for profit and the ethic of the gamble are interwoven in the culture that evolves from this enterprise.

The literature of mining and of the lure and lore of lost mines is strong and suggests a near-mystical symbolism in the link between industrial economies and nature perceived as exploitable resource. Probably the best known text in the literature of lost mines in the arid zone is Ion L. Idriess's *Lasseter's Last Ride* (1931). Lasseter perished while seeking to rediscover a rich reef of gold he had stumbled across years earlier in the Peterman Ranges of the Central Ranges bioregion. While focused on the details of Lasseter's search for the gold, and then on the search for the lost Lasseter, Idriess's book gives us occasional scenes portraying the ecology of the desert. For the most part, however, the book describes the desert as a forbidding space and its dryness as a formidable barrier. Lasseter's gold is hidden by little more than distance and aridity, yet it is effectively hidden nonetheless.

Numerous novels set in desert mining districts describe the desert and its residents in decidedly negative terms. In most cases the emphasis is on how the vast and hostile desert spaces serve to isolate the human community, which, combined with the inevitable greed associated with the search for mineral wealth, often results in a decline in morality, a combination Roslynn Haynes refers to as the Gothic Desert (Haynes 1998: 184-208). These elements can be seen in novels such as Kenneth Cook's *Wake in Fright* (1961), Randolph Stow's *Tourmaline* (1963), Thea Astley's *An Item from the Late News* (1982), and Janette Turner Hospital's *Oyster* (1996).

The impression one gets from much of this literature is that — to people of the coastal cities, who are the primary creators and consumers of this literature — the people of the arid inland are, like the desert itself, the wholly Other against which they can measure their own civility and sophistication. In order to generate their desired effect, these novels depend upon a non-ecological portrayal of the desert as vast, largely lifeless, and especially threatening. In this regard, Cook's *Wake in Fright* is typical. In the novel, a naïve Sydney school teacher, John Grant, has been teaching in Tiboonda, which is probably modelled on Tibooburra, along the ecotone of the Channel Country and the Simpson-Strzelecki Dunefields bioregions in the northwest corner of New South Wales. Looking about him in Tiboonda, Grant notes how the desert's aridity has sucked the life from both the landscape and the people. He observes that "there had been no rain for almost a year, the sun had withered every living thing except the salt-bush. The people had withered, their skins contracting and their eyes sinking as their stock became white bones" (Cook 1961: 6). Cook establishes a contrast between coastal Australia and the arid inland, illustrating how the inland is defined by its difference from the coast. This contrast is implicit in much literature about the desert, but Cook makes it explicit. He explains that the schoolteacher "was a coastal Australian, a native of the strip of continent lying between the Pacific Ocean and the Great Dividing Range, where Nature deposited the graces she so firmly withheld from the west" (p. 7). Summing up his descriptions, Cook tells us that Grant despises the desert, finding it "a variation of hell" (p. 7). Nothing in the novel ever suggests that Cook does not share the perspective of his character who, on his way home for the holidays, becomes trapped both by the desert's spaciousness and by its deceitful residents in the town of Bundunyabba, a fictional version of Broken Hill.

4. Traversal

While pastoralism and mining have brought numerous Settler Australians to the deserts, for the majority of people the primary orientation to the deserts, and the basis for much of the literature, is the traversal. Travelling through the desert and subsequently returning to more settled regions along the coast to recount the tale is the dominant

desert narrative. From an ecocentric perspective the problem with so
many of these narratives is that the desert is usually configured more
as an obstacle to be conquered rather than as a worthwhile place in its
own right.

The first English speakers to venture into much of the Australian
arid zone, the nineteenth-century explorers, serve as a prototype for
later traversal experiences. These explorers — Charles Sturt (1795-
1869), John McDouall Stuart (1815-1866), Robert O'Hara Burke
(1821-1861), William Wills (1834-1861), Ludwig Leichhardt (1813-
1848?), Edward Eyre (1815-1901), Augustus Gregory (1819-1905),
and Ernest Giles (1835-1897) word — remain important icons in
Australian culture and have continued to influence the way people
think of the arid lands and their own place, or lack of place, in them.
The first half of the twentieth century saw many non-fiction works
describing travels, traversals, and travails in the deserts of Australia
engaged in by scientific exploring parties, journalists, or adventurers.
Writers in this tradition include David Carnegie, John Walter Gregory,
H. H. Finlayson, Ernestine Hill, Francis Ratcliffe, C.T. Madigan, and
George Farwell.

Drawing upon this tradition, but more conscious of the tourism potential of the deserts, is Arthur Groom's *I Saw a Strange Land* (1950).
The book recounts Groom's visits to the MacDonnell Ranges, Finke,
and Central Ranges bioregions in 1946 and 1947. Groom had been
active in the development of the National Parks movement in coastal
Queensland. He visited the deserts because he "wanted to see if Central Australia's scenery was grand enough, the climatic conditions
moderate enough, to warrant tourist development in any large degree"
(Groom 1950: 12).

Operating out of Hermannsburg, Groom spent several months
bush-walking, often alone, to what have now become the major tourist
destinations in the region, including Glen Helen and Ormiston Gorges,
Palm Valley, Kings Canyon (Watarrka), Ayers Rock (Uluru), and the
Olgas (Kata Tjuta). His purpose was to familiarise his audience with
this 'strange land' and thereby, paradoxically, to reduce their estrangement from it. Indeed he seeks to convert strangeness from a
liability into an asset; the land's strangeness is the source of its appeal
to the tourists he hopes will visit the area; its otherness is what makes
the land worth visiting and protecting, not despising.

While camping at Ellery Gap he notes a threat that becomes a re-
curring theme throughout his book and that reinforces for him the
conviction that the central deserts are in need of the sorts of protec-
tions afforded by a national park system. After describing the
splendour of the landscape, he laments that "The wild grandeur was
marred only by prominent white signwriting on the red rock:
'KATHNER-HOPE CAMP, NOVEMBER 1945'" (Groom 1950: 48).
Developing this theme further, he ends this chapter by recognising
the harm that road access has brought to Simpson's Gap: "The place
was beautiful; and from a bank of sand I saw not so much the grandeur of it all, but empty beer-bottles in shallow water fouled by stock,
empty tins, and a gallery of names painted in large white lettering on
the smooth red rock. A white ghost gum had been shot at. It was all
evidence of vandalism — following upon road access from Alice
Springs" (pp. 77-78). Groom recognises the harm tourism can bring
and in his book seeks to cultivate an appreciation for the aesthetics of
the desert that will foster an appropriate ethic of care among his fellow
travellers.

Among the best known works in the traversal tradition, especially
outside of Australia, is Robyn Davidson's *Tracks* (1980). In this book
Davidson documents her sometimes[4] solo camel trek from Alice
Springs 2,700 km to Hamelin Pool on the Indian Ocean. Christy Collis
has argued for the uniqueness of this text in which, she proposes,
Davidson has reconfigured the tradition of the desert explorer's traversal. In *Tracks*, Collis argues, "Davidson initiated a traversal not of
physical but of cultural space, of a landscape constructed in over 150
years of non-Aboriginal spatial discourse as empty, dead, passive,
useless, flat, blank, and vacant" (Collis 1998: 179). In contrast to this
tradition, Collis proposes, *Tracks* "produces a desert space which is
inhabitable, active, alive, and part, rather than the ancient foe, of the
non-Aboriginal Australian subject" (p. 184).

I think in these claims Collis underestimates the degree to which at
least some of the previous post-settler Australians portrayed the desert
as inhabitable, active and alive, and overstates the degree to which
Davidson challenges the image of the desert as empty, dead, and
vacant. While many observers have certainly portrayed the desert as
so much empty space, there are some (such as Groom) who did not.[5]
Furthermore, though Davidson may have presented the desert as more

inhabitable than did some earlier writers, it was not, apparently, inhabitable by her, for she did not write about living in the desert, but, like the explorers and travellers before her, about crossing it. And at the conclusion of her trek, Davidson did not decide to inhabit the desert, to make it her home; in fact she moved to that most un-desert-like of places, England. The implicit message is that the desert remains a suitable place for an adventure, but not a suitable place for a home.

Overall, even if interestingly inflected through a nascent ecofeminist sensibility, *Tracks* remains more similar to than different from earlier desert narratives. Reflecting a feature common in the work of many desert travellers, the desert's main value for Davidson lies precisely in its difference from familiar places. For Davidson, entering the desert is about gaining release from conventional responsibilities. Indeed the motif of shedding burdens runs throughout the book. Shortly before she begins the trek, Davidson is accused by a friend of being a selfish "bourgeois individualist". Stung by the charge, she consoles herself with the reflection that when she begins her journey "it will all be over. No more loved ones to care about, no more ties, no more duties, no more people needing you to be one thing or another, no more conundrums, no more politics, just you and the desert, baby" (1980: 105). Ironically, this consolation does more to confirm than refute the charge that she is bound on a selfishly individualistic quest.

Nevertheless, while I see *Tracks* as more continuous with the tradition of earlier desert exploration narratives than does Collis, at least two features distinguish it. First, and this is no mean feat, it is better written than most works in this genre. Davidson narrates a compelling story in vivid language. I am also persuaded that, in its self-reflective subjectivity, the book may represent a tipping point in the evolution of desert narratives, opening up certain possibilities for reconfiguring the desert, especially but not exclusively by women, that were less available before its publication. In *Tracks* the struggle to complete the journey is as much overtly psychological as it is physical. Davidson's willingness to expose her emotional vulnerabilities is perhaps related to her gender. In *Craft for a Dry Lake*, Kim Mahood comments on her reaction to *Tracks* in a manner that underscores this factor:

> When I first read *Tracks* [...] my response to it was ambivalent. I found the whole thing too close for comfort. She articulated too clearly the complicated impulses and female messiness and fears I hated in myself. There she was, raw and visible,

a woman struggling as much with her own nature as with the practical and cultural obstacles involved in such a venture. (Mahood 2000: 231-32)

Especially notable in the exploration tradition for its intensive attention to a particular location is Roma Dulhunty's Lake Eyre trilogy: *The Spell of Lake Eyre* (1975), *When the Dead Heart Beats Lake Eyre Lives* (1979), and *The Rumbling Silence of Lake Eyre* (1986). Between 1972 and 1982, while accompanying her husband, geologist John Dulhunty, as he studied the hydrogeology of the lake, Dulhunty made extensive visits to Lake Eyre, the world's largest ephemeral lake, lying in the Stony Plains and Simpson-Strzelecki Dunefields bioregions. In her introduction to *The Spell of Lake Eyre* Dulhunty surveys the descriptions of the lake by earlier visitors. After summarising their various mostly negative reports, she replies:

> But what damning descriptions they all are! No mention of the joy of experiencing its salt-sea freshness out in the middle of the Dead Heart; nothing of its scientific wonder, its caprices and fitfulness. No word of the unbelievable mirages which parade over it in early black-frost mornings, or late afternoons in winter, casting their strange spells. (Dulhunty 1975: 7)

She continues in this vein for another half a page celebrating the beauty and wonder of Lake Eyre.

Unlike many writers who portray deserts as timeless or eternal, Dulhunty recognises that Lake Eyre is an ever-changing landscape. By returning to the same location over a long span of time, Dulhunty is able to observe the evolution of the landscape. Indeed she witnesses the bed of Lake Eyre change from a barren salt flat to an inland ocean teeming with bird life, and returning again to an empty salt flat. Dulhunty was not a professional writer, and her work suffers from the sorts of infelicities one might expect from an amateur author. Nevertheless, her Lake Eyre trilogy is one of the most sustained and intensive literary studies of a specific desert ecoregion, informed by both scientifically astute observations and a poetically imaginative eye; as such, it deserves more attention that it has so far received.

Non-fiction writers aren't the only authors addressing themes of desert traversals. Indeed such traversals have been a common subject for novelists. The most celebrated example, Patrick White's *Voss* (1957), tells the story of a desert explorer modelled loosely on the ill-fated Ludwig Leichhardt and his 1848 expedition intending to cross the interior from Moreton Bay (Brisbane) to Perth. Leichhardt's expedition vanished without a trace, a fact that certainly reinforced the notion of the arid interior as a foreboding place. White's novel is more an exploration into the psychology of such explorers than an inquiry into the characteristics of the desert country. Passages such as "the party entered the approaches to hell, with no sound but that of horses passing through a desert, and saltbush grating in the wind" (White 1957: 331) are psychologically evocative but hardly likely to overcome the prevailing antipathy to desert places.

Another novel involving a desert traversal is Dal Stivens's *A Horse of Air* (1970), a work that demonstrates some of the most ecologically astute fictional portrayals of the Australian deserts yet to appear. Both Stivens and his novel's main character, Harry Craddock, are amateur naturalists, and so the desert landscape is portrayed from the perspective of an ecologically informed and sympathetic sensibility. The novel involves Craddock's desire to find the elusive and possibly extinct night parrot. In search of the parrot, Craddock mounts an expedition into the Rawlinson Ranges of the Central Ranges bioregion and the adjacent Gibson Desert. What is most distinctive about Stivens's novel is that the deserts portrayed in it are extremely particularised and detailed. For example, the novel includes excerpts from the diary of one of the characters, Joanna, that include quite ecologically informed descriptions:

> The Rawlinsons — and other ranges — are giant sponges that trap the rains and feed them slowly to the rockpools and to the wide belts of bloodwoods (*Eucalyptus terminalis*) at their base. In some ravines they feed water to scattered clumps of tall river red gums (*E. camaldulensis*). Beyond the gums stretches the vast ocean of petrified combers, the sandhills, with their froth of spinifex, mulga (*Acacia aneura*), saltbush (*Atriplex nummularia*, mainly), mallees (*Eucalyptus* spp.), and scattered desert oaks (*Casuarina decaisneana*). (Stivens 1970: 112-13)

While I don't expect every novel set in the deserts to include the generic and specific Latin names for every plant mentioned, it is refreshing to read a novel that is so aware of the diversity and richness of plant life in arid lands.

Susan Hawthorne's novel *The Falling Woman* (1992) describes the journey of two lesbian lovers, Estella and Olga, through South Australia into the central deserts in a manner that provides an especially strong feminist portrayal of the deserts. Alison Bartlett argues that *The Falling Woman* "is particularly interested in the desert being a place in which a women's culture might be located" (2001: 119). The novel characterises the desert both in terms of the female body and in terms of the global history of women's culture. For example, at one point we read that "a bulbous rock" they encounter is "like the Venus of Willendorf" (Hawthorne 1992: 37).

As the novel progresses we can trace the women's course through Coober Pedy, Witjira National Park, and then to Kings Canyon, Uluru, and finally to Kata Tjuta, which the novel particularly identifies with the female body. "[T]he rocks", we're told, appeared "like an old woman with lumpy patches on her body, or like one of those ancient figurines that are all buttocks and breasts" (pp. 251-52). After arriving, the two women enter a V-shaped canyon which resembles a womb and which they identify as a place associated in Aboriginal culture with birthing. In general, *The Falling Woman* is more ecologically aware in its portrayal of the desert landscape than have been many previous novels. It is also alert to how the desert landscape changes as the two women travel through it; their desert is by no means an undifferentiated space.

One of the best-known recent works from the arid zone is Doris Pilkington-Nugi Garimara's *Follow the Rabbit-Proof Fence* (1996). This book also dramatises a traverse, but, since it is told from the perspective of Aboriginal girls whose home is in the desert, it reverses the usual valence of such traversals. The book tells the story of three 'half-caste' Mardudjara girls, Molly, Daisy, and Gracie, forcibly removed from their families by the government of Western Australia in 1931. The girls had been living in the desert at Jigalong, along the ecotone where the Great Sandy Desert, the Little Sandy Desert, and the Pilbara bioregions overlap. Taken to the Moore River Native Settlement near Perth, the girls find themselves in a landscape that, because of how wet it is, strikes them as alien. On the banks of the Moore River on a rainy day, we're told that

> The river and the flats on either side were full to overflowing. To the girls from the East Pilbara region, this chocolate-coloured river was a new and exciting spectacle, quite different from the normal pinky coloured salt lakes, creeks and rivers

back home. This sight only made Molly more aware that She was a stranger in this
part of the country [...]. (Pilkington 1996: 68)

This description configures the usually dry water courses of the arid
zone as normal. It is the well-watered landscape that is alien. In this
way, the book inverts the usual pattern of desert traversals, for it is the
arid inland that is the familiar and desirable home and the wetter coast
that seems alien.

Beginning in this unfamiliar country, the girls escape from the settlement and journey more than 1,000 km to their homeland. Along the
way, they pass through a diversity of increasingly arid landscapes, the
Avon Wheatbelt, Yalgoo, Murchison, Gascoyne, and Little Sandy
Desert bioregions. Pilkington pays close attention to these transitions,
recognising that in each new bioregion the girls face different challenges in finding food and water, but also that each new bioregion
indicates their progress homeward.

They had left the landscape of red loam, mallee gums, acacia trees and green
fields and found themselves in a very different countryside; one of red soil, tall,
thick mulgas, gidgies and the beautiful, bright green kurrajong trees that stood out
against the grey-green colours of the other vegetation. (p. 106)

Finally, they recognise their approach to their homeland in the new
colours and different vegetation of the landscape. We're told how they
"took in the familiar landscape of the red earth, the dry spinifex grass
and grey-green mulga trees. There was nothing to compare with the
beauty of these plains that stretched in all directions" (p. 123). Pilkington's recognition of the changing ecology of the land serves not
simply as a demonstration of botanical knowledge but is also fully
integrated into the drama of the narrative.

Another recent book that recounts a traversal through the desert by
a non-white woman is Eva Sallis's novel *Hiam* (1998). In this case,
the woman is not from an Aboriginal culture that is at home in the
desert, but a recent Arab immigrant who flees a domestic tragedy by
driving impulsively north from Adelaide towards Darwin. Alison
Bartlett proposes that *Hiam* presents a new way of seeing the deserts
(Bartlett 2001: 120). However, though this novel presents us with a
new kind of protagonist, I do not find that it really presents us with a
new way of perceiving the desert. While there is much of interest in

Hiam, an ecocentric reading indicates that it repeats common images of the desert. For example, Bartlett proposes that "Hiam's journey into the desert is not a conventional one of discovery; she is wanting to escape, she seeks self-annihilation. Her desire is the exact opposite to the traditional explorer narratives" (p. 120). This strikes me as a difficult argument to sustain, as clearly works such as *Voss* suggest that self-annihilation may well be strong motive in the explorer journeys. As David Tacey has suggested, "the real motivational force behind Voss and his explorers is the desire for death and disintegration" (Tacey 1995: 89). Bartlett argues that:

> It is Hiam's subjectivity as a Middle Eastern Muslim woman that determines [...] her spatial relations with the land, so that her description of "a pink lake. Monochromatically fairy-floss pink, with a small, iridescent centre", strikes me as an entirely new perspective in desert description. (2001: 120)

It is not clear to me why such a description need be predicated on Hiam's Muslim subjectivity, and, in any case, such descriptions are not new. In 1975, Dulhunty used quite similar language to describe the region around Lake Eyre, noting "the Dresden-china daintiness and fairy-palace beauty of salt-crystal formations glowing apricot in their centres; [and] the sunsets over the lake, flushed pink beneath the fiery beauty of an opal coloured sky" (Dulhunty 1975: 7). Rather than providing new perspectives modulated by her Muslim subjectivity, for the most part *Hiam* perpetuates the image of the desert as a void, a largely lifeless and undifferentiated place: "Red forever, seamless, shimmering, unlike anything she had ever imagined" (Sallis 1998: 37).

One might expect a writer with Sallis's background, a scholar of Arabic literature who has spent time in the deserts of Yemen, to have a more nuanced and sympathetic view of the desert, interestingly inflected by the perspective of the desert-adapted cultures of the Middle East; however, I found my expectations for such a new perspective disappointed. Whatever innovations *Hiam* contributes to Australian literature do not involve perceptions of the desert.

5. Polyvocal Bioregional Texts

I would now like to consider several recent works that I think do begin
to develop some new bioregionally informed perceptions of the desert:
Barry Hill's *The Rock: Travelling to Uluru* (1994); Pat Lowe and
Jimmy Pike's *Jilji: Life in the Great Sandy Desert* (1990); and the
painter Mandy Martin's various collaborative projects: *Inflows: The
Channel Country* (1996), *Tracts: Back o'Bourke* (1997), *Watersheds:
The Paroo to the Warrego* (1999), and *Strata: Deserts Past, Present
and Future* (2005). Though quite distinct, each of these works is
multi-voiced and/or multi-genred, incorporating voices of different,
sometimes complementary and sometimes conflicting, perspectives.
And they blend literary texts with the visual imagery of photographs
and paintings. Taken together, these works suggest the emergence of a
polyvocal bioregional tradition in desert literature and indicate fruitful
avenues for further development.

Barry Hill's *The Rock* provides a polyvocal cultural and natural
history of Uluru and its environs in the Central Ranges bioregion.
While the focus is on 'the Rock', as he calls it, Uluru is not isolated
from its cultural or natural context. Furthermore, in spite of Robyn
Davidson's hope that politics could be one of the burdens she sheds
when entering the desert, the messy contentions of politics are perva-
sive at Hill's Uluru. "Such politics", Hill says, "can't help but frame
any journey to the Rock today. It's a new kind of journey that requires
new ways of telling (and vice versa)" (1994: 2). The new way Hill
attempts to tell the story is by writing what he refers to as a "poetical
history", and to this end his text is highly intertextual, incorporating
numerous and conflicting stories about the land and its history.

In the first portion of his book, Hill analyses various writers who
have dealt with the Rock for their contribution to our understanding of
it. His book is both a journey to the Rock and a journey through the
literature and stories that have been produced about the Rock. Viewed
this way, Uluru and the desert around it are not so much vacant space
with a big rock plunked down in the middle, but a deeply storied
landscape. Some of these stories are tens of thousands of years old;
others are as recent as the latest tourist e-mail home. While Hill re-
spects and grants priority to the Anangu stories of Uluru, he does not

thereby denigrate the stories of all the others who have been to this place.

Hill is particularly interested in showing how Anangu knowledge and land-use practices relate to scientific understandings. While Anangu knowledge and beliefs are not entirely reconcilable with the scientific perspective, Hill seeks to show how these approaches complement and supplement one another. Throughout his book, Hill moves toward an integration of all the various sorts of desert dreamings — Aboriginal, settler, tourist, scientific — with his personal experience of country. His personal responses link the narrative, but the book shows how all these other perspectives inform and adumbrate his experiences.

Another work that utilises Aboriginal perspectives in its presentation of desert country is *Jilji: Life in the Great Sandy Desert*. This book includes text and photographs by Pat Lowe and paintings by the renowned Walmajarri artist Jimmy Pike. Lowe and Pike lived for several years on the northern edge of the Great Sandy Desert, and their book provides a detailed look at some aspects of the ecology of that bioregion as perceived by members of the local Walmajarri population. For example, at the beginning of the book, in a section titled 'The desert landscape', we have a painting by Pike followed by several photographs of similar terrain taken by Lowe. These images are then discussed in the text. Lowe first tells us that "Much of the Great Sandy Desert consists of Jilji — long rolling sandhills or ridges with flat country known as Parapara lying between them" (Lowe and Pike 1990: 1). Providing greater detail, she then explains how

> Here and there amongst the sandhills, a patch bare of growth called a Pilyurrpily-urr, stands out as a red landmark from a long way. Where the action of the wind has braided the crests, natural hollows occur as if scooped out of the sand. Such a hollow, smooth and without plant life, is called a Larralarra. A Kurrkuminti is a similar but deeper hollow, with grass and small shrubs growing in it. This kind of hollow provides good shelter from the wind, and was favoured by the desert people as a sleeping place during cold weather. (p. 3)

Furthermore, *Jilji* has one feature of a bioregional text that is lacking in every other work I've considered so far; it is a text involving local knowledge written primarily for a local audience. In the book's Preface, Lowe explains that because there are few resources concerning the desert available for use in the schools in the Kimberley, "it is primarily with such schools in mind that I have written this book" (n.p.). While the knowledge contained in the book is valuable, of even greater significance is the attitude to the desert that is evoked. The image of the desert in *Jilji* could not be further from the perception of it as a vacant, lifeless, hostile void. Subtle gradations in the landscape are identified and named, and nearly every feature discussed in the book is considered for its utility for human well being. *Jilji* is of humble literary ambitions, but works such as it will probably do more to make settler Australians feel at home in their arid continent than will many a literary work of much greater celebrity.

Finally, I'd like to consider a set of multi-genred and multi-voiced bioregionally based projects involving the collaborative work being done by the painter Mandy Martin in conjunction with a number of different writers. In *Tracts: Back o'Bourke, Watersheds: The Paroo to the Warrego, Inflows: The Channel Country*, and *Strata: Deserts Past, Present and Future*, Martin provides paintings while several writers — Paul Sinclair, Peter Haynes, Guy Fitzhardinge, Tom Griffiths, Libby Robin, Jake Gillen, and Mike Smith — bring their diverse perspectives to bear on understanding the various desert places under consideration. Additionally, *Strata* contains paintings by eight Ikuntji women artists living in the area as well as paintings Martin did in collaboration with Smith, Fitzhardinge, Gillen, and Robin. Each of these texts combines various sorts of environmental knowledge about a particular place with aesthetic visual interpretations of that place.

Tracts, Watersheds, and *Inflows* are all concerned with different regions in the arid country of southwestern Queensland and north-western New South Wales, areas located in the Mulga Lands, Channel Country, and Simpson-Strzelecki Dunefields bioregions. Each contains landscape paintings by Martin along with essays that address the ecological and social implications of the changing role of pastoralism in these landscapes. In his introduction to *Tracts*, Guy Fitzhardinge, a pastoralist and rangeland specialist, explains that "the Project seeks to provide a 'feeling' for the region and its ecology through the examination of a sample range of landscapes and seasonal conditions" (Martin and Sinclair 1997: 5). In *Watersheds* Fitzhardinge explains that many of the towns in the region are being abandoned as the pastoral enterprise fails. In response, he laments, proposals have been made "to use the west as a dump for nuclear waste, and imaginative policy makers can see it as a new industry for the west!" (Martin, Fitzhardinge and Griffiths 1999: 9).[6] Such a proposal reflects the still widely held image that these arid regions are worthless tracts of empty space, an image, unfortunately, that has been furthered by some of the literary texts I have considered earlier. Part of the mission of these projects is to envision positive alternative futures for the pastoralists and others living in this country, a future that, though still nascent and unclear, involves respect for the land rather than its use as a dumping ground for toxic materials.

Strata concerns a different location than the previous three texts. It focuses on Puritjarra, a rock shelter in the Cleland Hills of the Central Ranges bioregion near the western edge of the Northern Territory. Archaeologist Mike Smith's researches have discovered that the site has been periodically occupied for at least 35,000 years. In the book's Introduction, Martin, Robin, and Smith explain that

> This book is about diverse kinds of knowledge and ways of knowing place. [...] In this interdisciplinary project, we explore several knowledge systems, Indigenous, scientific and artistic — and by locating them in a common place we seek *co-understanding*, for valuing the different ways each of us sees a single place that is significant, but differently so, for each perspective. (Martin, Robin and Smith 2005: 1)

To foster this end, *Strata* broadens the range of visual representations. As in the previous texts, Martin contributes her own paintings, but she also collaborated on paintings with each of the writers of the text: archaeologist Mike Smith, environmental historian Libby Robin, pastoralist Guy Fitzhardinge, and plant ecologist Jake Gillen. Further broadening the aesthetic range, the project includes paintings by Aboriginal artists connected with the area: Narputta Nangala Jugadai, Daisy Napaltjarri Jugadai, Molly Napaltjarri Jugadai, Anmanari Napanangka Nolan, Eunice Napanangka Jack, Colleen Napanangka Kantawarra, Alice Nampitjinpa, and Linda Ngitjanka Naparulla. These paintings portray the features of the country that are of most significance to the local indigenous community, showing it as an ecologically rich and aesthetically pleasing homeland.

Projects such as *Strata* and *Jilji* that include Aboriginal paintings suggest we may be thinking of 'literature' and 'narrative' in too lim-

ited of ways. These paintings often embody story and depict a narra-
tivised landscape, and efforts that find ways to incorporate these sorts
of indigenous visual narratives into the larger vision of the desert
country will go a long way towards overcoming the still-too-pervasive
Anglo-centric bias that perceives desert country more in terms of
absence than of presence.

Notes

[1] Also known as 'stations' a term arising in 1815 originally "to describe an area inland
from the settlement at Port Jackson where government stock were grazed". Consult
the entry 'Station' in *The Oxford Companion to Australian Literature* (Wilde, Hooton
and Andrews 1994) for literary examples.
[2] Not to be confused with the Illawara people located in the area of Wollongong,
NSW.
[3] Perhaps the prototypical station-wife memoir is Mrs. Aeneas Gunn's 1908 *We of the
Never-Never*. It is set in 1902 in the Northern Territory on 'Elsey', a cattle station
where she (Jeannie) and her husband (the boss) lived for thirteen months. Predictably
for the time, Aboriginal portrayals are patronising, but Gunn's account of exploring
masculine territory, such as participating in cattle-musters, conveys a genuine affection for the Outback, the Never-Never.
[4] The publicity for the book calls the journey "a solo trek", but in fact less than half
the journey was solo.
[5] While the work of novelist Arthur Upfield (1890-1964) is largely unfashionable in
part to do with the portrayal of the central character a 'half-caste' detective, Upfield
populates the Outback with crime and mystery. He was the first foreign mystery
writer admitted to the Mystery Writers' Guild of America. Upfield's environmental
concerns can be found in *Gripped by Drought* (1932) and *Death of a Lake* (1954) both
novels are set in New South Wales.
[6] The first nuclear bomb was exploded in October 1952 over Monte Bello Islands off
the coast of Western Australia; followed by Emu Field and Maralinga (South Australia).

Bibliography

Primary Sources

Astley, Thea. 1982. *An Item from the Late News*. St Lucia, Qld.: University of Queensland Press.
Carnegie, David W. 1898. *Spinifex and Sand: A Narrative of Five Years' Pioneering
and Exploration in Western Australia*. London: Arthur Pearson.
Cook, Kenneth. 1961. *Wake in Fright*. New York: St Martin's.

Dulhunty, Roma. 1986. *The Rumbling Silence of Lake Eyre*. Seaforth, NSW: J.A. and R. Dulhunty.
——. 1975. *The Spell of Lake Eyre*. Kilmore, NSW: Lowden.
——. 1979. *When the Dead Heart Beats Lake Eyre Lives*. Kilmore, NSW: Lowden.
Davidson, Robyn. 1980. *Tracks*. New York: Vintage.
Ellis, Rex. 1998. *Outback by Camel*. Roseville, NSW: Kangaroo.
Farwell, George. 1950. *Land of Mirage*. Adelaide: Rigby.
Finlayson, H.H. 1935. *The Red Centre: Man and Beast in the Heart of Australia*. Sydney: Angus and Robertson.
Gregory, John Walter. 1906. *The Dead Heart of Australia: A Journey Around Lake Eyre in the Summer of 1901-1902, With Some Accounts of the Lake Eyre Basin and the Flowing Wells of Central Australia*. London: John Murray.
Groom, Arthur. 1950. *I Saw a Strange Land: Journeys in Central Australia*. Sydney: Angus and Robertson.
Gunn, Mrs. Aeneas. 1908. *We of the Never-Never*. London: Hutchinson.
Hawthorne, Susan. 1992. *The Falling Woman*. North Melbourne, Vic.: Spinifex.
Hill, Barry. 1994. *The Rock: Travelling to Uluru*. Sydney: Allen and Unwin.
Hill, Ernestine. 1937. *The Great Australian Loneliness*. Melbourne: Robertson and Mullens.
Hospital, Janette Turner. 1996. *Oyster*. Sydney: Random House.
Idriess, Ion L. 1931. *Lasseter's Last Ride*. Sydney: Angus and Robertson.
Lowe, Pat, and Jimmy Pike. 1990. *Jilji: Life in the Great Sandy Desert*. Broome, WA: Magabala.
Madigan, C.T. 1936. *Central Australia*. London: Oxford University Press.
——. 1946. *Crossing the Dead Heart*. Melbourne: Georgian House.
Mahood, Kim. 2000. *Craft for a Dry Lake*. Sydney: Anchor.
Mahood, Marie. 1995. *Icing on the Damper*. Rockhampton, Qld.: Central Queensland University Press.
Martin, Mandy, et al. 1996. *Inflows: The Channel Country*. Canberra: Goanna.
——, Guy Fitzhardinge and Tom Griffiths. 1999. *Watersheds: The Paroo to the Warrego*. Canberra: Goanna.
——, Libby Robin and Mike Smith. 2005. *Strata: Deserts Past, Present and Future*. Canberra: Goanna. Also available on line at: http://cres.anu.edu.au/strata/contents.html.
——, and Paul Sinclair. 1997. *Tracts: Back o'Bourke*. Canberra: Government Printer.
Pilkington, Doris (Nugi Garimara). 1996. *Follow the Rabbit-Proof Fence*. St Lucia, Qld.: University of Queensland Press.
Ratcliffe, Francis. 1938. *Flying Fox and Drifting Sand: The Adventures of a Biologist in Australia*. London: Chatto and Windus.
Ruhen, Olaf. 1957. *Naked Under Capricorn*. Philadelphia: Lippincott.
Sallis, Eva. 1998. *Hiam*. Sydney: Allen and Unwin.
Stivens, Dal. 1970. *A Horse of Air*. Sydney: Angus and Robertson.
Stow, Randolph. 1963. *Tourmaline*. London: Secker and Warburg.
White, Myrtle Rose. 1955. *Beyond the Western Rivers*. Adelaide: Rigby.
——. *From that Day to This*. 1961. Adelaide: Rigby.

——. *No Roads Go By*. 1932. Sydney: Angus and Robertson.
White, Patrick. 1957. *Voss*. New York: Viking.

Secondary Sources

Arthur, J.M. 2003. *The Default Country: A Lexical Cartography of Twentieth-Century Australia*. Sydney: University of New South Wales Press.
Bartlett, Alison. 2001. 'Desire in the Desert' in *Antipodes* 15(2): 119-23.
——. 1998. *Jamming the Machinery: Contemporary Australian Women's Writing*. Toowomba, Qld.: Association for the Study of Australian Literature.
Collis, Christy. 1998. 'Exploring Tracks: Writing and Living Desert Space' in McDonnell, Jennifer, and Michael Deves (eds) *Land and Identity*. Adelaide: Hyde Park: 179-84.
Environment Australia 2000. 2000. 'Revision of the Interim Biogeographic Region-alisation of Australia (IBRA) and the Development of Version 5.1 — Summary Report'. Canberra: Department of Environment and Heritage. On line at http://www.deh.gov.au/parks/nrs/ibra/version5-1/summary-report/summary-report3.html (consulted 14.01.2006).
Haynes, Roslynn. 1998. *Seeking the Centre: The Australian Desert in Literature, Art and Film*. Cambridge: Cambridge University Press.
McGregor, Gaile. 1994. *EcCentric Visions: ReConstructing Australia*. Waterloo, Ont.: Wilfrid Laurier University Press.
Stegner, Wallace. 1992. 'Thoughts in a Dry Land' in *Where the Bluebird Sings to the Lemonade Springs: Living and Writing in the West*. New York: Random House: 45-56.
Tacey, David. 1995. *The Edge of the Sacred: Transformation in Australia*. North Blackburn, Vic.: HarperCollins.
Wilde, William H, Joy Hooton and Barry Andrews (eds). 1994. *The Oxford Companion to Australian Literature*. Melbourne: Oxford University Press.

The Green Thumb of Appropriation

Mitchell Rolls

Abstract: A growing body of literature proffers Aborigines and their cultures as the healing poultice for an ailing and dispirited West. Whereas Aboriginal cultures were denigrated during the phase of territorial dispossession and were used as evidence in pejorative portrayals of Aborigines up until at the least the 1950s, they are now championed as a hitherto unrecognised fertile field that contains riches both needed and desired by Western cultures. In this body of appropriative literature Aboriginal cultures are moulded so as to fit whatever needs they are being asked to serve. Environmental concerns of one sort or another are common to much of this interest, including the interest shown in Aborigines by that which can be clustered under the New Age rubric. In this chapter I discuss two such texts, revealing the ways in which Aboriginal people and cultures are distorted so as to shape them according to the author's needs and desires. I conclude by discussing why it is that posing Aborigines as consummate environmentalists misrepresents Aboriginal cosmologies and ways of relating to country.

1. Introduction[1]

The harnessing of an Other to varied external agenda is commonplace, and the practice has long drawn criticism. Frequently this imagined Other stands in opposition to the perceived flaws of Western cultures and societies. Yet as Edward Said (1978: 2) argued in *Orientalism*, constructions of the Other transcend the "merely imaginative". Through their expression in a mode of discourse that is both incorporated by and disseminated from major social and cultural institutions, they gain material purchase (p. 2, and *passim*). Imbricated with the construction of the Other (and in some ways inseparable from it) is the search for the primitive. And this search too has long drawn criticism. Writing in 1973, the anthropologist Edmund Carpenter noted:

> This search for the primitive is surely one of the most remarkable features of our age. It's as if we feared we had carried too far our experiment in rationalism, but wouldn't admit it & so we called forth other cultures in exotic & disguised forms to administer all those experiences suppressed among us. But those we have summoned are generally ill-suited by tradition & temperament to play the role of alter ego for us. So we recast them accordingly, costuming them in the missing parts of our psyches & expecting them to satisfy our secret needs. (Carpenter 1973: 101-02)

More than three decades on, the anti-rationalist sentiment remains one of the principal factors driving the interest in primitivism. Indigenous peoples, the bearers of so many defining impositions, are with varying levels of adroitness and complicity re-imagined as the exemplars of a formerly denigrated but now celebrated primitivism. The assumption is that indigenous societies are by nature pre-logical, their lives ruled by the senses, the mythopoeic realm, and instinctual empathy with the cosmos. It is held that indigenous peoples have not yet learnt to separate themselves from the world in which they live and therefore remain at one with it, thus avoiding the sense of alienation and emptiness that many claim is bedevilling the modern Western self.

This concept of a people who are a passive extension of the natural realm and bearers of spiritualism unmarked by human agency is applied to Aborigines in an ever-growing body of literature. Not only does this literature emerge from divergent fields, it is provoked by divergent interests. These interests are sometimes made relevant to national, Western, or global concerns, and sometimes are overtly more selfish. Nevertheless, concerns common to much literature deploying imaginary Aboriginal cultures and their bearers as redemptive agents are environmental degradation, loss of habitat, loss of biodiversity, and much else within the range of familiar critiques of anthropogenic impact on the environment. That literature which can be loosely described as New Age is no exception. And it is to two such examples that I now turn. The first is more obviously constrained by its genre and would have few readers outside of that. The second, however, is less constrained but undeservedly so. Discussion of the two texts is followed by a consideration of the nature of the relationship between Aborigines and their environs and explanation as to how this relationship is often misunderstood. This has consequences for both Aborigines and the environment.

2. *Crystal Woman*

Lynn Andrews' *Crystal Woman: The Sisters of the Dreamtime* (1987) purports to be a response to an impending global environmental crisis and sensitivity to an ailing Earth. Andrews, who claims to be a shamaness apprenticed to a Native American from Canada, is an initiated member of the "Sisterhood of the Shields", a group of forty-four women representing different indigenous cultures. Their "purpose is to memorise and preserve the laws of magic and the various codes and traditions of shamanism from around the world" (Andrews 1987: xv). Assuming that all indigenous cultures possess within their ancestral lore a late twentieth-century Western environmental consciousness, and that all see the Earth as Mother, the group believe that their task is to return the world to a "state of wholeness" through the employment of the ancient knowledge they share. From Los Angeles, and the only non-indigenous initiate of the shield Sisterhood, Andrews gained entry because she has "walked the moccasin path as a shamaness in previous lifetimes", and because she is committed to recording the "ancient wisdom" as it pertains to contemporary needs (pp. xv-xvi). To a limited extent Andrews is attempting to present herself as a form of mythical Wild Woman. She is the warrioress in whom all the world's shamanistic traditions are coming to dwell. It is not surprising, therefore, that Andrews has been accused of appropriating and exploiting the cultural property of indigenous peoples, particularly Native Americans, the focus of much of her work.[2]

Crystal Woman is set in Australia, and Aborigines are the props for Andrews' adventure. The narrative supposedly tells of Andrews' journey to Australia to save nothing less than Aboriginal women's Dreamings and ceremonies from two evil male sorcerers who were attempting to destroy them (p. 6). She learnt of the Aborigines' plight whilst camped on the coast to the north of Santa Barbara with her Native American mentor for a morning medicine wheel and then an all-day prayer vigil that was dedicated to the iconic dolphin. The pair were rewarded with a visit from a dolphin school that appeared to perform a ritual for them. That evening, with her head resting on a eucalyptus tree, Andrews received a request for help from Aboriginal women in central Australia. The message had been relayed by dolphins through the tree. It is this that leads to Andrews' arrival at a secret location in central Australia and her participation in a women's ceremony that extends over many days. Through various rituals, ceremonies, magic, visions, crystals, terrifying ordeals, and periods away from the campsite surviving in the desert as a hunter/gatherer and being initiated as a "woman of High Degree", Andrews manages to restore the balance "between the men's and women's warrior clans" and release the women from the clutches of the evil male sorcerers. The survival of Aboriginal women's Dreamings and ceremonial life is thus ensured (p. 263), and by extension, a bulwark against Earth's further degradation is strengthened. Andrews positions herself not only as the white American woman saviour of helpless Aboriginal women but implicitly also as a successful crusader for the environment.

The theme of saviour is evident in her characterisation of two of the young women present at the central Australian campsite: the passive, feminine, attractive, happy, and slim Alice who warmly welcomes Andrews' presence is contrasted with the more chubby, brooding, and aloof Buzzie, who was "obviously threatened by a white" (p. 74). Buzzie, the only character in the novel to display a political consciousness, later tells Andrews that her taciturnity arises from her knowledge of the impact of colonisation upon her people and the resulting sadness she feels in her heart. Demonstrating a refusal to countenance the possibility that different cultures may not share a Western environmental consciousness as popularly understood, and that the way different cultures understand local environments might facilitate practices which would now be regarded as inimical to sound management of depleted ecosystems, Andrews rebuffs Buzzie by declaring that the "mamma earth is in great danger of dying" and that she has come to join the Dreamtime to assist the Earth's healing (p. 87). Thus the complex issues arising from colonisation and dispossession intimated by Buzzie are swept aside. The Aboriginal struggle is usurped by Andrews' concern for the environment. Her proclaimed attempt to 'preserve' Aboriginal women's Dreamings is not made in the interests of Aborigines but in the imagined and claimed potential service their cultural property has in halting feared global and catastrophic environmental devastation. Andrews demonstrates no awareness of how the Dreamings she claims to be preserving might facilitate the Earth's healing, or more to the point, how the Dreamings could possibly frustrate these ambitions. There is no real attempt to understand the relationship between Aborigines and their environs through anything other than an imposed variant of Western environmental sentimentality. This is typical of this genre of literature.[3]

Through the course of the novel Buzzie becomes an increasingly shadowy figure, and it is soon evident in the unravelling plot that the one young woman who dared voice criticism of whites and Andrews' attendance at Aboriginal women's ceremonies is the conduit for the dark forces threatening the spiritual if not actual lives of all Aboriginal women (see pp. 119, 157, 183). Consequentially then, Buzzie is further jeopardising the environmental health of the planet. When Andrews finally confronts the two warriors responsible for the forces endangering the women and removes from them the mystical agents producing their evil, Buzzie departs into the ether as the partner of one of the warriors and does not return (pp. 183-87). In this way her political consciousness, shown at first to be a malign force, is ultimately rendered futile. Thus we are left with Andrews, the shamaness and warrioress, initiated woman of high degree, Spirit Woman, and self-interested coloniser of Aboriginal cultural property, who through great risk to her own life (p. 226), emerges as both saviour of the Aboriginal women and, potentially, of Earth itself. The tacit message is that Aborigines cannot control on their own terms, nor exercise rights of exclusivity over, their cultural property, but must acquiesce to its use as a technology in the service of needs deemed greater than their own. Only on this basis will the dominant society allow Aboriginal cultures to flourish.

It would be possible to go through *Crystal Woman* on a point by point basis and challenge much Andrews claims she has experienced. The dedication to Guboo Ted Thomas for showing her Mumbulla Mountain, and the description of central Australian scenery suggest that she actually did visit Australia. The repeated references to following "deer" paths through the desert landscape speak of a visit of insufficient length to become familiar with the dominant fauna (see pp. 150, 184, 252). The lengthy descriptions of Aboriginal ceremonial and ritual life could have been taken from most anthropological texts, with Elkin's *Aboriginal Men of High Degree* (1977) a likely key source. Although stating that she has changed names and locales to protect privacy, Guboo Ted Thomas is named, and though from the

South Coast of New South Wales, he appears in visions giving advice peculiar to events allegedly being experienced in central Australia (p. 144). The use of the idiom "yea" in all Aboriginal dialogue at the end or in the middle of sentences as the sole signifier of Aboriginal English suggests unfamiliarity with this language and its speech patterns. Yet in the text she refers to writing down experiences as they happened (p. 65). One would think this would make the nuances of language easier to capture — something Andrews states she has attempted (p. xvii). The glossary reveals a lack of knowledge on a great deal more. "Alcheringa" is explained as "a teacher in the Dreamtime or a symbol" (it's not); "billy tea": "Australian tea made from herbs" (it's not); "corrsoborees", which I presume means corroborees: a "social dance" (they are not); "the Dreamtime": simply "sacred time" (it isn't); "Koori": "the Australian aborigine [sic] language" (it's not); "also refers to all borigines [sic]" (it doesn't); "kudaitja man": "a tribal executioner" (wrong) and so on (see pp. 267-69). These are not difficult terms for which to find meanings nor to explain. This lapse demonstrates further any lack of real interest in Aborigines and their cultures, except in so far as they can be deployed as imagined props supporting agendas other than their own.

Despite many indications that Andrews has imagined rather than experienced much of the account of her time spent with Aborigines, a prefatory page declares "This is a true story" (p. ix). As one of only two sentences on the page, it is positioned so that it cannot be missed by those who studiously avoid prefatory notes. Nor is there any indication suggestive of a reflexive post-modern irony. In the introduction Andrews explains how she intends spending her life learning and writing about the world's shamanistic practices, and that in order to do this one must become a shamaness. She then states that in the "Outback of Australia" Koori women taught her their ancient shamanistic traditions. In *Crystal Woman* she has "tried to write down faithfully the extraordinary events that took place" (pp. xvi-xvii). Thus it really is a "true story". However, perhaps partly in defence of any challenge to the text's veracity, Andrews hurriedly proffers the qualifying comment that what she has written about is not "traditional Koori training", but the initiatory experiences appropriate for a white apprentice. Then she discloses that it is actually "the story of a woman unravelling the mysteries of selfhood [...] a personal journey" (p.

xvii). This journey comes to the fore towards the novel's denouement when we learn of an unhappy childhood and of her failing the expectations of her parents (pp. 242-43). We also learn of several personal quirks that have always caused her problems, such as feeling responsible for others. These issues are worked through in an increasingly dominant sub-text to the story of her experiences valiantly saving Aboriginal women from the forces of destruction. The contradiction between solving the problem of feeling responsible for others whilst engaged in a struggle to successfully counter hostile forces threatening many others does not appear to be realised, but it does point to an issue of concern. Here is a book purporting to be a 'true story', but the 'truth' is in the mystical and hence unverifiable journey of Andrews' self-discovery, not in her actual experiences with Aborigines. The inclusion of Aboriginal cultural markers and the central Australian setting are to give the imagined personal journey of self-discovery through contemporary mysticism — if indeed this is what it is — the added appeal of the ancient and exotic Other.

Aborigines, mystically powerful but ultimately dependent upon the external agency of Andrews to free them from destructive forces, are turned into little more than fodder for fantasy and fiction, and a passive medium through which we (Westerners) can find ourselves. Typically the book concludes with the argument that for Aborigines to survive they must, under the guise of sharing, cede what little they have left — their cultural property. Andrews has a mystical Aboriginal figurehead whom she has just saved declare, "To survive, we must step forward and reach out to all the magicians around our mother earth. We must share our dream paintings and our hearts" (p. 264). The politics in this is subtle but the significance is clear. It expresses the theme underlying the entire narrative. Rather than arguing for equality so that Aborigines can themselves determine their future and protect against exploitation whatever aspects of their cultural heritage they desire, Andrews is declaring that in order for them to have a future they must subjugate their traditions to an emerging universal shamanism. Hence in a story that is ultimately about realising the self, Andrews is practising and advocating the effective colonisation of a last frontier — the intellectual property of the Other.

3. *Voices of the First Day*

Another text within the genre that purports to be a factual account of
traditional Aboriginal peoples and cultures is Robert Lawlor's *Voices
of the First Day: Awakening in the Aboriginal Dreamtime* (1991).[4]
This text is couched within scholarly pretence; hence much of its
fantasticalness would be less apparent to a general reader than Andrews' *Crystal Woman*, a novel whose appeal might be constrained to
fellow travellers and spiritual questers. *Voices of the First Day*, on the
other hand, adopts a more overtly ethnographic pose.[5]

Lawlor, an American, was hoping to become an artist. An injury
sustained when mixing toxic chemicals for a plastic sculptural work
led him to pursue other interests. His publications based on these
interests include books entitled *Earth Honoring: The New Male Sexuality* (1989) and *Sacred Geometry: Its Philosophy and Practice*
(1987). Unconsciously following what he calls his own "songlines",
he spent six years living with Dravidian villagers in southern India
before arriving in Australia in the late 1970s. When *Voices of the First
Day* (1991) was published, Lawlor was living on Flinders Island, a
small island in eastern Bass Strait. The back-cover blurb describes
him as an "artist, translator and international lecturer".

The front cover of *Voices* boasts an eye-catching photograph of an
Aboriginal bark painting from Arnhem Land. It is immediately recog-
nisable as being of the so-called traditional style. Inside, one finds the
extensive use of reproductions of Aboriginal art and motifs, illustrations of Aborigines in allegedly authentic but highly romanticised
tribal pose,[6] and depictions of sacred *Tjuringa*[7] and assorted traditional tools. These are supported by many photographs, mostly taken
from Baldwin Spencer's collection. They predominantly depict Aborigines performing various rituals and ceremonies, or some other
aspect of the hunter-gatherer lifestyle, such as making fire or spear
throwing. It is a handsome publication that promises accessible rather
than recondite anthropology. This notwithstanding, the use of end
notes and the inclusion of a bibliography lends the book an air of
scholarship and appears to authenticate the descriptions given of
Aboriginal life. Though designed to appeal to a popular audience, it is
a work that is asking to be taken seriously.

Closer reading, however, reveals that the book is not so much about Aborigines, but more typically about the crises held to be bedevilling Western cultures. In this respect it closely follows the pattern of the counter-culture's construction of Asia described by Diem and Lewis (1992: 57-58). Lawlor finds fault with his own culture, imagines principles and practices that would serve to counter such failings, and then projects these onto Aborigines before reclaiming them as evidence legitimating his own beliefs.

For Lawlor, the West is a monolithic, homogenous culture "engrossed in its own destruction" (p. 7). In contrast, Aborigines, representatives in this text of all that is good, are said to be the bearers of "archaic consciousness". This is likened to a germinating seed that first appeared in the 1960s through the spreading and deepening cracks in Western civilisation (pp. 6-8). Wanting to nurture this shoot, Lawlor puts his book forward as an "invitation to enter, as in a dream, a lost memory of our race as well as a fresh imagining of the earth's cycles of death and rebirth" (p. 8). This "memory" is contained in the Dreaming, which, because it embodies "the remembrance of the origin of life" (p. 14), is a rich storehouse that potentially holds the keys to our survival. In order to reveal these keys, Lawlor positions Aboriginal culture as the antithesis of all he finds wanting in the West. To this end he asserts that

> *Everything* in Aboriginal life — childrearing; food gathering, sharing, and cooking; marriage, infidelity, taboos, and the structure of family, clan, and tribe; burial practices; methods for dealing with crime — defines a world view utterly different from ours, yet urgently relevant to our need to transform the way we exist in the world. (p. 151, my emphasis)

Thus it is that, rather than resembling anything actually experienced by any Aboriginal group either in the past or the present, Lawlor's Aboriginal culture embodies his prescriptive remedies for an ailing West. Confirming this is his introductory qualification that he is not advocating a return to the hunter-gatherer life (a point which is not so evident throughout the text) nor making an emotional plea. He is merely hoping to rekindle imaginative ways through which to approach the human condition (p. 9). Hence the hunter-gatherers he creates can be shaped according to that vision rather than being given integrity unto themselves. In this way *Voices of the First Day* is an explicit example of the attempt to procure "a non-West which itself is a construction of the West" (Nandy 1983: xii).

Lawlor, like most who seek solace or some form of restorative function in elements of Aboriginal culture, argues that Aborigines lived (and live) harmoniously with the natural world. In this guise Aborigines emerge as conscious caretakers of their environment, not destructive exploiters. The emphasis is on presenting them as living in a non-interventionist spiritual affinity with nature. Through Aboriginal cultural mechanisms or belief systems, it is argued, the environmental crises facing Australia and more generally the Western world could be addressed. In this respect "the Aborigine" has usurped the position formerly occupied by Native Americans:

> Late in the 1960s the North American Indian acquired yet another stereotypic im-
> age in the popular mind: the erstwhile "savage," the "drunken" Indian, the
> "vanishing" Indian was conferred the title of the "ecological" (i.e., conservation-
> ist-minded) Indian. Propped up for everything that was environmentally sound,
> the Indian was introduced to the American public as the great high priest of the
> Ecology Cult. (Martin 1978: 157)

Integral to this construction of the Native American, or the Aborigines as their successor in this role, is how nature itself is perceived. Thorslev (1972: 284) reveals how the characteristics imposed upon the symbolic Wild Man in response to society's needs reflect these changing perceptions. When nature was regarded as a benevolent and moral force, it was peopled with the Noble Savage, but when a hostile presence, "red in tooth and claw", its children were threatening brutes (see also White 1972: 27). These constructions continue. For example, in the 1960s the environmental movement gathered both momentum and increasing support. Responding to nature's apparent degradation, the movement stressed nature's supposed redemptive qualities. The movement also needed an agent that could demonstrate harmonious non-exploitative coexistence between humankind and their environ-ment. The ideal of the Native American was employed for this task. As noted in 1970 by Rennard Strickland, "[t]he idea of ecology de-mands the ideal of the Indian" (qtd. in Martin 1978: 160).

However, as Native Americans increasingly expressed their weari-ness with being caricatured as ecology's 'high priests', the extensive period of Aboriginal occupancy in Australia came to be better understood. It was soon apparent to many of those seeking evidence of the possibility of living harmoniously with the environment that no better exemplars for the Ecological Being could or would be found. Here in Australia was 'the world's oldest culture' inhabiting 'the oldest land'. As Annette Hamilton (1990: 22) comments, "the litany of 'a culture over 40,000 years old' stands for the notion of sustainable continuity against the destruction of 200 years of white settlement". And to this image of Aborigines as primal environmentalists at one with the natural world, those seeking the antithetical Wild Man as cultural critic added the crucial element of agency. Aborigines were not unwitting, but knowing and deliberate conservationists.[8]

The portrayal of Aborigines as consciously determined 'Ecological Man', is adopted by Lawlor. He argues that "hunter-gatherers do not disfigure and exploit the natural environment" (p. 54). More specifically, when assessing the practices of food procurement, he claims that "in 100,000 to 150,000 years the Aborigines' impact on the fragile environment of Australia has been minimal" (p. 65; see also pp. 232-33, 237). In fact "no other culture has had such a gentle effect on the natural environment as that of the Aborigines" (p. 233). Whilst he does acknowledge that the practice of "fire-stick" farming has environmental consequences, rather than assessing this in terms of damage or the possible introduction of significant ecological change through promoting fire-resistant species as the dominant vegetation amongst other repercussions, the stress is on its beneficent promotion of existing flora. Fire encourages the growth of the "many edible plant species" that will not germinate without it (p. 311). That the prevalence of such species is almost certainly a marker of Aboriginal influence upon the 'fragile environment' is not considered (see Lewis 1982: 63; see also Pyne 1991: 71-150).

To support his claims Lawlor turns to Tasmanian Aborigines and imposes upon them the evidence he requires. Accepting that Palaeolithic societies may have caused environmental degradation in other parts of the world by employing fire as a tool (p. 86), he argues (incorrectly) that Tasmanian Aborigines not only did not make fire, they may have restricted its use to sacred purposes only due to foresight as to its ecological consequences (pp. 81, 86). He asserts that although 'fire-stick farming' was once practised it had ceased, and the inference is that the cessation occurred thousands of years before present (pp.

80-81). However, the factors indicating that Tasmanian Aborigines were still regularly firing tracts of country at the time of colonisation are many, and all of the sources that Lawlor has used as reference material document these (see Clark 1983: 19-20;[9] Ryan, 1996: 17, 21, 23, 24, 38, 73, 95; Flood 1983: 213-15; Roth 1899: 97-98). For instance, Lesueur, the artist aboard Baudin's expedition of 1803, sketched a family setting coastal grasses alight (see Lewis 1982: 60, figure 2). I refer to this particular example because Lawlor cites from the volume in which it appears a number of times; therefore, he is almost certainly aware of it.[10] Furthermore, Lyndall Ryan (1996: 17, 21, 23, 24, 38) makes no fewer than five references to the practice in her opening chapter, a chapter that we know Lawlor has read, for elsewhere he cites it as a source for other information; and Josephine Flood (1983: 213-14) summarises other research in detailing not only the fact that Aborigines continued to burn country at the time of colonisation, but that their employment of fire brought fundamental changes to Tasmania's vegetation in a number of areas. Hence from his own sources Lawlor must be aware that Tasmanian Aborigines had not ceased 'fire-stick farming' as he claims. As Edmund Carpenter (1973: 102) noted, those we summon to play "the role of alter ego for us" are generally ill suited to do so, "[s]o we recast them accordingly".

In order to press his point about Aboriginal environmental responsibility and sense of unity with all life forms, Lawlor steps into the realm of absurdity. The caption added to one of Spencer's photographs of an Aborigine in northern Australia killing a file snake reads: "The Aborigines live so in tune with nature that they utilise the most painless methods for killing their game" (p. 60).[11] The basis upon which such a claim is made is not given, perhaps for the obvious reason that its substantiation is impossible. For instance, how painless for an animal is spearing? do Aborigines only spear an animal if they can be certain that they will not cause it excessive pain? is a quick death of prey sought, if indeed it is, because of sensitivity to its suffering, or is it to avoid expending more energy in the potentially long and fruitless chase of a wounded animal? and so on. Furthermore, in contrast to Lawlor's unsubstantiated assertion, Roth (1968: 53), one of his sources, cites two accounts that found Aborigines insensitive to the distress of wounded animals and birds, and states that an end to their suffering was not sought. More contemporaneously, Lee Sackett

(1991: 238) found that men who were certainly capable of tracking animals did not do so if they ran or hopped off after being wounded. Barry Hill (1993: 8) gives an account of being on a kangaroo hunt with Aborigines using rifles where wounded animals were 'traditionally' clubbed to death, whereas if the interest was to quickly end their suffering they would have been shot. Mervyn Meggitt (1965: 15) reports observations of animals being deliberately subjected to painful procedures so as to ensure their utility. The women of southern Queensland who became dependent on camp dingoes would break their forelegs in order to prevent them from leaving. Although many reports exist of the affection Aborigines showed towards dingoes, this did not extend to alleviating their suffering if they were sick or injured, nor in intervening to prevent their prolonged death by starvation if disability for whatever reason left a dog unable to forage for itself or compete for camp scraps (Meggitt 1965: 16-17). One could go on listing similar examples almost endlessly. Is such behaviour the hallmark of a people 'so in tune with nature' that only the most painless methods of killing game are employed?[12]

More generally, the fashionable propensity to describe peoples such as Aborigines as living a utopian existence untroubled by many of the problems confronting the West not only hinders our understanding of these peoples and cultures, but also has the potential to work against their interests. As Fred Myers (1988: 264) asserts, "When we seek to show that [hunter-gatherers] are freer, less violent, more egalitarian, or less territorial than ourselves, we distort their reality, defining it largely in terms immediately meaningful to our own debates" (See also Torgovnick 1991: 8-9; Lovejoy and Boas 1965: 7). He goes on to say that "such constructions may also affect them politically". *Voices of the First Day* reads like a script written for the very purpose of illustrating the veracity of this argument. Lawlor first establishes the present as a condition where the Western world, perceived as monolithic and homogenised, is engendering the social, psychological, sexual, and ecological conditions that will inevitably lead to its own destruction. This theme, in one form or another, is the premise for his entire project. Even when not overtly stated, it is directly shaping the narrative. The various proposals to deal with some of these issues, as put forward by scientists, academics, and the green movement amongst others, are summarily dismissed as perpetuating the current crises. They are incapable of introducing the necessary structural changes, for their solutions are offered within the rationalist framework that is responsible for the problems identified (pp. 149-51, 386-87). What is needed instead is "a deep concurrent linguistic, neural, psychophysical, and spiritual transformation at the very core of our being" (pp. 386-87). Through *Voices* Lawlor wants to "open our minds" to the concepts that he believes can bring about this transformation and which allegedly offer humankind the greatest prospect of survival, together with emotional, spiritual, social and sexual security, and fulfilment. Aboriginal religions, spiritual beliefs, and assorted cultural practices are literally bent to this cause. He presents a utopian society in which the constituents live a ceaselessly exuberant and joyous life in a paradisiacal garden, where song and dance spontaneously erupt. Even the wildlife is drawn into this fairy-tale vision. "Unlike the aggressive predatorial placenta mammals that emerged in other parts of the world, marsupials are peaceful, nocturnal creatures, which do not prey on humans or any other species" (p. 280). This is the "world of the picnic", that lost but reclaimable imagined world that so beckons the primitivists (White 1972: 26, 27).[13]

It is in this Arcadian fantasy that Lawlor wants to imprison Aborigines. Whilst he makes empathetic noises about the impact of colonisation on Aboriginal cultures (p. 248), his support for land rights is not based on the recognition of past or present injustice, nor prior ownership, nor the necessity of restoring to Aborigines an economic base, nor even the profound symbolic significance of reinvesting land title with Aborigines, irrespective of how the land comes to be used. Rather, it is a necessary step in "preserving" a "way of life" that, like original seed stocks, may function as a warehouse of essential attributes necessary for the survival of humankind:

> It is important to recognise that the Aboriginal way of life retains the seed of human culture. It is of great importance to humanity to retain and protect this seed. The thwarted attempts by Aboriginal leaders and communities to obtain land rights over some of the uninhabited regions of Australia so that they can practice their traditional way of life is a significant issue for our entire civilisation. (p. 138; see also pp. 386-87)

Besides the fact that no Aborigines are calling for land so that they can resume a traditional life as envisaged by Lawlor — according to Lawlor this would necessitate a life without such things as housing, clothes, reading, writing, agriculture, or competitive games — this passage confirms that his "unwavering respect" (p. 11) for Aboriginal peoples is not based on the respect due to different cultures as valued by those supposedly within them. In other words, the cultures are not accorded respect for their significance unto themselves, but in their utility for the "deteriorated and purulent condition" of the West (p. 386). As is readily apparent, it is not contemporary Aboriginal cultures that Lawlor employs in this service. The fact that Aborigines have creatively incorporated new "ways of living" into a continuing and vibrant cultural heritage is not allowed for (see Kolig 1981: 1, 5-6, 177; Thomas 1994: 177). Instead, Lawlor implies that the enforced changes to the Aboriginal socioeconomic base expunges their ancestral lore and the needed restorative "perceptual modes" (pp. 386-87). Thus in order to save the planet and therefore themselves, Aborigines, who now experience a lifestyle that differs from the one they could have expected to lead prior to colonisation, must return to the illusory state that Lawlor has decreed represents their traditional existence. So the West can sup from the supposed origins of human culture as the need dictates, Aborigines are to be denied any opportunities other than ceaselessly replicating a fantasised rendering of their past in reserves set aside for this purpose (pp. 386-87).

It is not necessary to list the many factors that render Lawlor's proposal impossible. In addition to the primitivism in which he seeks to permanently imprison Aborigines is the problem that the people whom he wants to staff his remote centres of "seed culture" do not exist, nor have they ever. It is possible to demonstrate on an almost page-by-page basis that the Aboriginal culture Lawlor describes is nothing more than a phantasm. In the 391 pages of narrative in which he claims that respect for Aborigines guided his hand, this is all that is ever encountered. Lawlor may "shudder to think how this compassionate, humane, and dignified culture was ripped apart by the blind greed and punishing desperation of a colonialist convict mentality" (p. 248), but in reality it is his own culture that he is shuddering for. The peoples and the culture that he conjures in *Voices of the First Day* are the products of his disillusionment, fleshed out upon the distorted skeletons arbitrarily wrenched from anthropological publications. The Aborigines in Lawlor's text, and the culture they bear, have no actuality beyond the shaping force of his disillusionment.

4. *Messengers of the Gods*

Australian authors too approach Aborigines and their cultures with similar interests, needs, and desires as those aforementioned and in the work just discussed. Surprisingly, perhaps, proximity to Aboriginal cultures has not stemmed the tide of local publications exhorting the utility of imagined Aboriginal cultural contrivances in redintegrating a supposedly fractured and ailing West, nor to a more sensitive or better informed interest. An added incentive underlying the appropriative approach of settler Australians is the widely promulgated myth that they are alienated from the land they inhabit and hence are spiritually un-homed. In the appropriative body of local literature, Aboriginal cultures are described as containing the mechanisms that settler Australians could use to address these needs.[14]

Annette Hamilton (1990: 16) reminds us, "an image of the self implies at once an image of another, against which it can be distinguished". This applies equally to the image one has of one's culture. James Cowan is one local author (though he once stated he did not like being called an Australian author [see Rolfe 1995: 88], preferring to see himself as a citizen of the world) who finds in Aboriginal cultures oppositional values to those he identifies as belonging to his own.[15] His understanding of Western culture as a materialistic carapace bereft of a life-nurturing and nourishing spiritual underbelly creates an image that demands its contrary, and the space for it to fill. As this space is already enclosed by Western materialism, rationalism, and empiricism, Aborigines in Cowan's work fill the void as spiritual incarnations. They are religious beings, not economic ones (see Beckett 1988: 207).

In *Messengers of the Gods: Tribal Elders Reveal the Ancient Wisdom of the Earth*, Cowan (1993) gives voice to the above sentiments. Westerners, who have been "seduced by the sirens of the laboratory" (p. 2), find themselves "at a loss for answers to the problems confronting us in the area of economics, social justice, the environment, agriculture, disease, overpopulation, and pollution" (p. 1). Indigenous peoples, however, do not suffer the same problems for they live in a "balanced relationship with their regions, which in turn support them 'with a certain benign grace'" (p. 2). Whilst exploiting the environment for their survival, they compensate through "engaging in an unremitting dialogue with nature itself" (p. 2). It is the "earth-wisdom", a possession of "traditional people throughout the world, to which we must now turn if we are to treat what is clearly nature's ailing condition" (p. 3). Cowan proceeds to advise that he learnt that the substance of these "important truths" was contained in "the art of myth and story" (p. 94), the subject of *Messengers of the Gods*.

It should be clear from the above that Cowan's interest in Aborigines (and other indigenous peoples) is at least in part precipitated by an array of popular concerns — the environment, pollution, and so on — and the desire to construct a cultural foil so as to better reflect those concerns. The cosmologies of indigenes, as imagined by Cowan, are not therefore accorded respect on their own terms, but for their supposed utility in addressing the West's alleged failings and needs. More parochially, according to Cowan, immersion in the cosmologies of Aborigines would not only assist in the development of a more environmentally responsible ethic of living with the land, it would also assist settler Australians like Cowan overcome their supposed alienation from the land. This too he makes clear in *Messengers of the Gods*. Spending time with Aborigines in the Kimberley region in Australia's remote North West, Cowan was introduced to a number of significant Aboriginal sites and sacred caves. At one such overhang, Cowan's Kimberley experience was consummated in a spiritual epiphany:

> I had become part of the Dreaming, my ancestors those Sky Heroes who had made rivers, mountains, and deserts. The earth was in my bones, each fibula and rib a blend of its elements. For the first time I no longer felt like a [...] stranger in this land. (p. 197)

On a number of grounds this is a troubling claim. In 1993, Aboriginal land rights remained a contentious issue. Furthermore, Australia's High Court judgment of 3 June 1992 in Mabo and Others v. the State of Queensland determined that Aborigines held native title over their land as a result of their prior occupation of the Australian continent. The enabling legislation for this determination, the Native Title Bill, was introduced in the Federal Parliament in November 1993 amidst heated and acrimonious debate. Cowan's claim to have become part of the Dreaming and to belong to the land as Aborigines do renders vulnerable Aboriginal claims of a unique relationship to land, a rela-

tionship upon which their claims to native title and land rights partially rests.

5. The 'Ecological Aborigine'?

The popular portrayal of traditional Aborigines as the exemplars of an
environmental consciousness, as such a term is understood today and
as promulgated in Lawlor's *Voices of the First Day*, is beset with
problems.[16] Yet it is a portrayal that is often presented as if it is a truth
needing no substantiation. As Erich Kolig (1987: 119-20) notes, the
view that Aborigines "have a non-exploitative, purely spiritual relationship with the land, which makes them reluctant to extract the
land's natural wealth for material profit, or to allow others to do so" is
a stereotype widely held. As with most stereotypes, there is little of
substance behind it.

> The apparent harmonious and non-exploitative relationship that Aborigines en-
> joyed with their physical surrounds should not be simplistically read as evidence
> of their being conservation-minded, if what is meant by this is that they took de-
> liberate steps to conserve species and maintain the environment in a condition that
> did not in any way reflect the intervention of humankind. (Kolig 1987: 120)

As Kolig argues, "objectively seen, the concern of Aborigines in pre-
European times was certainly not to preserve the natural environment
for posterity to enjoy" (p. 120). Contrariwise, he gives evidence that
suggests Aborigines were indiscriminate harvesters of resources. They
were not concerned about depleting a resource through quantities
taken (see also Sackett 1991: 238; Strehlow 1947: 49-50). They were,
however, 'unintended' conservationists in that technological limitations guarded against over-exploitation (Kolig 1987: 121-22). Lesley
Head (1990: 452), who has conducted detailed research on historical
and contemporary land use and resource management in the East
Kimberley region, reached a similar conclusion. Technological and
population limitations, in conjunction with detailed local knowledge,
ensured what is now considered responsible resource management. It
was not a product of the application of practices specifically intended
to conserve resources as understood in European terms, which is the
understanding generally implied if not overtly stated. Furthermore,
Kolig (1987: 122) makes the significant point that Aboriginal belief

systems actually work against the development of a conservationist ethic. "Practical concern with conservation is simply superfluous in a view on nature predicated on man's ability to critically intervene and increase *ad libitum* the numbers of any diminished species". Tonkinson (1978: 31), one of Lawlor's key sources on how pre-contact tribal life was supposedly lived, also makes this very point. The group he studied did not practise protective measures or show much concern over issues of exploitation. Rather, they relied "on occasional small rites to ensure continued supplies of needed plant and animal foods". The relationship between Aborigines and the environment, therefore, whilst knowledgeable and profound, does not readily nor necessarily provide a blueprint for sound ecological management.

Furthermore, there appears to be a profound misunderstanding or ignorance as to how Aboriginal cosmologies actually accommodate (and accommodated) the surrounding environs. "Caring for" and 'looking after country' is how many Aborigines describe the relationship they have with their land. And many of those that do, particularly in central, northern and remote regions, believe they retain the knowledge that enables them to 'care for country' in a traditional way. This means, however, that rather than envisaging country as it was and attempting to 'care' for it in such a way that would promote an environment as free as possible of alien influences, country is accepted as it is. Partly this is because in vibrant and responsive oral cultures "the new [...] becomes over time that which always existed" (Birckhead 1992: 302). It is also partly to do with how country, and more specifically, ecology, is understood. Within the more traditionally-oriented Aboriginal cosmologies, changes to the environment are seamlessly incorporated into a broader culturally specific understanding of ecology. As a consequence, a range of issues that cause consternation and alarm to environmentalists cause no such perturbations to many Aborigines, and if they do so, it is for different reasons. In disregard of this fact, it is Western notions of conservation that we find underlying arguments deploying Aborigines as consummate environmentalists.

The discrepancy between the 'Aborigines are conservationists' claims — whether made by Aborigines or others — and more traditionally-oriented Aboriginal practices and cosmology can be readily illustrated. A case in point is a detailed report charting 'Attitudes and Perceptions amongst Aboriginal People of central Australia' to Land

Management (Rose 1995). It found, for example, that introduced feral animals are not perceived as constituting a problem by many Aboriginal groups. This includes those animals responsible for causing considerable change to ecosystems. Significantly, nor are these animals regarded as not belonging to country. Whereas it is recognised that feral animals might once have come from elsewhere, their status has changed to one of belonging. When groups in central Australia were asked about feral pests such as horses, camels, donkeys, rabbits and foxes, they pointed to the demonstrable fact that as "these animals were living on country [...] [and had] successfully survived and bred there", they too, like native flora and fauna, "belong to country" (Rose 1995: 109; see also Povinelli 1993: 128). In this way several animals widely regarded as pests have become integral to Aboriginal cosmology. Some central Australian groups maintain a pussy cat Dreaming.[17] The Pintupi, amongst others, consider cats to be food, not pests. Fusing Christian instruction — Jesus rode on a donkey — and Aboriginal beliefs, some groups have donkey Dreamings. Other desert groups maintain camel Dreamings. Similarly, in her *An Aboriginal Mother Tells of the Old and the New*, Labumore (Elsie Roughsey 1984) tells of the seamless inclusion of the pastoral industry into the ancestral legends of the Lardil (Mornington Island). She writes of witnessing the subjects of some of these legends, the Cave People, who in resplendent dress and with stockwhips and cattle dog were mustering their own herd of bullocks on horseback (Roughsey 1984: 134-35). The literalness of such observations, and the veracity of the legends themselves, is repeatedly attested to. In Central Arnhem Land there is a widespread belief that the buffalo is a manifestation of one of the most significant mythological beings of the region, the Rainbow Serpent (Bowman and Robinson 2002: 200; Altman 1982). Whilst settler-Australian conceptions of the buffalo have changed (and continue to do so) since the animal's introduction in the early nineteenth century, free-ranging buffalo are considered a feral population, and rigorous management and eradication practices are based on that conception (Bowman and Robinson 2002: 198-99).

Whilst many feral (amongst other introduced) animals do not have a Dreaming — nor for that matter do all native flora and fauna, a point consistently overlooked — this is not regarded as a reason why anything should be eliminated from country. In fact the presence of feral animals provides evidence of the productivity and therefore health of country. Eliminating them would be nonsensical and against good management practices. In fact, rather than killing feral animals, some feel that National Park rangers should instead be 'looking after' them (Rose 1995: 110, 114; see also Bowman and Robinson 2002: 202-03). As Bruce Rose (1995: 108) summarises in his report,

> The reasons for feral animal control programs are very unclear for many people. Most of the people spoken to do not feel that feral animals damage country or interfere with native animals. By far the majority of those spoken to do not see any reason to distinguish between feral animals and native animals in terms of the effect they have on the country.

Yet feral animals do have an effect on the country, but where this effect is apparent, other factors are privileged as causal. Significantly, in terms of environmental impact, there is no distinction between feral and native animals. The fouling of waterholes and cloven-hoofed damage to fragile topsoils leading to windblown erosion, dust storms and loss of fertility is more usually attributed to a lack of rain than to the impact of feral animals, who, like native flora and fauna, are now considered an integral part of a natural system (see Rose 1995: 111, 43-55).

Land degradation too is regarded as a natural occurrence, not something demanding of interventionist management practices bent on either stabilisation or rehabilitation. In fact the notion of degradation is not readily accepted. Instead, observed changes to the land and its ecology are naturalised. This does not mean the extent of change is unrecognised or misunderstood. To the contrary, the breadth and depth of environmental knowledge Aborigines have gained is well documented, and there is no doubt that they are acute observers of the environment in which they live and have lived (see for example Reid, Kerle and Morton 1993: 79-132). Change brought about by pest species and/or overgrazing is witnessed, but rather than blaming, say, overgrazing, factors such as too little rain are suggested, or that the traditional owners have been absent from country and hence not 'looking after' it. In this latter respect land "degradation is seen as the result of non-use rather than overuse" (Rose 1995: 47, 43-54; see also Burbidge in Low 2002: 56).

Furthermore, contrary to popular attributions, the practice of 'look-ing after' country in a traditional setting did not and does not privilege the conservationists' explicit objectives of conserving habitat and biodiversity. In fact the goals of these objectives are neither well understood nor accepted by many of the more traditionally-oriented Aboriginal groups. The practice of 'looking after' country is instead concerned with satisfying a range of other obligations and performing a number of pre-determined actions, all of which have variable conse-quences for the environment in terms of conservation. As Lesley Head (2000: 225) argues, "[f]or Aboriginal people [...] traditional land use is that undertaken with the appropriate social authorisations, according to law; the technology involved is a secondary issue, and the actual impacts that are the outcome are variable". Healthy country, therefore, is not country subordinated to the goal of maintaining habitats nor biodiversity, but one where, amongst a range of other practices, "hu-man stewards are undertaking appropriate actions such as burning and ceremonial activity" (D.B. Rose qtd. in Head 2000: 230; see also Rose 1996: 63-72). Irrespective of what is achieved by these activities, neither have as their primary objective the maintenance of biodiver-sity. Nor is biodiversity an accidental and consequential corollary of burning and ceremony. Nor for that matter, is preservation of habitat.

Thus the apparent harmonious and non-exploitative relationship that Aborigines enjoyed with their physical surrounds should not be simplistically read as evidence of their being conservation-minded. As discussed, Aboriginal cosmology mitigates against the argument and/or self-assertion that Aborigines are guided by an environmental consciousness as such a consciousness is popularly understood today. This is significant because many who champion an Aboriginal rela-tionship to country argue it is traditional knowledge and the fact that Aborigines 'care for country' that is responsible for Aborigines being conservationist-minded. Clearly this is wrong. Something other than, or in addition to, traditional knowledge is influencing these attribu-tions and self-assertions. Acculturated Western environmentalist idealism is re-hewn as innate, quintessential Aboriginal knowledge.

Unfortunately, the popular stereotype of Aborigines being exem-plars of an environmental consciousness, and the heartfelt expressions of Aborigines self-identifying with this peculiarly Western notion, is widely accepted. Despite the manifest inaccuracies, we see and hear in much discourse, popular and other, including the work of Lawlor's discussed here, the imputation that if only the Western world adopted the same attitude as Aborigines towards the land and its resources, an environmentally responsible lifestyle and (ultimately) political economy would result. Whilst Aboriginal apperceptions of the environment "may render perceptible something authentic in nature" (Rolston 1990: 70) which otherwise would have remained obscured, and there is no doubting their profound understanding of local environments built through age-old accretions of intimate observations and interactions, Aborigines are not natural conservationists in the way that term is popularly understood today. Theirs is not a life of harmony with nature and unity with all living things. There is an abundance of refuting evidence. As Lee Sackett (1991: 240) argues, "Aborigines can be painted as exemplars only through selectively accepting abetting evidence and opinions while studiously ignoring contrary data and judgments" (see also Anderson 1989). Ignoring this data in order to create a people as a tool through which to critique the West's record of ecological mismanagement, or as strategic or naïve oppositional self-affirmation, locks Aborigines into yet another construction of who they are or once were. The complex, differing, and changing ways of Aboriginal interaction with the environment are subjugated to an imposed and/or appropriated Eurocentric model of what conservation and responsible environmental management means. This is not to criticise those Aborigines who on the basis of introduced cognitive changes articulate an environmental consciousness however modified through the processes of adoption and adaptation. It is to argue that such a consciousness does not have its derivation in the cognition immanent to traditional cosmologies.

The inaccurate portrayal of Aborigines as conscious primal ecological beings not only operates to the detriment of Aborigines but also to the detriment of the environment. This is because the idea that Aborigines are eco-environmentalists ignores the structural causes — both within Aboriginal and settler-Australian society — of environmental change. The interrelationships between epistemologies, the practices they sanction and environmental effect — both directly and indirectly — are of significance. So too is an understanding of "the relationship between nature and society in the production of knowledge" (Gandy 1996: 31). Understanding these relationships is crucial to developing a comprehensive understanding of causality underlying foreseen and unforeseen, intended and unintended, environmental impacts (Gandy 1996: 36, and *passim*). An explication of these relationships might also reveal "the kind of nature we hope to make" (Demeritt 1994: 28) and provide a better framework for more informed and less ideologically driven negotiations towards that end. Obviously then, it is here, rather than in imagined Aboriginal cultures, societies, and identities, that something resembling conservationist management practices might be determined. Or at least practices that could possibly assist in constructing the sort of natures we desire.

Notes

[1] This chapter contains revised extracts of work first published in the *Journal of Australian Studies* and the *Feminist Law Journal*, which are reprinted here with the permission of the publishers: Rolls (2000; 2003).
[2] Andrews' work has been witheringly dismissed as "Barbie has a dream". Yet Web sites featuring readers' reviews of her work reveal similar sentiments to those expressed on sites reviewing Marlo Morgan's egregious *Mutant Message Down Under* (1994). Women especially respond enthusiastically to Andrews' "beautiful" and "spiritually uplifting message" of feminine renewal, power, and spirituality. See for example http://www.earthwisdom.com.wwwboard/dir/philo/messages/24.html (11 June 1997). In the narcissistic playground of the do-it-yourself Web-based *Pleiades Book Review* site, many readers aware of the controversy aroused by Morgan's (1994) text urge us not to be concerned but instead listen to the spiritually uplifting message of living in worshipful harmony with nature and the cosmos and knowing and trusting our inner selves. See http://www.pleiades-net.com/choice/books/MM.1.html (22 May 1997). See Rolls (2002) for a critique of Morgan's novel. See also Povinelli (1998: 9-16).
[3] See for example Morgan (1994); Lawlor (1991); Schaef (1995).
[4] See Rolls (2000) for a lengthy critique of this text.
[5] See Rolls (2002) for discussion of how texts such as these, including the egregious *Mutant Message Down Under* (Morgan 1994), are increasingly accepted as credible ethnographic accounts of Aboriginal cultures and people. Lawlor, for instance, is regarded as a credible author and commentator on Aborigines and their cultures (see also Rolls 2000: 211-12; Povinelli 1998: 11, 15-16).
[6] See for example p. 124, fig. 81; p. 157, fig. 91; p. 203, fig. 110; p. 204, fig. 111; p. 214, fig. 116; p. 218, fig. 118; p. 256, fig. 128; p. 304, fig. 155; p. 308, fig. 158.
[7] An Arrernte term for a sacred (usually) stone or wood incised object signifying many things. In some rituals they are used to represent ancestral beings from the Dreaming.

[8] See Griffiths (1996: 255-77) for an informative discussion of the differing perceptions of wilderness, the sometimes antagonistic struggle between those seeking to
preserve cultural and natural heritage, and how Aborigines are caught in this debate.
[9] Lawlor's bibliography gives 1986 as the year of publication for this book. I have not
been able to locate this edition. I am confident that in the complete absence of any
substantiated evidence that would have led Clark to change her account, the 1986
edition would contain no revisions that would support Lawlor's argument that the
Tasmanian Aborigines did not practice fire-stick farming at the time of colonisation.
[10] Not only do some of the papers in the collection edited by Williams and Hunn
(1982) refute Lawlor's general claims about Aborigines having no environmental
impact through their use of fire (see Lewis 1982), most of the information that he
attributes to articles in this publication is either not found in the cited sources or
considerably distorts the given data (see Lawlor's Chapter 17, pp. 307-11, end notes
15, 18, 19, 21, 22). Careless referencing makes some assertions difficult to check
against the attributed sources. For instance, the information attributed to Williams and
Hunn (1982: 91) is actually taken from pages 72-73 (see Lawlor 1991: 310, note 19).
Whilst in this specific instance most points are in accord with Lawlor's rendering of
them, he still introduces significant evidential changes without informing the reader
upon what basis he has done so.
[11] In *Mutant Message Down Under* Marlo Morgan (1994) makes a similarly silly
assertion. Morgan proclaims that wildlife Aborigines procured for food was killed
instantly so that it did not suffer, including a camel with the thrust of a single spear
(pp. 103, 120, 174).
[12] The notion that living 'in tune with nature' engenders sentimentalising fauna and
sensitivity to its suffering is common to most of the literature in which some form of
this phrase is propounded as something to aspire to. For example, Monica Furlong
(1996: 154-55) writes of her shock at witnessing young Aboriginal girls removing
budgerigar nestlings from their nest with no intention of returning them nor concern
for the nestlings' welfare. Furlong attributes the girls' behaviour to human failings.
She is unable to grasp that their behaviour is perhaps a manifestation of the very
qualities she was seeking to find in Aboriginal cultures. Furlong misunderstands the
full implications of her advocacy of the notion of oneness with all living things. See
Rolls (1998: 59-60, and *passim*) for analysis of this event and critique of Furlong's
text.
[13] This depiction demonstrates Lawlor's reliance upon out-dated constructs of Aborigines developed under the scientific paradigms he spurns. The fact that Aborigines
did not have to contend with fierce animals (nor compete with 'higher races') was a
popular Darwinian theory as to why their wits had supposedly remained dulled (see
Spencer 1914: 33).
[14] See for example, David Tacey's *Edge of the Sacred: Transformation in Australia*
(1995). For a critical response to Tacey's text see Rolls (1998b; 1999/2000).
[15] Cowan is a prolific author who has written many books on various aspects of
Aboriginal culture, including myth and art. His *Two Men Dreaming: A Memoir, a
Journey* (1995) is an autobiographical venture into Pintupi culture and the self. His

novel *A Mapmaker's Dream: The Meditations of Fra Mauro, Cartographer to the Court of Venice* (1996) won the Australian Literary Society Gold Medal in 1998. (See Rolls 2001 for a critique of Cowan's Aboriginal oeuvre.)
[16] See Rolls (2003) for a more extended critique of this portrayal.
[17] It was long thought that in Central and Northern Australia the feral cat might have pre-dated European settlement. This possibility, however, has recently been discounted. DNA testing shows that all feral cats in Australia have the same origin. They are all descended from British-introduced cats. The regional differences in coat colour are an example of rapid environmental adaptation. See Gary Steer and Alice Ford (Directors), 'Ten Million Wild Cats', Australian Broadcasting Corporation, Television, (Film Australia), Broadcast 24 October, 2002.

Bibliography

Primary Sources

Andrews, Lynn V. 1987. *Crystal Woman: The Sisters of the Dreamtime*. New York: Warner Books.
Cowan, James. 1993. *Messengers of the Gods: Tribal Elders Reveal the Ancient Wisdom of the Earth*. Milsons Point, NSW: Vintage.
Lawlor, Robert. 1989. *Earth Honoring: The New Male Sexuality*. Rochester, NY: Park Street Press.
——. 1987. *Sacred Geometry: Its Philosophy and Practice*. London: Thames and Hudson.
——. 1991. *Voices of the First Day: Awakening in the Aboriginal Dreamtime*. Rochester, NY: Inner Traditions.
Morgan, Marlo. 1994. *Mutant Message Down Under*. New York: HarperCollins.

Secondary Sources

Altman, J.C. 1982. 'Hunting Buffalo in North-Central Arnhem Land: A Case of Rapid Adaptation among Aborigines' in *Oceania* 52: 274-85.

Anderson, C. 1989. 'Aborigines and Conservationism: The Daintree-Bloomfield Road' in *Australian Journal of Social Issues* 24(3): 214-27.

Beckett, J. 1988. 'The Past in the Present; the Present in the Past: Constructing a National Aboriginality' in J.R. Beckett (ed.) *Past and Present: The Construction of Aboriginality*. Canberra: Aboriginal Studies Press.

Birckhead, Jim. 1992. '"Traditional Aboriginal Land Management Practices" at CSU—The Cultural Politics of a Curriculum Innovation' in Birckhead, Jim, Terry De Lacy, Laurajane Smith and Helen Brindley (eds.) *Aboriginal Involvement in Parks and Protected Areas: Papers Presented at a Conference Organised by the Johnstone Centre of Parks, Recreation and Heritage at Charles Sturt University, Albury, New South Wales, 22-24 July 1991*. Canberra: Aboriginal Studies Press: 297-306.

Bowman, D.M.J.S., and C.J. Robinson. 2002. 'The Getting of the Nganabbarru: Observations and Reflections on Aboriginal Buffalo Hunting in Northern Australia' in *Australian Geographer* 33(2): 191-206.

Carpenter, Edmund Snow. 1973. *Oh, What a Blow that Phantom Gave Me!* New York: Holt, Rinehart and Winston.

Clark, Julia. 1983. *The Aboriginal People of Tasmania*. Hobart: Tasmanian Museum and Art Gallery.

Demeritt, D. 1994. 'Ecology, Objectivity and Critique in Writings on Nature and Human Societies' in *Journal of Historical Geography* 20(1): 22-37.

Diem, A.G., and J.R. Lewis. 1992. 'Imagining India: The Influence of Hinduism on the New Age Movement' in Lewis, James R., and J. Gordon Melton (eds) *Perspectives on the New Age*. Albany: State University of New York Press: 48-58.

Elkin, A.P. 1977. *Aboriginal Men of High Degree*. New York: St Martin's Press.

Flood, Josephine. 1983. *Archaeology of the Dreamtime*. Sydney: William Collins.

Furlong, Monica. 1996. *Flight of the Kingfisher*. Hammersmith, London: Harper-Collins.

Gandy, M. 1996. 'Crumbling Land: The Postmodernity Debate and the Analysis of Environmental Problems' in *Progress in Human Geography* 20(1): 23-40.

Griffiths, Tom. 1996. *Hunters and Collectors: The Antiquarian Imagination in Australia*. Melbourne: Cambridge University Press.

Hamilton, Annette. 1990. 'Fear and Desire: Aborigines, Asians and the National Imaginary' in *Australian Cultural History* 9: 14-35.

Head, Lesley. 1990. 'Conservation and Aboriginal Land Rights: When Green is Not Black' in *Australian Natural History* 23(6): 448-54.

——. 2000. *Second Nature: The History and Implications of Australia as Aboriginal Landscape*. New York: Syracuse University Press.

Hill, Barry. 1993. 'Travelling Towards the Other' in *Overland* 130: 8-15.

Kolig, Erich. 1981. *The Silent Revolution: The Effects of Modernization on Australian Aboriginal Religion*. Philadelphia: Institute for the Study of Human Issues.

———. 1987. *The Noonkanbah Story*. Dunedin: University of Otago Press.

Lewis, Henry T. 1982. 'Fire Technology and Resource Management in Aboriginal North America and Australia' in Williams and Hunn (1982): 45-67.

Lovejoy, A.O., and G. Boas. 1965. *Primitivism and Related Ideas in Antiquity*. New York: Octagon Books.

Low, Tim. 2002. *The New Nature: Winners and Losers in Wild Australia*. Camberwell, Vic.: Viking/Penguin.

Martin, Calvin. 1978. *Keepers of the Game: Indian-Animal Relationships and the Fur Trade*. Berkeley, CA: University of California Press.

Meggitt, Mervyn J. 1965. 'The Association between Australian Aborigines and Dingoes' in Leeds, Anthony, and Andrew Peter Vayda (eds) *Man, Culture and Animals: The Role of Animals in Human Ecological Adjustments*. (Publication No.78). Washington, DC: American Association for the Advancement of Science: 7-26.

Myers, Fred R. 1988. 'Critical Trends in the Study of Hunter-Gatherers' in *Annual Review of Anthropology* 17: 261-82.

Nandy, Ashis. 1983. *The Intimate Enemy: Loss and Recovery of Self under Colonialism*. Delhi: Oxford University Press.

Povinelli, Elizabeth A. 1998. 'The Cunning of Recognition: Real Being and Aboriginal Reconciliation in Settler Australia' in *Australian Feminist Law Journal* 11: 3-27.

———. 1993. *Labor's Lot: The Power, History, and Culture of Aboriginal Action*. Chicago: University of Chicago Press.

Pyne, Stephen J. 1991. *Burning Bush: A Fire History of Australia*. New York: Henry Holt and Company.

Reid, J.R.W., J. Anne Kerle and S.R. Morton. 1993. *Uluru Fauna: The Distribution and Abundance of Vertebrate Fauna of Uluru (Ayers Rock-Mount Olga) National Park*. Canberra: Australian National Parks and Wildlife Service, Canberra.

Rolfe, P. 1995 'Please Don't Call Him an Australian Author' in *The Bulletin* (10 January 1995).

Rolls, Mitchell. 2003. 'Black Is not Green' in *Australian Studies* 18(1): 41-65.

———. 1998. 'Monica Furlong and the Quest for Fulfilment' in *Australian Feminist Law Journal* 11: 46-64.

———. 2002. 'New Age: New Orthodoxy — The Institutional Authorising of Balderdash' in *Journal of Aboriginal Studies* 1: 22-34.

———. 2000. 'Robert Lawlor Tells a "White" Lie' in *Journal of Australian Studies* 66: 211-18, 284-86.

Rolston, Holmes III. 1990. 'Science-Based versus Traditional Ethics' in Engel, J. Ronald, and Joan Gibb Engel (eds) *Ethics of Environment and Development: Global Challenge and International Response*. London: Belhaven Press: 63-72.

Rose, Bruce. 1995. *Land Management Issues: Attitudes and Perceptions amongst Aboriginal People of Central Australia*. Alice Springs: Central Land Council.

Rose, Deborah Bird. 1996. *Nourishing Terrains: Australian Aboriginal Views of Landscape and Wilderness*. Canberra: Australian Heritage Commission.

Roth, H. Ling, et al. 1968. *The Aborigines of Tasmania*. Hobart: Fullers Bookshop.

Roughsey, Elsie (Labumore). 1984. *An Aboriginal Mother Tells of the Old and the New*. Ringwood, Vic.: McPhee Gribble/Penguin Books.

Ryan, Lyndall. 1996. *The Aboriginal Tasmanians*. St Leonards, NSW: Allen and Unwin.

Sackett, Lee. 1991. 'Promoting Primitivism: Conservationist Depictions of Aboriginal Australians' in *Australian Journal of Anthropology* 2(2): 233-46.

Said, Edward W. 1978. *Orientalism*. New York: Pantheon Books.

Schaef, Anne Wilson. 1995. *Native Wisdom for White Minds: Daily Reflections Inspired by the Native Peoples of the World*. Milsons Point, NSW: Random House.

Spencer, W.B. 1914. 'Chapter II: The Aboriginals of Australia' in Knibbs, George Handley (ed.) *Federal Handbook: Prepared in Connection with the Eighty-Fourth Meeting of the British Association for the Advancement of Science*. Melbourne: Commonwealth Government: 33-85.

Strehlow, T.G.H. 1947. *Aranda Traditions*. Melbourne: Melbourne University Press.

Thomas, Nicholas. 1994. *Colonialism's Culture: Anthropology, Travel and Government*. Princeton, NJ: Princeton University Press.

Thorslev, P.L. 1972. 'The Wild Man's Revenge' in Dudley, Edward J., and Maximillian E. Novak (eds) *The Wild Man Within: An Image in Western Thought from the Renaissance to Romanticism*. Pittsburgh: University of Pittsburgh Press: 281-307.

Tonkinson, Robert. 1978. *The Mardudjara Aborigines: Living the Dream in Australia's Desert*. New York: Holt, Rinehart and Winston.

Torgovnick, Mariana. 1991. *Gone Primitive: Savage Intellects, Modern Lives*. Chicago: University of Chicago Press.

White, H. 1972. 'The Forms of Wildness: Archaeology of an Idea' in Dudley, Edward J., and Maximillian E. Novak (eds) *The Wild Man Within: An Image in Western Thought from the Renaissance to Romanticism*. Pittsburgh: University of Pittsburgh Press: 3-38.

Williams, Nancy M., and Eugene S. Hunn (eds). 1982. *Resource Managers: North American and Australian Hunter-Gatherers*. Boulder, CO: Westview Press.

Under the Mountains and Beside a Creek:
Robert Gray and the Shepherding of Antipodean Being

Mark Tredinnick

Abstract: This chapter explores the agricultural and literary metaphors of pastoralism; it takes a traditional ecocritical approach, focussing on how the land has affected the poet and his writing. In Australia, whose economy has so long depended on the pastoral industry, there has developed a different kind of pastoral poetry, exemplified by the poetry of Robert Gray. Drawing on his experience of the North Coast of New South Wales, Gray's poetry has matured as he has become an exemplar of what Martin Heidegger terms the "shepherd of being".

1. Prologue

> Pastoral: (Latin) pertaining to shepherds
> J.A. Cuddon, *Penguin Dictionary of Literary Terms & Literary Theory*

Since modern Australia rode to prosperity and nationhood on the sheep's back, it is said; and since the feet of millions of sheep — like four times as many roving jackhammers — have done unspeakable damage to soils never in their long history acquainted with hard hoofs, we need to consider the kind of pastoral this dry continent now needs us to write.

Clearing the land for pastoral enterprise has been almost the definitive Australian project. Paddocks (increasingly saline and eroded) are our inheritance, part of our sense of Australian self; and it has long been too easy to look at them as though they are how the country always went. It can take a lifetime to learn to listen like shepherds until we hear those paddocks for what they really are and what they were before — and what they need of us, by way of poetry and pastoral care.

This chapter focuses on the erosion of a pastoral conception of land through the poetry of Robert Gray. It is about his arrival home in country (and in a poetic) made strange by a lifetime's listening.

2. The Erosion of the Pastoral — an Introduction

What else could Robert Gray have become but a pastoral poet? He did not stand a chance. True, there are vocations other than poetry that might have found such a boy born on a banana plantation in the midst of dairy country at the edge of a country town in northeast New South Wales — dairy farming, shearing, school-teaching, shopkeeping, gambling, the ministry, accountancy. But if it was going to be poetry, it was always going to be pastoral. When an interviewer asked Gray what memories he had of childhood, this is what he said:

> [All my childhood memories] have to do with nature — being exhilarated by the light and vitality and vividness of the bush, up there on the northern coast of New South Wales. After having to leave the plantation, which was just below the for-est-line on a beautiful hillside, we rented a house that came with a small dairy farm, which my father ran. This was also in a very striking piece of countryside, under the mountains and beside a creek. (Spurr 1995: 32)

Gray might be seen as a pastoral poet in two senses — his subject matter and his approach to it. He writes landscape, frequently pad-docks and shorelines, the working landscapes of dairy farmers and fishermen and poet-scholars like himself; the locus of much of his work is, in other words, the traditional territory of pastoral poetry. Gray writes other places, too, especially Sydney Harbour, by which he has long lived. But even when it is the city Gray's poems witness, he seems to hold places up as precious stones, as archetypal realms, as dreams, where one longs to belong but feels one cannot. He writes gritty, hip idylls, many of them rural, some of them urban.

But if not all his subject matter is strictly pastoral, Robert Gray's stance, his attitude toward the world, and his mood in its company, certainly might be so called. British poet, rock-climber, and ecocritic Terry Gifford tells us that pastoral is "a discourse of retreat" (Gifford 1999: 45). Conventionally, in the pastoral, the poet retreats from the social realm to the more than merely human, to the countryside, where a kind of idealised former world is still hard at work, and he seeks wisdom there. The pastoral poet locates virtue in nature, outside the world of men, except to the extent that those men are shepherds, country folk, fishermen, cowboys, oarsmen and ferrymen, sometimes poets. But mostly shepherds. Although there are few shepherds in Gray's poems, one could argue that it is a poetry of retreat that he has been writing all these years, if one means by *pastoral* a sensibility that inclines to find wisdom and truth in the world itself, beyond the merely human realms of reality, though inclusive of them. In his poetry, the real world — true humanity, true society, and true poetry — is naturally constructed. We are, in all our folly and poverty and brilliance, set down within a wide, old, long field of truth — it is the world as it was before and will be after us; it is the world as it mani-fests in us. Nature in that large sense, in all its mystery, ruin, and transcendence.

Pastoral, writes Gifford, traditionally takes the poet (and his read-ers) on a journey from the court to Arcadia and back to the court, renewed (Gifford 1999: 47). But Gray is a country boy — he grew up in Arcadia, as it were. If he writes his places a little like the Chinese poet-philosophers wrote their mountain-side retreats, the way Gary Snyder writes his, or Wordsworth his, still Gray's pastoral is the less rarefied, more locally inflected kind that a child of the land is prone to write. Gray comes from the places he retreats to. So his retreat is always also a coming home. It is home he writes. It is the place where, as Robert Frost said, they always have to take you in.

Pastoral ranges, as Leo Marx put it, from the sentimental to the mindful, the simplistic to the complex (Marx 1964: 72). And Robert Gray's poetry is very much at the mindful and complex end of the pastoral spectrum — it is ecologically aware and locally literate. At least, it has become more and more so through the course of his work, in ways and for reasons suggested here.

It should also be noted, as an aside, that in Australia *pastoral* de-scribes the work of raising sheep or cattle — as opposed to crops — on the land, and *pastoralist* is the name that cattle- and sheep-men (and women)[1] use for themselves. They are the ranchers. Everyone else is just a 'farmer'. Pastoral is their work, and not much of it has to do with Arcadia — though it has always had, at least in the inside country, a lot to do with clearing forests to make pasture, with making over a scrubby landscape into something resembling a sheep or cattle run. Pastoralism takes place all over Australia, as it does in America, from the grassy (once also heavily wooded) ridges of the Great Divide to the vast pastoral leases of the rangelands of the country's heart — even in the most arid reaches of the inland, where, if the rains get it right, some of the best cattle-fattening grasses in the world rise up out of the apparently dead earth. So pastoral, outside literary circles at least, has a certain tough swagger in Australia. And if it has contributed to the wreck of certain stretches of marginal country, it is also the place where one will find the fiercest love for and the deepest wisdom about the land.

Pastoral is part of our sense, true and false, of who we are in Australia. Although the term carries echoes, perhaps even to a landholder on Cooper Creek, of brooks and meadows and water nymphs, its primary meaning — the life one makes out of raising cattle on a dry continent — has adapted to local conditions and describes a tougher and sturdier aesthetic than the same word does in literary circles.

'Pastoral', then, has a complex set of associations in Australia, and few of them have to do with shepherds and shepherdesses. Australian pastoral poetry only rings true to Australian places when, as in the work of David Campbell and Judith Wright, and increasingly of Robert Gray, it picks up the frequencies of Australian pastoral landscapes, where, more than anywhere else, the business of reconciliation with country and with Indigenous people is being played out; where the experiment in large-scale Western land use is being tested and found wanting; and where the price for all that tree-felling, for all that overstocking and all that plundering of the rivers and the aquifers is being paid.

In a powerful essay, 'Getting off the Sheep's Back: Farewell to Arcady', George Seddon (2003) has argued that just as the pastoral attitude in farming practice has impoverished Australian landscapes, subjected them to erosion, and effaced the land's older histories, so in literature, the dominance of a pastoral attitude to landscape has diminished Australian places in Australian imaginations. Like Gifford, Seddon argues that we need on the land and in our writing a new kind of engagement with country, something more than merely pastoral, more aware of how the land really works and the kind of care it needs. Pastoral itself has been eroded in Australian conditions so that it is no longer sustainable. Arcadia does not work here. It is just not possible to run that many sheep on pastures that green on soils like ours, under dry skies like ours — and if the writing pretends you can, it rings false.

I suggest that an eroded — a sclerophyll, a drought- and fire-adapted — pastoral is precisely what Australia needs in order to see and serve and save the land. And that is the kind of pastoral — or post pastoral — Robert Gray is now writing; and that is what the land has done to him. It has eroded his sense of place until it is this contingent, unsettled, uncertain, enduring love. What this erosion yields in literature is what it has yielded in his writing: landscapes given back to themselves, to their pasts and futures, and a practice of pastoral care that wants to write and serve the land as it has been since the beginning, not just the way it has been since white men cleared and fenced it and tidied it of its indigenes.

Robert Gray began writing in a straight pastoral mode, party, without meaning to be, to the land clearing, to a Colonial, simplifying, idealising (and destructive) apprehension of Australian places. He was just working hard to notice and give witness. One hears an older-style uncomplicated pastoral in his very first published poem, 'Back There', and in 'Journey: North Coast'. By reading that early poem against a late prose poem, it is possible to see that time and weather have abraded Gray's poetry and complicated his practice of attention to country. Over time, his poems have grown less pretty, less nostalgic, messier, more discursive, more aware (or, if they were always aware, then more expressive) of three enfolded aspects of his country: the land's long pre-pastoral history with Aboriginal people; the sublime, as opposed to the merely beautiful, the sometimes dead-set deathly aspects of Australian places; and his own untenable, subjunctive, yet finally adequate inhabitation of the earth. (Martin Harrison [2004] has noted, too, how, in revisions Gray made to his body of work in the 1998 *New Selected Poems*, the poet has worked back into earlier poems suggestions of what I call his eroded pastoral sensibility; part of the poet's development, part of his erosion, is a deepened appreciation of the problematic 'human presence' within the world the poet witnesses; his post-pastoral vision is, if I may use my words for what Harrison so delicately notates, putting people back, is populating and personalising his pastorals.)

Gray's coming into this more complex awareness of the land —
and his place, and the place of all humans, within it — is his own. But
it is not his alone. For it is representative also of a deepening into this
place, a complicating of one's sense of self and country, that many
Australian poets and writers, myself included, have undergone these
past dozen years, out of which a new Australian poetic is coming. One
cannot do Australian pastoral the same way anymore, not if one wants
it to witness truthfully in a land our pastoralising forebears stole and
began rapidly undoing not so very long ago. 'Post' is what our best
pastoral is becoming — various, changeful, complicated, sclerophyll,
drought-affected, stark, just here and there lush. And, in my estima-
tion, Gray's pastoral is our very best.

Also, by looking at some of Robert Gray's recent prose (part of a
memoir he is writing about his father and his childhood), we will note
how easily an older pastoral aesthetic returns to our apprehension of
our place, how readily we start fencing the paddocks, clearing the
trees again, letting the land slip away, in our sentences, when we
loosen our lyric engagement with country.

3. Who the Poet Has Become and How

Robert Gray has written eight volumes of poetry from *Creekwater
Journal* in 1974 to *Nameless Earth* in 2006. His work is admired by
poets like Kevin Hart, Les Murray, and Geoff Page. There is scarcely
a poetry prize he has not won, a residency he has not done. His poems
are read at school. I sometimes meet people in my classes, even in
corporate Australia, who say they have heard of him! But Gray does
not yet have an international reputation — the kind that Les Murray
has, or Kevin Hart or John Kinsella. This may have to do with having
failed to win traction among the literary scholars. It may also have to
do with his being, as Martin Harrison puts it, the "dogged opponent of
reader-hostile 'experimentalism' and of the empty American-
influenced 'internationalism' which many of his generation of Australian poets engaged in" (Harrison 2004: 37). It may have to do with his
poetry's unfashionable 'sensuous materialism' — unfashionable, that
is, within the academy; for sensuous materialism — that is, the description of the actual world — is always popular among readers. It
may have to do with "the poet's undoubted repugnance towards mere

manner and emptily trendy gesture", which Gray sees manifest in so much of the work of his contemporaries (Harrison 2004: 37). His is not a particularly erudite, pyrotechnical, or sophisticated poetry. It makes sense, and there are *places* in it. These can be drawbacks these days. So Gray seems a poet readers read and poets respect and critics ignore or disparage.

In his work there is no fat, no affectation, no games, no posturing. He is looking for the unsayable essence of the world and its moments, and for that one has to leave a whole lot of poem out. Think of a Japanese watercolour, and you have his landscape poetry. Indeed, *painterly* is another adjective needed in order to know his work. He is an accomplished drawer and painter. His last two collections included some of his sketches, though he mostly draws to help him to find and begin to say the unsayable thing he is after. He sees the world in line and tone and gesture; and he speaks poems the way a painter paints.

In most of the writing of the first half of his writing life — these "slim volumes [...] full of treescapes, seascapes, chiaroscuros and metaphors of vision" (Poacher 2003: 223) — Gray uses visual imagery almost to the exclusion of the other senses. In intimate detail, with an emphasis on line and form and colour and texture, Gray witnesses with his eye. Listen to these early haikus:

'13 Poems'

A waterbird lifts
out of dead grass; its slow flight
is water lapping.

[...]

Sultry night. The moon
is small and fuzzy, an aspirin
in a glass of water.

Chopping wood,
I strike about at mosquitoes
with the axe.

Smokestack, evening sky;
And the smoke, a woman's long hair,
who pauses underwater. (Gray 1974: 17-21)

In his poem 'In Thin Air', from his 1993 collection *Certain Things*, Gray reflects that he imagined his work as "a hymn to the optic nerve", and so it may be read; but he has learned, he says, lately, and from a woman, that "other senses [...] will have all they deserve". Geoff Page has dubbed Gray "Australia's premier imagist" (qtd. in Poacher 2003: 223). Among our poets, Page means, Gray is the most painterly, the most pictorial, and also the most clearly in debt (a debt he acknowledges) to William Carlos Williams: "no ideas but in things", Williams famously enjoined. In his later work, perhaps, consciously, Gray is exploring the world through his other senses: in 'A Poem of Not More than Forty Lines on the Subject of Nature' from *Afterimages* (2002), for instance, there is much to find of heft and sound and felt-sense and dream as there is of form in space and light. This is one of the ways in which the work of "Australia's premier imagist" has grown, in which his witness has become more resonant.

Gray, perhaps too glibly, is thought of as a poet of spare haikus (every collection has a sequence) and of long, free verse, meditative lyrics of place and philosophy ('Mr Nelson', 'Dharma Vehicle', 'On Climbing the Stone Gate Peak', 'At the Inlet'). This is forgivable: Gray works his most lasting imagist magic in these two forms. But he is a master of many poetic forms. In his versifying, he is quietly virtuose and nimble. From the start (*Creekwater Journal*, 1974), he brings together two or three poems in each of his forms he works in — haiku sequences, prose poems, shorter and longer lyric poems, rhymed quatrains and tercets, long-lined Jeffers-like schemes — to make his tidy mosaic volumes. And lately he has explored more traditional rhythm and rhyme schemes — for example, the rhyming quatrains, in the rhythm of a ballad, of 'Black Landscape' (originally published in *Piano*, 1988, a collection whose title alludes to sound, another sense):

All of the high country, that year, had been burned out
with the headline blackness of war.
Soon afterwards we came travelling through the place,
along a ridge's blade-edge by car. (Gray 1998: 158)

Paradoxically, it is by returning to traditional forms, with their rigours, and by speaking in a prosier (which is to say, more syntactically correct, more verb-rich and more prolix) voice that Gray witnesses the nature of his Antipodean realities, in particular of the pastoral and coastal landscapes to which his heart always returns him, and the way his mind and body wonder/wander here. It could be that a certain kind of lyric prose is what Australian places need, for it is how they speak; and it could be that, as is often the case in art, the most lasting originality of perception and expression happens when one takes old forms and makes them new (this is what Pound meant by his enjoinder to make it new) — rather than inventing new forms. Australia presents the poet and the pastoralist with just about the oldest, most enduring forms one can imagine. Here tradition, in art and land management, has been practised continuously longer than anywhere on earth.[2] One needs a bit of respect for tradition to make sense of this place. It takes both a feeling for the old and a tough freshness of perception to witness what is actually going on here — not least in oneself.

4. The Shepherd of Being

But what did Robert Gray say, in 'Poetry and Living', he looks for in a poem? What does he think poetry can do? Two things. First, poetry "can be the most complete mode of apprehension [...]. Poetry can be, and should be, what Francis Ponge has spoken of — a rational language that will resonate also in the body" (1982: 122). Notice that Gray speaks of "apprehension" here, not merely of visual perception. And, with Ponge, he understands poetry is an activity, in the writing and in the reading, that marries sense with mind; poetry is thoughtful and embodied witness. It is (multi-)sensual contemplation of the world and one's work within it. And one can see how he sets about that task endlessly in his own work.

Second, seeking a definition of the kind of relationship the poet wants with his subject matter and with his readers, Gray employs a phrase he translates from Heidegger: the poet is "the shepherd of being". The poet, Gray believes, must, most of all, *care* for things, for what they truly are. The poet's duty of care is to shepherd the essence of the things he turns to into the kind of being they can only have in the witness a poet can make. The poet cares with mind and sense and word. Noticing things without using them: this is how poetry can be useful to humanity and serve the world. Caretaking is what it can model: the tough, unsleeping, tender care of the shepherd. It is hard to imagine a more pastoral metaphor for the work of poetry itself.

In Gray's conception, then, poetry itself is pastoral. It *is* shepherd-
ing. The poet shepherds reality into words.

But true poetic witness is an especially demanding kind of husbandry. For what the poet cares for is the integrity of the world's
forms, their life independent of whatever use he may wish to make of
them. If one cares like this, the being one attends to may keep on
becoming something else, the world may keep on becoming more and
more itself, and less and less what one thought it was. And it may
demand of the poet a different kind of work of witness, of shepherd-
ing: different prosodic devices, less of what he wants, more of what
the land wants. The flock may change the witness into what it needs
him to be to bear witness to it. And it may erode and alter his very
work. So it has been with Gray. The world is not the place he thought
he knew. And only caring for it as he has in his poetry would have
allowed him to discover that.

It is chiefly in this way — through his evolving, eroding practice of
care for things — that Gray is a pastoral poet. Despite his particular
affection for pastoral places, people, and things, and his sad, tender,
nostalgic mood (and pastoral is, above all, a mood — *that* mood),
Robert Gray is a poet of things and thingness, as Martin Harrison
might put it. Nature is not a retreat, not a resort, for him — at least it is
that less and less. Nature is just what is. And nature is every*thing*. It
includes, for instance, himself and all of us — Mr Nelson, Gray's
mother and father, the abattoir, the light on the harbour, the flight
through storm, the nation's first peoples. And just what nature's nature
is goes on changing and eluding him and changing him by virtue of
his sustained sensuous and mindful attention. And so the poet has
grown and the poetry has changed, while the world has gone on becoming more and more the same.

5. Retreat/Return

The very first poem in Robert Gray's very first book (*Creekwater
Journal*, 1974) describes his going home:

'Journey: the North Coast'

Next thing, I wake up in a swaying bunk,
as though on board a clipper

lying in the sea,
and it's the train, that booms and cracks,
it tears the wind apart.
Now the man's gone
who had the bunk below me. I swing out,
cover his bed and rattle up the sash —
there's sunlight rotating
off the drab carpet. And the water sways
solidly in its silver basin, so cold
it joins together through my hand.
I see from where I'm bent
one of those bright crockery days
that belong to so much I remember.
The train's shadow, like a bird's,
flees on the blue and silver paddocks,
over fences that look split from stone,
and banks of fern,
a red clay bank, full of roots,
over a dark creek, with logs and leaves suspended,
and blackened tree trunks.
Down these slopes move, as a nude descends a staircase,
slender white gum trees,
and now the country bursts open on the sea
across a calico beach, unfurling;
strewn with flakes of light
that make the whole compartment whirl.
Shuttering shadows. I rise into the mirror
rested. I'll leave my hair
ruffled a bit that way — fold the pyjamas,
stow the book and wash bag. Everything done,
press down the latches into the case,
that for twelve months I've watched standing out
of a morning, above the wardrobe
in a furnished room. (Gray 1998: 2)

One can feel Gray's gift for description here. Though it moves with uneven rhythm and narrates a simple homecoming, 'Journey' is essentially a descriptive poem. The imagery is easy and not particularly arresting. But it is vivid and tidy. I have never been able to forget the feel of that so cold water, joining through my hands in that basin. Nor the sound and dance of the poem and the country it tells: the swaying bunk, the swinging man, the boom and crack of the train as it tears the wind apart, the train's fleeing shadow, the shuttering shadows (it is a visual image, but listen to it), the clattering sash, the country bursting open, the whirling compartment.

There's real country here, but it is uncomplicated, and the imagery Gray uses belongs to the books he's read and the kitchen his mother kept: these are the "bright crockery days" of memory (that nostalgic note already); these slender trees are nudes descending a staircase. The beach is calico (a perfect choice of colour and texture, but a particularly interior, colonial, and housekeeping kind of reference). In the whole poem only the "gums" and, at a stretch, the "blackened tree trunks" mark this as an Australian poem. When I realised this, I was shocked. The poem evokes for me the north coast of my country, but somehow it does it without many images that place it there. It does it by its coastal and sclerophyll feel, not to mention its title. But the country it really inhabits and sings is the country of common European memory, only slightly inflected with an Australian accent. This is a pastoral; it could be happening anywhere there are pastures edged with trees and opening onto the sea.

This is a landscape not really seen or heard; its own being is not deeply felt and limned. This is landscape as a furnished room passed through at speed, filled, appealingly, with slender nudes: It is a young man's poem. Only the man who's gone disquiets this poem of excited return. And not for long. There's just a small suggestion in this reference that the young man knows this room is not really his own, or not his alone. There was someone else here before.

Then the country bursts open — but not to the poet, just to the sea. The country is still closed in its being from the man, yet what he sees of it and how it makes him feel, he loves. That love carries the boy home and it carries the poem. (Poet and philosopher Kevin Hart, Gray's contemporary and friend, says he has reread this poem countless times over the years — this poem and many others, of course. "It is easier to quote poems by Robert that I love than to say why I am so drawn to them", Hart admits [1999: 9], though he too notes Robert's "care for things", his tenderness of attention, and his gift for curious and intricate image, not profoundly evident in the above poem. Hart quotes "The night as filled with rain as a plank with splinters" to illustrate Gray's real gift.)

6. Arrival — a Stranger House

Between that poem and 'A Poem of Not More Than Forty Lines on the Subject of Nature' (*Afterimages*, 2002) stretch almost thirty years, and one can tell. Between the poems lies a career made of lines as quintessentially Australian as the one Hart quotes, a hundred fresh ways of getting close to the very being of eucalypt leaves and the light upon the harbour.

'A Poem' is the work of an older poet. It is jaded pastoral: of *arrival,* this time, not passage. Between the poems the poet has lost his pastoral innocence. The erosion of his witnessing self, of this shepherd, exposes to him a more animate, broken, yet enduring and resonant landscape. His familiar places sound strange in him now. The poet, who arrives in this poem to a place very like the one he has always belonged, is not the same as the one who was coming home in 1974.

Both poems begin with a waking. The first wakes to light, the second to an animate darkness, and in this later waking, though one feels the poet's weariness and unease, one discerns a fuller awareness of things beyond the waker, and a connection between them all. Gray's world has grown less pretty, his poetry less clean and simple.

'A Poem of Not More Than Forty Lines on the Subject of Nature'

I'm woken to rain blown against this one room, beneath the cliffs of forest, on a slope above the valley that has welled with night.

All evening the rain riddled the lamp's beam that leaned outside as if to brace the shack. Now what I hear is only the aftermath, shed thickly by the branches and settling like fishing lines through the sea, many small weights sounding separately on the tin.

The night creatures have streamed forth again, to exult after the storm. It was a bird that with a shout opened my sleep, and that I dreamed forbore, in its natural economy, although it hung above me glaring.

I hear insects, as constant as the water that runs off the slopes, and imagine those whirling articles tied into a form, like the finely entwined column beneath a tap when it's left to run in a certain amount.

> Lying here half awake I feel this shack is a room within some great
> house that creaks and strains about me, an abandoned place. It seems
> I am listening for someone who is responsible to come back. I have
> to remember that no one needs to come — it is going on as it has
> always done.
>
> This is a house, though, where I lie. I could find within it, through
> certain rooms, through many of the rooms, things that seem laid out
> for me. It is a house we have inherited, but as though by default. A
> strange house, not made with hands.
>
> I go outside to urinate from under the small awning. Now
> autumn's sky is clear, and looks shaggy, ice-encrusted. Twisting
> above the ranges, all jammed-together, dilated stars. So still is the
> night, and so heavily laden, that it seems I can hear from far off the
> roar of its rampaging terrible machinery.
>
> We are on a planet that lies face-up beneath these burning faces
> like an ace. (Gray 2006: 10)

Notice, first, *where* the poet is. He is back there where he was as a child (though not exactly in that same house above that same valley), and where much of his poetry seems to reside, at this edge between pasture and timber, between the tame and the wild: he is just below the forest on the slope above a cleared valley. (Recalling his childhood country in the passage quoted earlier, Gray said he grew up "just below the forest-line on a beautiful hillside" and then "under the mountains and beside a creek".) But night has welled in the valley, and the place is no longer the same. It has become strange to him. He is no longer at home, though he is more fully present, one feels, in this terrain. The poet hears things which go on tonight, he realises, as they always have, but which he never knew and which seem laid out for him now. The place is at once empty and darkly, insistently alive, silent with threat and suggestion. He hears things inside — over, beyond and under — what he hears and sees. He hears the roar of the night's "terrible, rampaging machinery". The house of the night above the valley is haunted, and its emptiness creaks and strains, as once the train did, about him.

This house — the place about him — has come to him by default. Similarly, we stumble into our particular place on earth. And there it is going on about us. It is someone else's house that has come to us.

Nature is for Gray no safe harbour any more. It is no idyll. Nor is it a place, the poet knows, from which the human can be banished. Nature in its indifferent way includes us. Nature has become for Gray a strange house — a stranger's house. It is not his, it is not ours, and yet it is where we must live, our only home. In 'A Poem' one finds the poet reasonably at ease, if not quite at home, within this teeming, empty, unsafe house; and here in the night, in all the rooms of the house, are the voices of the men and women who used to be here — along with all the living beings ("the night creatures") whom we cannot hope to know, and yet which we can hear beyond hearing. The land, this house, goes on "as it all began", regardless of the man, and yet cognizant enough of him to lay things out for him, if that man or woman learns to stay and listen.

Echoes of his first poem resonate in this late poem, as though Gray had it in mind. Apart from the waking and the creaking and booming about him (which was the train in the early poem, and is now the whole place, an interesting shift, suggesting that the land itself has grown animate for the poet), there is the abandonment of the space (to him, by default) by the previous tenants. The insects in the night now "whirl", where the compartment did before, in the light of day. The same verb elaborates here an awkward and unsettling image of the infestation of emptiness.

Here, the poet's sleep, the poet himself, is *opened* up by the place: by a bird and a dream of a bird standing over him, glaring but not attacking. In 'Journey' the *country* itself bursts open, but not upon the poet. The "so clear" water in the early poem, part of a small moment of personal domestic economy, has become a sky "so clear" the poet can discern in its clarity the awful spinning of the planet, the machinery of the world — a quality of a massive and overbearing natural economy in which the poet is dwarfed. And this time the poet does not rise to wash but to urinate. He is connected in this way with the whole streaming night — which is also, suddenly, miraculously clear.

Gray's closing line, in which stars have become "burning faces" and the whole world a prone body, spinning helplessly beneath those faces' glare, is sharp with threat and beauty. This place is haunted by the dead with their fiery eyes; the whole world is.

This is antipodean sublime. The country Gray has always inhabited and shepherded in verse has turned out to be something much more strange, something much less lovely than he had thought. It has aged back into itself, and Gray's witness has aged until he can discern it. By 'country' I mean the familiar setting of his poems, I mean the shack at the edge of the eucalypts, above the valley, and I mean Australia. The poem may be read as Gray's acknowledgment that the whole continent has come to us by default, that there is hell to pay for the beauty laid out for us, that our belonging, our sleep within it, will always be troubled. And nothing and no one can really make it right: "no one needs to come". That is just the way it is going to be.

The country is inhabited by everything beyond our control and ken, and by the sleepless generations who came before. Except that the place itself is quite all right: it goes on as it began, and takes us with it, part of its cargo of night creatures, of rain, of ranges and moving trees. It is good to remind oneself properly where one is, who was here first, and how it all goes on and on regardless.

There is even less in this poem than in 'Journey' to suggest an Australian place. One can expect more identifiers of Australian places (eucalyptus leaves, paperbarks, kangaroos, currawongs, white-faced herons) in almost any other Gray poem. All the same, there is a sense of an Australian night welled in an Australian valley here; it is eucalypts that creak and strain against sandstone scarps. But without the body of the poet's work that has gone before and gathered itself in this place, this could be almost anywhere.

Finally, note that this poem is made of prose. Gray has always written one or two prose poems in each book, so there is nothing new in that. This stretch of prose is manifestly a poem — but how to know this? There's a compression of language, a texture, a rhythmic quality (albeit irregular), richness and strangeness of imagery, and a refusal to explain that are characteristics of the poem. This is uttered — this is a mind at song.

7. Prose and Prosody

Robert Gray is writing a memoir. Its first chapter appeared in late 2003 in the journal *Heat* ('The Waters Under the Earth'). The chapter is mostly about his father. Something about writing prose — *as prose,* not as poetry — changes Robert Gray's voice. It is hard to recognise the writing as the work of the same man who wrote the other lines shared here. While the prose of the memoir is elegant, it is strikingly different from the prose, for instance, of 'A Poem'. It has little of its edge. It seems to be a throwback to an older kind of pastoral — the kind Gray's father tried to live out, the kind, in his reading, Robert Gray grew up with. It has a formality, reticence, and propriety about it that remind me — and I mean no disparagement — of the prose of Beatrix Potter and Rudyard Kipling and Kenneth Grahame. And what makes this so striking and surprising — since a certain delicacy, an Anglophone particularity of diction and syntax, inhabits his poetry — is how out of register it is with the poetry Gray has recently been writing. It seems that the poet, writing prose (as opposed to a prose poem), writes almost entirely out of a different aspect of himself, from the same well of his inherited being, from which he drew his earlier pastorals. It is mostly a function of diction.

Gray's prose does not seem to belong within the same lyric practice from which his poems come. It probably never occurred to him, as it occurs to few Australian writers of non-fiction prose, that it should, that there might be such a thing as a lyric essay. We have no such tradition. But prose, memoir in particular, doesn't have to be so, well, prosy. Think of Annie Dillard's *An American Childhood*, Joan Didion's *Where I Was From*, or John Haines' *The Stars, The Snow, The Fire*. In other words, one can write extended prose works out of a poetic space. Gray does not do that here. And I do not think in Australia we have often written prose out of the ruthless attention to the world (even of our own childhoods) that poetry insists upon; and so our prose, when it is otherwise any good, often ends up sounding as though it had been written by someone more like Robert Gray's father than his son the poet:

> When I was a child, my father had another plantation, in a different part of the district, about three miles inland from the town, and his solution to his transport problem was to own an ex-racehorse (a very fine animal, it was said), which would bring him home, slumped in the saddle. God knows how he climbed on board, let alone stayed there. Getting him seated must *have been done with much staggering about and hilarity*, among his helpers, in the backyard of the pub. The horse trotted back, joggling its dozing rider, along the side of the road, through occasional headlights [...]. (Gray 2003: 63)

The italicised phrase concentrates the tone of voice I am talking about.

Gray's memoir does not express the same state of being in the world his poetry does. He is being, in a sense, his father; he is not being *here and now*, as he is so powerfully in his poetry. He is not being-with the land.[3] What he is doing is remembering, and memory (expressed in prose, anyway) seems to have a different syntax and diction for him. So it is his father, or at least, a bookish kind of self, who writes these sentences, as though they were a continuation of all those books his father, and young Robert himself, read in that house among the paddocks, when he was finding out he could write. He has become his father in the telling.

This may be no accident of remembering, no accident of writing prose. Gray may be consciously affecting his father's diction. That was the way his childhood spoke, and whether he intends it or not, he is being true, in his prose, to his childhood country, which ran to that older pastoral rhythm.

In any event, his prose draws out and concentrates a courtly, English tone of voice that has always been there beneath his poems — the waters, to use his metaphor, that run beneath his earth. And this is what I wish to point up — not for a moment as a failure of his writing, but as an instance of a literary inheritance that persists in many Australian writers concerned with what our country is and who we are within it. The different music that plays in this prose plays in the lives and works of many writers and readers and plain old citizens, notwithstanding their attempt to deepen into the real music of the Australian land they inherit.

Gray sounds like the gentleman his father, like many of his generation, and many cultured Australians still, writers among them, aspired to be. "The gentleman was proverbial in this country", Gray writes, "until the nineteen-fifties, invoked in homes, in schools, in the streets […]. Those who experienced this ideal through their imaginative reading, as my father did, were surely the most susceptible to it" (2003: 60). If that is true, it was true not only for Gray's father, but for Gray himself, and for pretty much any Australian who grows up among books and imagines he or she might someday like to write this place.

How is it that a poet can write poetry in a voice increasingly indigenous to his country, while at the same time writing prose that speaks more of England? What has happened is that an unconformity in his life's geology — between the father he has spent his life trying not to be and the poet the landscape has made him into — has been exposed by the passage of time, and the weathering of his witness — by the land's genius for finding us out. It is a split many recognise in themselves. It is the unconformity between the bookish selves, which are Anglophone and Eurocentric, steeped in older world pastoral habits and intonations, and the antipodean selves, which are in love, more and more, with a land that will not be caught in the language learned in school.

Sometimes this unconformity within Australian writers sits there as part of their work, unsettling it, unexpressed. This is how it was in Gray's earlier poetry. Sometimes it is exposed by the erosion of one's deepening belonging, and one is forced to speak of it: one is forced to find the language of and for the disjunctive sense of oneself in this land, of this land in oneself. And that is what Gray is attempting in his recent poetry. But in this memoir, Gray's internal unconformity has also been inadvertently exposed, down to the colonial bedrock upon which his antipodean sandstones have been deposited. It speaks, despite himself; yet it speaks truthfully of who he is. It speaks the truth about a kind of belonging to this Australian earth that is not limited to Gray. It does so even more truthfully and thoroughly than he may have intended.

For this reason especially — the way it speaks, more than it means, of the multiple, divided self he is and many of us are — Gray's emerging memoir is a beautiful and important work. In it, Gray is coming, at the age of sixty, to own the shadows, as well as the light and the vistas, of his growing up. He is allowing himself to be his father's son. At the same time, he is uncovering in his poetry the violence and grief that underlie the country of his writing — all those cleared coastal paddocks, those paperbarked creeks, the city and its harbour lights. In his prose he remains the man his father and all those books made him, and he speaks, still, like a visitor here; in his poems, he is the land itself, and he speaks its language. This contradiction — no, this counterpoint — is where many Australian writers of place (in poetry and prose) find themselves just now: this is where the pastoral stands, dancing a little awkwardly to two different musics, failing and falling and trying again. This is the unconformity, this is the disjunction, out of which we write Australia now. This is how we shepherd her and how we must — uncertain of our selves, trying to be who we are while listening for what the place needs us to be.

Notes

[1] See for example Jill Ker Conway's *The Road from Coorain* (1989).
[2] See Les Murray's land claiming and the reworking of the Aboriginal song cycle (chapter 1).
[3] See Ruth Blair's discussion of the concept of 'belonging with' the land below (chapter 9).

Bibliography

Primary Sources

Gray, Robert. 2002. *Afterimages*. Sydney: Duffy and Snellgrove.
———. 1993. *Certain Things*. Port Melbourne, Vic.: Heinemann.
———. 1974. *Creekwater Journal*. St Lucia, Qld.: University of Queensland Press.
———. 2006. *Nameless Earth*. Manchester: Carcanet.
———. 1998. *New Selected Poems*. Sydney: Duffy and Snellgrove.
———. 1988. *Piano*. Sydney: Angus and Robertson.
———. 2003. 'The Waters Under the Earth (from a work in progress)' in *Heat* 6 (New Series): 57–72.

Secondary Sources

Conway, Jill Ker. 1989. *The Road from Coorain*. New York: Knopf.
Cuddon, J.A. 1999. *Penguin Dictionary of Literary Terms and Literary Theory* (rev. C.E. Preston). London: Penguin.
Gifford, Terry. 1999. *Pastoral*. London: Routledge.
Gray, Robert. 1982. 'Poetry and Living: An Evaluation of the American Poetic Tradition' in Kirkby, Joan (ed.) *The American Model*. Sydney: Hale and Iremonger: 117–36.
Harrison, Martin. 2004. 'Robert Gray and the Revision of the Senses' in Harrison, Martin (ed.) *Who Wants to Create Australia?: Essays on Poetry and Ideas in Contemporary Australia*. Sydney: Halstead: 37–44.
Hart, Kevin. 1998. 'Gray's Images are Both Fresh and Tender' in *Australian Author* 30(3): 7–11.
Marx, Leo. 1964. *The Machine in the Garden: Technology and the Pastoral Ideal in America*. New York: Oxford University Press.
Poacher, Jeffrey. 2003. 'A Hymn to the Optic Nerve: The Poetry of Robert Gray' in *Heat* 5 (New Series): 223-29.

Seddon, George. 2003. 'Farewell to Arcady: or Getting Off the Sheep's Back' in *Thesis Eleven* 74: 35-53.
Spurr, Barry. 1999. *The Poetry of Robert Gray*. Glebe, NSW: Pascal Press.

The Poetry of Judith Wright
and Ways of Rejoicing in the World

Veronica Brady

Abstract: Poetry, as W.H. Auden said, "makes nothing happen". But it can alter our ways of seeing and thus of being in the world. The poetry of Judith Wright, for example, can "persuade us to rejoice" in the world — another task of poetry as Auden sees it — thus helping us to fulfil the essential task of people in a relatively new settler society like Australia to learn to dwell in rather than merely build on the land. From the beginning of her career she set herself to this task, challenging the 'masculine' separation of self and world to explore a deeper 'feminine' relationship with it, setting the self within the larger life of the universe and celebrating its beauty and terror.

Poetry, as W.H. Auden famously said in 'In Memory of W.B. Yeats', "makes nothing happen". But he also said that

> it survives
> In the valley of its saying where executives
> Would never want to tamper

since its great task is to "persuade us to rejoice" (Auden 1976: 197-98), that is, to put us in touch with deeper sources of meaning by ridding us of a purely instrumental sense of the world in general and of place in particular in order to respond to the deeper possibilities it presents. According to Mircea Eliade, it is a particularly urgent task for people in settler societies who find themselves in unfamiliar territory to make this transformation, from chaos into 'cosmos' and learn to live according to its rhythms (Eliade 1974: 10).

But this is not the way most settlers saw — or indeed still see. For them space was an empty container to be filled with sheep, cattle and crops, towns and cities, or to be mined for minerals, an empty stage on which "Nature's painted curtains are drawn aside to reveal heroic man at his epic labour on the stage of history" (Carter 1987: xv). But growing problems, terrors even, with which imperial history confronts us suggest that we may need, as Eliade said, rather than any further 'making' of this kind of history, to redefine our notions of place and time to situate ourselves in the universe as a whole (Eliade 1974: 153). This is something that many of our poets, along with other artists, have attempted to do from the beginnings of settlement. Judith Wright is one of them. In her view the land has "presented herself as the most difficult of technical problems", in the sense that to its early settlers it seemed hostile, "the outer equivalent of an inner reality, the reality of exile" (Wright 1966: xi). Her task as a writer, then, she believed was to "be at peace" with it. But for that "it must first be observed, understood, described and as it were absorbed" (p. xi). Significantly, she began this work at a crisis point in our history when the country was threatened with invasion and she felt her "own blood and bone", "beloved and imperilled" (qtd. in Brady 1998: 88).

'The Moving Image', the first poem in her *Collected Poems*, is about the collision she senses between the time of imperial history in which she sees

> no end to the breaking —
> one smashed, another mocks from your enemy's eye —
> [...]
> nothing but the tick of the clock and a world sucked dry (Wright 1994: 4)

and the time of the land and its "song [which] all life is learning", as it

> grows around us, before us, behind,
> there is sound in the silence; the dark is a tremor of light.
> It is the corn rising when winter is done. (p. 5)

For the rest of her career she was to dedicate herself to this music, aware that

> [t]he language and culture I was brought up in [...] had nothing to do with the land my relatives had taken. It was wholly imported, a second skin that never fitted, no matter how we pulled and dragged it over the landscape that we lived in. Nor, of course, did we ourselves fit. That fact was growing more obvious as the land changed under our hand. (qtd. in Brady 1998: 121)

The task therefore, to draw on Heidegger's distinction, was to learn to dwell *in* rather than merely to build *on* the land (Heidegger 1975: 145-61).

Her early poems, however, were about the New England tableland where she had grown up and where she identified with the land — feeling that, as she says in 'For New England', "the long slopes' concurrence is my flesh / who am the gazer and the land I stare on" (1994: 22). There was also a sense of exile, ancestral memory as "sullenly the jealous bones" recalled the "other earth" that was also "shaped and hoarded in them" (p. 22). The colonial self wants to conquer and possess the land. Only then "will my land turn sweetly from the plough / and all my pastures rise green as spring" (p. 23).

To do that, the first step was to let go "the long commentary of the brain" (p. 16), the "one-sided masculinity and narrowness of thought" which, she was coming to see, led "nowhere but to a world scarcely worth living in that, clearly, [...] was on a slide to its own destruction" (qtd. in Brady 1998: 121). This meant embracing a different kind of logic, the 'feminine', what Hélène Cixous (qtd. in Moi 1991: 112) calls the "economy of the gift" which is open to the other, giving and receiving, and lives from within, listening, as another poem has it, for and to "the word, that, when all words are said, / shall compass more than speech" (Wright 1994: 16).

Wright's experience of motherhood drew her into this economy. In 'Woman to Child', for instance, the self becomes one with the ongoing creative process of the cosmos:

Then all a world I made in me;
all the world you hear and see
hung upon my dreaming blood.

There moved the multitudinous stars,
and coloured birds and fishes moved.
There swam the sliding continents. (p. 28)

Poetry thus became Heidegger's "the topology of Being" since it "tells Being the / whereabouts of its actual presence" (Heidegger 1975: 12). It moves beyond a concern with the individual subject to become part of the folklore of humanity as a whole, challenging the separation of the physical and the psychic which is characteristic of

Western culture today, which, to refer to Cixous again, is essentially 'masculine', living according to the "economy of the proper, preoccupied with property, propriety and appropriation" (qtd. in Moi 1991: 111-12).

Romantic as this may seem, it nevertheless echoes current scientific thinking which sees the physical universe as more open, subtle, and supple than has been thought, regards humanity's place in it as more problematic and tends to study relations rather than single objects. Similarly, in her poetry, Wright was increasingly aware of actual living forces and interdependences at work in the world and of human beings as part of a wider process and subject to its laws, rejoicing in it, however, rather than deploring it: "[W]ho wants to be a mere onlooker? Every cell of me / has been pierced through by plunging intergalactic messages" (Wright 1994: 422).

Poetry of this kind has little to do with mere self-expression. Its task rather, as Rilke said, is to name the world, but "with an intensity the things themselves never / hoped to achieve" (1966: 1058),[1] recognising in them a power beyond the self which is often awesome and sometimes terrible but demands expression:

> The voice is not our own
> and yet its tone's deeper than intimate,
> comes from elsewhere and compels obedience.
> [...]
> [W]hen, expected and entreated long,
> the question comes, we cannot hesitate,
> but, turning blindly, put all else away. (Wright 1994: 210)

That, I suggest, is why in Wright's poetry, her nature poetry especially, one often senses a certain bafflement, a feeling of being overpowered by what it is attempting to depict. 'Nameless Flower', for instance, opens with a fairly confident description — "Three white petals float / above the green" — and asserts that "I'll set a word upon a word / to be your home". But self-confidence diminishes as wonder increases, and the poem concludes with something like defeat:

> Word and word are chosen and met.
> Flower, come in.
> But before the trap is set,
> the prey is gone.

The words are white as a stone is white
carved for a grave;
but the flower blooms in immortal light,
Being now; being love. (p. 130)

The encounter here is peaceful enough. But other poems are not. In 'Dust', written in the midst of drought, the "sick dust, spiralling with the wind" is accusatory:

our dream was the wrong dream,
our strength was the wrong strength.
Weary as we are we must make a new choice. (pp. 23-24)

As the devastation of the environment became more apparent, it is the poet herself who identifies with the land to make the accusation. 'At a Public Dinner', for example, presents 'developers' as cannibals:

No, I'm not eating. I'll watch the champing jaws,
solemnly eating and drinking my country's honour,
my country's flesh. The gravy's dripping red,
a nourishing stew for business. She's a goner. (p. 312)

'Jet Flight Over Derby', describing flight over eroded country in the north-west, "worn red lands", continues this indictment. Yet it is to them, not to the "bird-tracked air" in which she is merely a "travelling eye" that she commits herself. Her body

knows its place,
and longs to stand on land,
[...]
I am what land has made
And land's myself, I said. (p. 279)

She has known this from childhood:

Most children … are brought up in the 'I' tradition these days — the ego, it's me and what I think. But when you live in very close contact with a large and splendid landscape you feel yourself a good deal smaller than just I. (qtd. in Brady 1998: 469)

And she refuses to resile from this commitment:

And therefore, when land dies?
opened by whips of greed
these plains lie torn and scarred.
Then I erode; my blood
Reddens the stream in flood. (p. 280)

Here she has much in common with Aboriginal people. As one of
their leaders Patrick Dodson observes, "many Australians don't know
how to think themselves into country, into the world. We Aboriginal
people find it hard to think without the land" (Keeffe 2003: 35).[2]
Another angry poem written about the same time, 'Australia 1970',
which opens with the angry apostrophe

Die, wild country, like the eaglehawk,
dangerous till the last breath's gone,
clawing and striking (p. 287)

further echoes the sense of the land as a living power, expressed by
two Aboriginal women from the north-west: "Country knows who is
walking about in it. It can feel who is there. It knows if a stranger
comes, and it can get angry. Start a bushfire or something" (Landine
2003: 68).

At the same time Wright was aware, as she says in 'At Cooloola,'
that she came "of a conquering people" and was one of the "invaders".
But precisely because "no land is lost or won by wars, / for earth is
spirit" (1994: 140), she sensed an unpaid debt to the land's First
Peoples. As she put it in 'Nigger's Leap, New England', a meditation
on a nineteenth century massacre, it was "their blood channelled our
rivers, / and the black dust our crops ate was their dust" (p. 15). But
over time, as she made Aboriginal friends, especially with the poet
and activist Oodgeroo Noonuccal (Kath Walker), a common grief for
the land drew them together.[3] As she wrote to Oodgeroo in 'Two
Dreamtimes':

If we are sisters, it's in this —
our grief for a lost country,
the place we dreamed in long ago,
poisoned now and crumbling. (p. 316)

She also came to realise that in wounding the land and its First Peoples we had also wounded ourselves so that "[s]omething leaks in our blood / like the ooze from a wound", speaking from "a depth that rhymes our pride / with its alternative" (pp. 354-55).

To conclude then, Judith Wright's poetry becomes a point of entry into the life of the cosmos away from the chaos of contemporary history. It also challenges the complacent belief that human consciousness is the absolute centre of existence, suggesting rather that, as Lévinas has it, "it is [...] in the laying down by the ego of its sovereignty [...] that we find ethics and also probably the very spirituality of the soul, but most certainly the question of the meaning of being" (Lévinas 1989: 85). That meaning exceeds our understanding and control. But it is to be affirmed and celebrated — as one of Wright's last poems, 'Rockpool', insists:

I hang on the rockpool's edge, its wild embroideries:

admire it, pore on it, this, the devouring, the mating,
ridges of coloured tracery, occupants, all the living,

the stretching of toothed claws to food, the breeding
on the ocean's edge. "Accept it? Gad, madam, you had better."
(Wright 1994: 419)[4]

If it is true, as Auden said, that "poetry makes nothing happen", it may nevertheless "persuade us to rejoice" even in the dangerous times in which we live. Wright's poetry makes what she calls the "size and silence" (Wright 1966: xii) of Australia and its painful recent history a gift to our times, reminding us that, to quote Lévinas again, it may be necessary "to prefer that which justifies being than that which assures it" (1989: 85).

Notes

[1] "Are we, perhaps, *here*, only to say House. / Bridge. Fountain. Gate. Jug. Fruit-tree. Window. — / at most: Pilar. Tower ... But to *say*, — you understand, / O to *say*, with an intensity the things themselves never / hope to achieve." (Rilke 1966: 1058).

[2] For an alternative perspective challenging Patrick Dodson's general identification of Indigenous people with the land see chapter 5.

[3] For a discussion of Oodgeroo Noonuccul's work see chapter 11.

[4] The quotation is Samuel Johnson's reply to a rather silly woman who said to him that "on the whole I accept life".

Bibliography

Primary Sources

Auden, W.H. 1976. 'In Memory of W.B. Yeats' in *Collected Poems*. New York: Random House: 197-98.
Rilke, Rainer Maria. 1966. 'Ninth Elegy' (tr. Jessie Lemont) in Mack, Maynard, et al. (eds), *The Continental Edition of World Masterpieces*. Vol. 2. New York: Norton: 1058-59.
Wright, Judith. 1994. *Collected Poems*. Sydney: Angus and Robertson.
———. 1966. *Preoccupations in Australian Poetry*. Melbourne: Oxford University Press.

Secondary Sources

Brady, Veronica. 1998. *South of My Days: A Biography of Judith Wright*. Sydney: Angus and Robertson.
Carter, Paul. 1987. *The Road To Botany Bay: An Essay In Spatial History*. London: Faber and Faber.
Eliade, Mircea. 1974. *The Myth of the Eternal Return; or, Cosmos and History*. Princeton, NJ: Princeton University Press.
Heidegger, Martin. 1975. 'Building Dwelling Thinking' in *Poetry, Language, Thought*. New York: Harper and Row: 145-61.
Keeffe, Kevin. 2003. *Paddy's Road: Life Stories of Patrick Dodson*. Canberra, Aboriginal Studies Press.
Landine, Catherine. 2003. 'Sentient Country, Deferential People' in Cameron, John (ed.) *Changing Places: Reimagining Australia*. Double Bay, NSW: Longueville Books: 68-77.
Lévinas, Emmanuel. 1989. 'Ethics as First Philosophy' in Hand, Seán (ed.), *The Levinas Reader*: Oxford: Blackwell: 76-87.
Moi, Toril. 1991. *Sexual/Textual Politics: Feminist Literary Theory*. London: Routlege.

Ecopoetics of the Limestone Plains

Kate Rigby

Abstract: The Limestone Plains is the name given by British explorers in the 1820s to the area in the Southern Highlands of New South Wales, where the city of Canberra would later be built. Watered by the Molonglo, a tributary of the Murrumbidgee, and ringed by wooded hills, this area was a significant meeting place of several Aboriginal tribes, whose fire-stick farming practices had shaped its flora and fauna over the millennia. In the nineteenth century, the Canberra area provided a living for pastoralists and selectors, whose activities altered the local ecology and had a devastating impact on Indigenous people. The city that was founded on the Limestone Plains in 1913 in turn displaced this rural way of life, although remnants of pastoralism persisted beyond the urban fringe into the twenty-first century. Canberra's 'bush capital' was conceived as a city in and of the landscape, and it remains a place where town and country interpenetrate to a remarkable degree. As well as providing something of a haven for wildlife, Canberra and its surrounds have also nurtured numerous writers. In this essay, I will investigate the ways in which explorers and settlers construed the Limestone Plains as a locus of pastoral dwelling, before proceeding to consider how some more recent writers have responded to this place in literary form by attending to the more-than-human world that persists both within and beyond the city.

1. Kamberri: Old Country

Located in the Southern Highlands of New South Wales, the 'Canberra rift', as my natal home place is known to geologists, is a rolling plain lying 1800 to 2000 feet (545-606 m.) above sea level, bordered to the north and east by hills rising to another 800 feet, some of which, such as Mount Ainslie, were once active volcanoes (Abell 1991). From the top of Red Hill, a series of higher mountains along the western fall of the Great Dividing Range is seen resting blue-black along the horizon to the south and west, while the smaller Gourock Range is visible to the southeast. When a cutting was made to create the road that circles Capital Hill, which now houses the political centre of the nation, a massive geological unconformity was revealed. As John Cameron explains, this line that cuts across the dips and folds of the layered rock represents "a gap in geological time". It was

> formed when a layer of mud was deposited under the sea and compacted and heated to form the State Circle slate around 440 million years ago. It was then raised up above the surface of the sea and eroded. About ten million years later, it sank down again below the surface of the sea and a layer of sand was deposited on top of it, but not parallel with, not on the same inclination or surface as the original sediments. These were later compacted to form the Camp Hill sandstone. (Cameron 2003: 55)

It seems strangely fitting that the new Parliament House, where disjunctions and disagreements within the polis are also brought to light, should be sited at this place of unconformity within the very earth's crust.

This is old country, the outcroppings of granite and porphyry that litter its hillsides bearing witness to aeons of weathering that have left the soil thin and nutrient poor, and the climate is generally arid. When the rains do come, though, often in torrents after years of dry, the Canberra plain used to be amply watered by the Molonglo River, a major tributary of the Murrumbidgee. This is in turn part of the presently beleaguered Murray-Darling River system that is so crucial to the ecology of south-eastern Australia. Where the labile river, named 'the Thunderer' in the language of the Indigenous Kamberri in acknowledgement of its boisterous ways when in full spate, used to wend its fickle way, a placid lake now fills the flood plain, named 'Burley Griffin' after the architect who designed the federal capital. The climate here is one of hot dry summers and icy cold winters that bring frosty mornings and biting winds down off the Snowy Mountains. The dramatic electrical storms and hail that regularly beleaguer the Canberra area are legendary. When the first European explorers found their way here in 1820, this tough old land, in collaboration with the resourceful Aboriginal people who had dwelt here for 40,000 years or more, had nonetheless given rise to a rich diversity of plant and animal life across three main ecotopes: open grassland on the central plain; savannah woodland dominated by a Yellow Box-Red Gum alliance on most hills and ridges; and dry sclerophyll forest on the slopes of Mt. Ainslie and Black Mountain, where Red Stringybark and Scribbly Gum predominate. Dense wet sclerophyll forest is to be found on some slopes of the mountain ranges to the southwest, with Alpine woodland gracing the peaks.

Just over a century after the first white settlers arrived on the Limestone Plains, in 1927, the year of the opening of the first federal Parliament House in Canberra, John Gale, the founding editor of the *Queanbeyan Age*, published his *History of and Legends Relating to the Federal Capital Territory of the Commonwealth of Australia*. Recalling his first impressions on arriving in the area in 1855, Gale writes that he was instantly

> enamoured with the landscape outstretching east and west and south before me [...] the rolling downs at my feet, the blue haze-covered alpine peaks away to my right, mountainous country south and east of me, and the sheen of the meandering river bisecting the immediate downs — evoking the mental, if not vocal, exclamation: 'What a magnificent site for one of Australia's future cities!' (1977: 5)

Gale had himself been instrumental in developing and promoting the federal capital case for the tiny hamlet of Canberra, consisting of little more than a post-office and a few shops, a church and a school, surrounded by small farms and larger pastoral properties, and it seems likely that his memory of that first moment was coloured by subsequent events. Certainly, when Charles Throsby Smith and his party, the first recorded Europeans to set foot in the heartland of Kamberri country, ascended Black Mountain, as it would later be known, on December 7, 1820, their thoughts were not of future cities, let alone a national capital, but of the profits to be made from the land. They too admired the view. Yet it is evident from the emphasis on soil, grassland, and open forest in Smith's journal (1820) that the prospect it afforded them was primarily pastoral and pecuniary: crossing "scrubby Country for about a Mile", the small band of explorers found themselves in "a most beautiful country [...] a very extensive Plain, Rich Soil and plenty of Grass — Came to a Beautiful River", and next day to "a most beautiful Forest as far as we could see thinly wooded [...] in the Valleys a fine Rich Soil".

As the subsequent naming of the plain to the south of Black Mountain indicates, the early colonists were also on the lookout for potential mineral resources, and they were excited to find evidence of a valuable building material in the area. In fact, the limestone was not in great supply, although a kiln was operative in Acton by the middle of the century. In the 1850s and 1860s, gold was discovered not far away in Major's Creek, Araluen Creek, and Kiandra, and, in the following century, the silver-lead-zinc ore deposits in the vicinity of Captain's Flat to the south-east of the city proved profitable (although their extraction came at considerable cost to the ecology of the Molonglo River in this area). As far as the so-called Limestone Plains themselves were concerned, however, there was little gain to be had from minerals, apart from the gravel that would later be dredged from the river to make aggregate for concrete and roads, and, more pleasingly to the eye, the Black Mountain sandstone that was used in the early 1840s to build Canberra's first church, lovely little St Johns. As for the soil, it turned out to be far from "rich", with the exception of a few pockets of alluvium along the Molonglo and Ginninderra Creek, where fruit and vegetables and fodder crops could readily be grown (and where market gardens and nurseries thrive to this day). For this reason, the Canberra area has never supported large-scale commercial grain crops, although it was here, in the 1880s, that William Farrer (1845-1906) of 'Lambrigg' performed the experiments that helped to revolutionise wheat farming in Australia in the twentieth century. Still, Throsby Smith was right about the grasslands, which were indeed luxuriant, and it was this that soon attracted 'settlers' (mostly absentee landlords initially), with their sheep, cattle, overseers, and convict labourers. The grass was succulent purplish-green kangaroo grass, but it did not last long under grazing, quickly giving way to wallaby grass and spear grass, along with sundry invasive exotics (Gillespie 1991).

What none of the newcomers recognised, though, is the extent to which this landscape of grassy downs and forested hills, which pastoralists found so beckoning, had been carefully crafted over the millennia by its Aboriginal inhabitants into a richly 'nourishing terrain'.[1] Neither 'wilderness' nor 'artefact', this geo-cultural landscape was the outcome of a felicitous partnership between the *autopoiesis* of the more-than-human natural world and the *ecopoiesis* of an Indigenous human culture. Tragically, here as elsewhere in Australia, it was the places that had proven particularly congenial for ceremonial gatherings or making camp, and that had consequently been most carefully maintained, which were the first to be appropriated by settlers. On the Limestone Plains, these included a major corroborree site on the Molonglo River at Acton, which was taken by John Joshua Moore's overseer in 1924, and the sandy rise upriver at Pialligo, that afforded a "cool, soft and dry" warm-weather campsite (Gammage 2002: 19-20), which Robert Campbell's stockman James Ainslie claimed the following year. The first resident landholder was James Macpherson who called his property 'Springbank' after the water source on the Molonglo flats that never ran dry. Whereas Campbell renamed the Pialligo campsite 'Duntroon' in memory of a place far away in his natal Scottish Highlands, Moore showed an (admittedly ambiguous) respect for Indigenous designations in appropriating for his property the name that he transliterated as 'Canberry', thereby holding it in settler memory so that it could later be bestowed upon the capital city that would eventually be built here.

Along with their new regimes of land use, the colonisers also brought a set of assumptions about the natural world in general, and that of Australia in particular, which contrasted starkly with Indigenous understandings. Back in Europe, the Romantic movement that swept Britain and Germany around 1800 had proclaimed a panentheistic appreciation of nature as a locus of the holy, along with a new awareness of the power of place, informed in large part by experiences of dislocation and alienation arising from colonial expansion abroad and modernisation at home (Rigby 2004b). In the eyes of the squatters, by contrast, colonial land would appear to have had a primarily pecuniary value, at least initially. Thus, for example, Samuel Shumack, the son of the first selector on the Limestone Plains, observes approvingly in his memoirs that Robert Campbell recognised that "this unknown land under proper management would, in the future, become one of the greatest producing emporiums of the world" (1967: 3). Campbell was a merchant who had been granted 4000 acres (1615 ha.) in part compensation for the loss of his ships, "the fruit of some years' seal hunting in the South Seas" (Gale, 1977: 10), which had been requisitioned by the Governor to bring food to the starving colony in 1806 (native tucker evidently being perceived as inappropriate fare for Europeans). As a potential 'emporium', the colonised land is construed as a source of goods to be bought and sold (formerly seal skins, these were now primarily fleeces for the woollen mills back in England), not as a locus of dwelling. While the unfamiliar wildlife was seen as there for the taking and more valuable dead than alive, the primary commodities that Merchant Campbell looked forward to trading were to be 'produced', not by earth and sky as a locus of more-than-human agency, but rather by 'proper management' on the part of suitably knowledgeable humans (Indigenous knowledge and land-use practices evidently being discounted in this reckoning).

While the colonists' relationship to the earth, the divine, and their fellow mortals was clearly very different from that of the Kamberri, they were obliged to make their dwelling place under the same sky, sharing with them a vulnerability to the vagaries of the weather.[2] The non-annual climatic patterns that are characteristic of Australia generally, together with the unexpected ways in which the land responded to the colonists' activities, and the dramatic weather events that they encountered on the Limestone Plains, provided settlers with ample opportunity to encounter nature, not as a passive ground but as the locus of an independent, and not necessarily congenial, agency, perhaps even as a Trickster of sorts.[3] Certainly, the "mystic charm" that James Gillespie ('The Wizard') attributes to Lake George in a poem of that name from 1872 (Gillespie 1994: 124) must have been enhanced by the disappearing act that it performs from time to time. Among the early poets of the Canberra region, Bertha Boyd, 'The Poetess of Argyle', calls attention to the unpredictable and potentially violent manifestation of Australian skies in her poem of 1868, 'Australian Dewdrops' (1994). Having described the onslaught of a mighty thunderstorm (in a distinctly melodramatic manner conned from Tennyson), she proceeds to reflect:

> Such is Australia: calm the morn
> That woke the dancing leaves to day,
> With dewy blossoms newly born,
> And birds that on the branches play.
> The golden wheat upon the hills,
> The ruby cherries on the bough,
> With gentle tinkling of rills
> And emerald lawns; where are they now?
> Driven and whelm'd 'neath hills of sand,
> The gardens of their treasures swept,
> The crane stalks grimly o'er the land
> Where late the quail her feast-time kept. (pp. 55-56)

Yet, this sky, too, for all its seeming waywardness, Boyd assures us in her concluding lines, is still a locus of divine love, imaged as descending from on high in the light of the setting sun:

> All now is changed, but from above
> The setting sun's last ray is cast,
> And calmly beams with peace and love:
> That formidable cloud hath passed. (p. 56)

For all their belief in a divine Creator in a heavenly beyond, there is no doubt that the newcomers to the Limestone Plains were also capable of recognising agency, and sometimes also a trace of divinity, within the natural environment. Nonetheless, whereas Indigenous Australians had developed a mobile and flexible mode of dwelling that was well adapted to the unpredictability of the climate, as well as to other aspects of local ecology, the newcomers persisted in endeavouring to impose forms of land use that had been developed under very different environmental conditions. This misfit proved particularly problematic for the smallholders who selected land here from the 1860s and who, quite literally, continued to plough on, working the land in a manner that assumed a regular cycle of four seasons (as well as considerably deeper and richer soil than was generally to be found in most of the country), with the result that their labours were frequently foiled by a natural environment that continued to defy their expectations. To some extent, their perseverance in the face of such setbacks had biblical warrant. Although the topos of the Promised Land plays a considerably more muted role in Australian settler culture than it does in North America, for those "toilers who really laid the foundation of Canberra" (Shumack 1967: 83), many of whom had come here to escape dire poverty and, in the case of Irish nationalists or German 'Old Lutherans', political or religious persecution, the Exodus narrative could readily be called upon to provide reassurance that their endeavours to gain a foothold in this new world had God's blessing. This biblical warrant is recalled in the epitaph cited in the afterword to Shumack's autobiography: "The Lord your God hath given you this land to possess it" (1967: 170). That this possession was hard won, entailing much struggle with a recalcitrant earth under a capricious sky, could also be understood in biblical terms, namely as an inevitable outcome of the Fall, whereby the very ground was cursed by God on account of human sin (Gen. 3: 17-19).

2. "Awful yarns about snakes and death adders": Miles Franklin

Famously, God's curse is also said to have fallen upon the serpent as the agent of Eve's temptation (Gen. 3: 14-15), and it seems likely that this biblical anathema played a part in the utterly merciless treatment that the settlers meted out to snakes.[4] One of the stories that Shumack tells is particularly revealing in this connection. Shortly after their arrival on the Limestone Plains, he recalls how a certain George Flint took pleasure in frightening them with

> awful yarns about snakes and death adders [...]. We also heard strange tales about kangaroos that would attack and carry you to a waterhole and drown you. For a time we believed these tales, but after I had killed my first snake, a four-foot black one, we were no longer afraid. (1967: 31)

Here, the agency of colonial nature, cast as hostile, is clearly recognised but not necessarily respected. In slaying his first snake, the youngster from County Cork enacted a kind of *rite de passage*, in which the monstrous otherness of the colonial earth is symbolically overcome.

Snakes also figure significantly in the autobiography of Miles Franklin, who is undoubtedly the most renowned author of the late selection era[5] in the Canberra area, her novel *My Brilliant Career* (1901) being recognised as a classic of Australian literature. Franklin was born in 1879 at Talbingo, the grazing property of her maternal grandmother, Sarah Lampe, near Tumut, and spent her first ten years on a station, 'Brindabella', in the mountains overlooking the Limestone Plains. The name of one of the peaks in this range, Mt. Franklin, recalls her family's residence here. The Franklins also owned a neighbouring run, whose name was made familiar to Australian readers by the series of books that Franklin wrote under the pseudonym 'Brent of Bin Bin'. While the nostalgic nationalism of these tales of squatters and 'cockies' ('cockatoo farmers' being the colloquial expression for selectors) was already looking dated when they appeared between 1928 and 1956, the feminist and environmentalist consciousness that can be traced through much of Franklin's writing, including her *Childhood at Brindabella*, which was only published posthumously in 1963, was remarkably forward looking. Young Miles evidently enjoyed considerable freedom to roam in a still only partially domesticated natural environment, which she recalls as the greatest gift of her childhood:

> Santa Claus, the displaced European with his cotton-wool beard and minus the enchanting reindeer, is a bore [...] the open air furnished with miles of flowers, streams, orchards and mighty trees was my nursery-playground, and there was a variety of living toys. [...] To grow up in intimate association with nature — animal and vegetable — is an irreplaceable form of wealth and culture. (1963: 68)

It is noteworthy that although Franklin's comment on Santa Claus suggests a resistance to the importation of European cultural traditions to Australia, her endorsement of a childhood spent close to nature is thoroughly Wordsworthian. Her appreciation of the forested hill country in which she grew up was heightened by the trauma of being taken away from it when she was on the cusp of puberty, which meant that her affection for this lost home place became entwined with her grief at the inevitable passing of childhood. Tellingly, it is her disappointment with the "flatter, more lightly timbered country" of the disenchanted world of the Monaro Plains that prompts one of Franklin's most beautiful descriptions of the magical Brindabellas. In her new home, Franklin writes, there were no

> gorges and mighty rocks like castles and cascading streams draped with tree-ferns and maidenhair and flowering shrubberies along their banks. No lyrebirds gambolled across the track to flute in eucalyptus aisles across a big singing creek [...] no permanently running creeks, only weedy waterholes. (1963: 96)

Although the Franklin children were not permitted to own pets, they were encouraged to care for orphans and strays, and they were also expected to help look after the farmyard animals. Franklin recalls that their fowl houses were "as commodious as a man's hut", and the children were not allowed to confine or cage any creatures for their own pleasure (1963: 69-70). Franklin developed a particular love of the pigs, with whom she liked to wallow, dreaming of a pre-lapsarian world in which the animals had not yet learnt to flee from humans, but rather associated with them as equals (1963: 79). When told the story of St George and the Dragon, her sympathies were with the latter, and although she herself had a great fear of snakes, she disapproved of the settlers' "unrelaxing [...] war" against them. One of her most persistent childhood memories was of a close encounter with a blacksnake beside a creek wreathed in maidenhair fern. Returning to the same spot many years later, "doting and gloating on every rise and hollow of that cherished way", she discovered that the banks of the creek had been denuded of acacias and close cropped by the sheep that had followed the cattle and horses: "The place was bare and flat and unrecognisable; the creek was stripped of its exquisite shrubs, but it had not changed its course" (1963: 121-22). Moreover, its serpentine *genius locus* was still there. For her uncle, though, the war was evidently still raging, and he "skilfully mangled" the beautiful snake (1963: 122). Yet when she returned alone the next day, Franklin was blessed with a third serpentine encounter at this same spot, affording her the welcome opportunity to apologise to this embodiment of the abiding alterity of the Australian environment for the tyrannical behaviour of her own kind. She was, she says, "relieved to leave it undisturbed in enjoyment of his native earth, which he perhaps was worthier to infest than I" (1963: 123). This too was a *rite de passage* of sorts: one that, in turning aside from the patriarchal path of mastery in favour of a respectful recognition of the other, opens the way to reconciliation with the colonial earth (if not yet, or at least not explicitly, colonised people).

By the time Franklin's autobiography was published, the fly-infested sheep stations on the Limestone Plains below her home in the Brindabellas had been transformed into a remarkable 'bush capital'. This is the world into which I was born in the early 1960s, and to which I will return at the end of this essay. Before then, though, I would like to linger a little longer beyond the margins of the city, where elements of the older rural world of the Limestone Plains held on right up until the end of the millennium.

3. Monaro Pastoral: David Campbell

The pre-eminent poet of the pastoral landscape of the Monaro in the latter part of the twentieth century was David Campbell. As he writes in his 'Autobiographical Sketch', he was "born in a brass bed on a sheep station [...] not far from Gundagai, the town most often celebrated in the early songs and ballads of shearers, bullockies and bush-rangers" (1981a: 5). Descended on both sides from pioneering families, Campbell "was heir to a collective memory that went back to the early days of settlement", and wrote "with authority, insight and sureness about the land his forebears had done so much to pioneer" (Walsh 1987: 18). Having read English at Cambridge in the late 1930s, then done a stint as a fighter pilot in the Pacific during the War, Campbell returned with his wife and two children to the Monaro to farm his father's grazing property, 'Wells Station', just to the north of the city. There he built a house looking across Canberra to the Brinda-bellas. In the early 1960s, the Campbell family moved to another station, 'Palerang', near Bungendore to the east of Canberra, then, around 1968 when his first marriage ended, David and his new wife moved back closer to the city, settling at 'Folly Run' outside Quean-beyan, while retaining his wife's house in town.

Although Campbell would later become an influential figure in the burgeoning literary scene of the federal capital in the 1970s, one of his poems from the late 1950s, 'Looking Down on Canberra', is sugges-tive of his disdain for the human-all-too-human life of the polis. In the manner of many a pastoral poet from Virgil to Wordsworth and be-yond, Campbell proclaims that his place is among the hills, there to "think and sing in solitude":

> The thousand voices of the town,
> The worn phrase, the ruined word,
> In this clear mountain silence drown,
> Leaving the sweet song of a bird
> And coupled stone. (1989: 62)

Much of the poetry that Campbell wrote from this vantage point of rural retreat can be seen as renewing the pastoral tradition that had previously been translated into an Australian context by the bush balladists, of whom Banjo Paterson, himself a Monaro man, was Campbell's favourite. Chris Wallace-Crabbe (1987) refers to Camp-bell's verse as "squatter pastoral", although he observes that, not unlike the songs of imaginary shepherds that had been written for, if not by, English country squires by the likes of Robert Herrick in the seventeenth century, his poetry is peopled not by the privileged squat-tocracy, from whose ranks Campbell himself descended, but by bushmen and selectors. One of Campbell's most striking pastoral works from his Wells Station days is 'Cocky's Calendar', a twelve part cycle of poems, corresponding (generally rather obliquely) to the months of the rural year, whereby each individual poem echoes the structure of the whole in its arrangement of three four-line stanzas. In its title, this work looks back to the beginnings of English pastoral in Edmund Spenser's *Shepheardes Calendar* of 1579. In its aesthetic, though, it is closer to Yeatsian symbolism. Thus, for example, the hawk that hovers over its prey in the opening and closing stanzas, holding "all of time in his still stare" (Campbell 1989: 79), becomes a figure for the poet whose song penetrates beneath the surface of things, disclosing within the perishable entities apprehended by the senses something of the eternal.

The poetic 'I' of this work is as much a metaphysician as a farmer, and a decidedly 'cocky' one at that, for whom (after the fashion of Fichtean Idealism), the perceived world is but a thing of his own mind's making:

The hawk, the hill, the loping hare,
The blue tree and the blue air,
O all the coloured world I see
And walk upon, are made by me. (1989: 74)

This potentially solipsistic emphasis on the world-creating power of the human mind, which is continued into the first two stanzas of the second poem, suggestively entitled 'Red Cock', is nonetheless countered by an acknowledgement in the third of the countervailing force of the more-than-human world upon the poet's mind:

About my heart the land is dumb
And quietly the habit grows
Of peace, but fires like lions come
And fill my blackened heart with crows. (1989: 75)

Although Campbell claimed that his generation were much taken by Donne and the seventeenth-century metaphysical writers, and "found Shelley and the romantics a bit old hat" (1981b: 27), the metaphysics informing this work are in fact thoroughly Romantic, emphasising the continuity of human thought with the more-than-human rationality inherent in nature: "that sweet Intelligence / That hovering far-sighted love / That sees me and in whom I live" (1989: 74).[6] This geo-cosmic Intelligence is not conceived of monotheistically as a transcendent deity, though, for this metaphysician-farmer's "marble acres lie / Open to an empty sky", as we read in the third poem, a pantheistic 'Prayer for Rain', in which hare and man alike are said to participate (1989: 75). Where Campbell's poetic vision draws away from the Romantics, though, is in his resistance to the privileging of the human voice. In this, his thinking appears to have been informed by the aesthetic theory articulated by A. D. Hope in *The Cave and the Spring* (1965). For Hope, as Campbell explained in a conversation with Roderick Shaw at Palerang in the early 1960s, poetry was pre-eminently a work of "celebration", in which the poet is "aligning himself with the energies of nature and of the world [...] you're with the world and one of the voices that is expressing it — just the same as a tree with its leaves" (1981b: 31). This, then, is a participatory ecopoetics, rather than one in which a silent earth is held to wait upon the human word to give it voice.[7]

The countryside of 'Cocky's Calendar' is recognisably Australian, but only just. This is a place where rain is often scarce, where, in the autumn, "tongued like snow, if snow could cry, / The cockatoos flake from the sky / With one black crow amongst their white / As a re-minder of the night", while in early spring, lovers disport themselves under wattles on hillsides that "smoulder into gold" (1989: 75 and 77). In general, though, Campbell is less interested in rendering the par-ticularity of place here than in recasting the landscape as a terrain of symbolic significance, and his lexicon draws heavily on the language of Elizabethan pastoral, effectively Europeanising the Monaro Plains of the poem in a way that is analogous to the European colonisation of the land itself. By the late 1960s, however, Campbell was striking out in new directions. His greatest pastoral work of this period is 'Works and Days', which answers to 'Cocky's Calendar' by replicating its structure, as well as continuing its engagement with earlier pastoral literature. Here, though, the lines are longer and looser, the rhyme less regular, the tone more reminiscent of Banjo Paterson than W.B. Yeats, and the register considerably more colloquial. In place of the pathos and classical allusion of such lines as "But O the flakes that fell last year / No rain will wash from Tempe's hair", Campbell now offers us a more mundane reality, in which the glory of the harvest is celebrated in a decidedly down-beat and vernacular register: "Towards dusk by the dump, some sheila's singing a song" (1989: 76, 103).

Recalling in its title the ancient origins of European pastoral in Hesiod, 'Works and Days' recasts the cycle of the rural year into a thoroughly south-east Australian mould. Paying greater attention to the particularity of place, Campbell also strives to be true to the historicity of the world that he discloses in this work. This is no timeless rural idyll, but a landscape in the grip of modern industrialised farming, as we are reminded in the opening line: "The tractors are out turning the red soil". As "Brodricks, Masters and Harrisons" continue to plough up the earth, "Valley and town are red with a mist of dust", and when it comes to sowing in the winter, you find "Dust and super [i.e. superphosphate fertilizer] pitting your eyes like blindness" (1989: 102). Despite the deployment of heavy machinery and chemical weaponry, life on the land is nonetheless still shown to be vulnerable to forces beyond human control, notably the weather, and dependent upon the able assistance of dogs and horses. Livestock, too, while ultimately bred for profit and destined for the knackery, are accorded their own agency, and a resistant one at that. Thus, in the final lines of the poem, the cattle are said to "stand four-square and bawl / In yards with threatening horns as the floats back in" (1989: 107), while the fabled merinos are referred to, not without affection, as a constant source of exasperation:

> Sheep! They're not dumb, they know every trick in the book:
> Bale up, go down, dig in, at the cry of "Sheep!"
> Ask the penner-up. Ask Paterson: merinos,
> He wrote, made our men sardonic or they would weep! (1989: 104)

Here, as in 'Cocky's Calendar', crows are called upon to darken the rural world, reminding the reader of the suffering that is also to be found here, but Campbell is now far more explicit about what they do to his sheep during lambing: "When a ewe's / Cast, crows take the eye first (foxes the tongue) / And their beaks are poison" (1989: 104). Crows haunt much of Campbell's verse, forming an integral part of his vision of life, "where goodness without evil is not goodness" (1981b: 31).

'Works and Days' is without doubt Campbell's greatest tribute to the pastoral world of the Monaro. Poignantly, as fellow Canberra poet Robert Brissenden remarks, it is also something of "a farewell to the pastoral phase of his life" (1987: 3). In *The Branch of Dodona* (1970), where it first appeared, 'Works and Days' is preceded by a poem entitled 'My Lai', which opens the collection. Here, a Vietnamese farmer discloses how his works and days have been devastated by the blight of war, reminding us that while Australian farmers were assaulting their land with weapons of mass production, Australian conscripts were helping to lay waste to the lush countryside of Vietnam:

> I was milking the cow when a row of tall bamboo
>> Was mowed by rifle fire
>> With my wife and child in the one harvest,
>> And the thin blue milk spilt and ruined. (1989: 126)

In the face of this evil, of another order entirely than that which bedevilled lambing season in the guise of ever-present crows, Campbell felt that it was no longer possible to continue to "sit and sing in solitude" of life on the land. Meanwhile, the land itself, far from offering a place of withdrawal from the political, had been recognised as a site of political struggle. Also included in *The Branch of Dodona* is 'Kuring-gai Rock Carvings', a cycle of poems that also reframes 'Works and Days' by recalling the Indigenous mode of being and dwelling that was torn apart in the creation of the pastoral landscape that Campbell had inherited. Here, as in his later poems such as 'The Anguish of Ants' and 'Bellbirds', which bewail the disappearance of native woodland and forests, Campbell turned his attention to counting the cost of the continuing process of colonisation of a more-than-human Indigenous world, with which his own farming practices had been complicit. For Campbell, an engagement with the political, and with the life of the polis, had become inevitable, and there was no longer any question of perpetuating the time-honoured gesture of pastoral retreat.

4. The Culture of the Bogong Moth Eaters: Marion Halligan

What then of the city, and political heart of the nation, which, by the early 70s was beginning to sprawl out beyond the margins of Limestone Plains, transforming ever more of the surrounding sheep stations into suburbs? Michael Thwaites, Canberra's most loyal lyricist, has nothing but praise in his 'Psalm for an Artificial City':

> When enemies cry against you
> with vipers' tongues shooting malicious darts
> sneering "unreal, alien, artificial",
> rejoice, be glad
> grapple their empty slanders to your soul
> and glory, glory in being artificial
> as are those Aboriginal artefacts
> strewn in your valleys, shaped by human hands
> aeons before such things as cities stood.
> […]
> Be glad that Burley Griffin,
> before surveyor's pegs, huts, buildings, highways,
> long before fountain, lake that bears his name,
> stood on this ground
> lifted his eyes to the hills, sun, mist, and cloud,
> the singing light, the beckoning Brindabellas
> and willed his plan the servant not the master
> of a chosen place. (1993: 26)

Judith Wright, who was also active in the Canberra literary scene in the 1970s, as well as campaigning for Aboriginal rights and conservation, was more equivocal. In the opening poem of her 'Brief Notes on Canberra' (1975), 'City and Mirage', Wright emphasises the gap between Griffin's glorious vision and its inadequate realisation: "Shoddy officials / argue his job away, confuse his plan. / Mirages, changed to lakes, lap sewage. / Cities are made of man". Yet the neo-classical aspect of the vision itself, which Wright also foregrounds here in the "reflected image" of "arena, amphitheatre, gallery / on gallery of quivering marble" (1994: 351), was itself arguably in tension with the Griffins' aspiration to create a city that was environmentally attuned. While the layout of central Canberra is based on the natural land and water axes formed by the hills and the river that flowed between them, its strictly geometric design embodies a modernist aesthetics of abstract universalism rather than responsiveness to the particularity of place.

For all that, it is, as Thwaites observes in 'A Message to my Grandson', in large part thanks to "Burley Griffin's genius, working / After his death, enlisting trees, hills, water / As friends (he hoped) not subjects to his plan" (1993: 12), that Canberra can truly to be said to be "a city in the landscape and of the landscape" (Taylor 1999: 79).[8] Under the influence of John Sulman, a keen proponent of the Garden City movement, who took over from Griffin as Chairman of the Federal Capital Advisory Committee (1921-24), Canberra also became an exceedingly leafy city, rich in parks, gardens, and open space.[9] Although most of the trees that were planted on the formerly treeless plain were exotic and largely deciduous, the larger hills remain forested, and many smaller rises throughout the city retain rock-strewn grassy woodland. When I was growing up there in the 1960s, Canberra's suburban gardens tended to be miniature manicured versions of England's green and pleasant land (except for drought years, when water restrictions left them drab and brown); but wherever you lived, the bush was never far away.

A tension nonetheless remains, for although Canberra's town planners sought to allow a space for nature within the city, the overall impression is one of containment and control. This is particularly evident in the damming of the Molonglo to create Lake Burley Griffin, which is undoubtedly very beautiful, but entirely lacking in the tricksterish character of the changeable river. Similarly, although Canberrans are more than happy to enjoy a view of the Brindabellas, and sometimes like to venture out there for a hike, they recoil in horror from the Bogong moths that stray through their windows each spring, drawn off route in their journey to aestivate in rock crevices in the mountains by the glow of the city. The 40,000 lights of the new Parliament House burn especially long and strong, and millions of moths meet their death there when they have the misfortune to alight on poisoned window-ledges. In thus reviling as a pest a creature that once provided an annual feast for several local tribes, contemporary non-Indigenous Canberrans are evidently still far from embracing the Indigenous earth as a nourishing terrain.

Both the lake and the moth figure significantly in Marion Halligan's novel, *The Point* (2003). The title refers to the imaginary restaurant on an equally imaginary promontory of Lake Burley Griffin that provides the central locus and tropological focus of Halligan's tale. Based on one of Marion Mahony Griffin's beautiful drawings for her husband's prize-winning entry in the Federal Capital Competition of 1911, The Point is an octagonal building, and seven of its eight walls are made entirely of glass. In its unusual contours, this fictional locale exemplifies the Griffins' fascination with geometric configurations of space, which has lent the city that they designed a distinctly classical and cosmopolitan aspect, while its glass walls exemplify their commitment to attuning their artfully constructed urban spaces to the surrounding landscape. Halligan nonetheless emphasises that the diners' view is ultimately severely restricted. Reputed to be the best restaurant in town, The Point caters largely to jet-setting businesspeople, politicians, diplomats, journalists, and other well-heeled professionals, a microcosm of the privileged demographic of the capital city. These are, as the narrator observes, "those who possess, and are perhaps themselves possessed. Outside are the dispossessed". At night, when the restaurant is illuminated like a lantern, "the dispossessed see themselves, and the others, the insiders". For the insiders, though, the glass walls function more like a mirror, such that they "see only themselves" (2003: 1-2).

The cuisine that is concocted here by the ever-innovative *chef de maison*, Flora Mount, is emphatically cosmopolitan and postmodern, featuring such kitsch 1960s dishes as oysters Rockefeller and chicken Kiev, revisited with a subversive twist, and erstwhile working class staples, like tripe, reinvented as an exotic delicacy. Witchetty grubs, something of a cliché of bush tucker, are also on the menu. This surprising inclusion does not necessarily signal respect for Indigenous traditions or bioregional specificities, however: on the contrary, it merely demonstrates that for Flora and her cosmopolitan clientele, anything from anywhere is now available to be transformed into a postmodern work of culinary art. Towards the end of the novel, however, Flora imports a new political agenda into her cooking feats in what she terms the "virtuous globalisation" of the Slow Food Movement (2003: 267). It is while she is pondering her contribution to a forthcoming Slow Food dinner that the tragic denouement of the novel is brought about by the unexpected intrusion into the elegantly cosmopolitan and exclusively human world of The Point of an abject other-than-human native: namely, a Bogong moth, which flies into her kitchen one night through an open window. Recalling the feasts of old, Flora decides that moth cakes would be the perfect dish to add local colour to her eclectic menu, and sets about catching the other hapless Bogongs that had followed the first into her domain. Flora's second-hand knowledge, though, is inadequate, and, ironically, her time is short. In her haste, she makes a fatal mistake. The rock she takes inside on which to roast her moths is a river stone, a remnant of pre-lake days, which explodes when she heats it, causing a conflagration that kills the cook and destroys her restaurant, as well as injuring the destitute teenage girl sleeping outside.

Flora Mount's moth cake project, undertaken in the absence of Indigenous instruction, and for the benefit of an urban elite, might be taken as emblematic of a false reconciliation: although well-intentioned, it looks more like appropriation. In the city outside the book, though, real places of reconciliation are now beginning to be created. One such is to be found on the Acton peninsula. Here, the grounds of the Humanities Research Centre and the Centre for Cross Cultural Research are graced by an artwork composed of three totem poles honouring the Bogong moth and thereby also the culture of the moth eaters. The Bogong is a particularly apt emblem of reconciliation in the Canberra region, for it was the feast provided by the moths that possibly helped to gave rise to its name: Ngambra means 'meeting place'. If it is truly to be so once again, however, in an age of almost universal dislocation, we will need to bring down the walls separating the dispossessed from those who possess, and, in extending a welcome to the stranger, we will also need to hone our skills of translation and mediation.

Let me conclude then by returning to the words of a contemporary Canberra poet of Greek extraction, whose own work mediates between the poetic idioms of Classical Greece and settler Australia. In 'Your Life So Far', Timoshenko Aslanides offers this affirmation of the possibility of becoming native to a new place:

> Regardless of where you might
> Have been born, you are beginning to be Australian.
>   You are beginning to get up in the morning
> And marvel at sunrise which pastes the colour of wheat

Over a demonstrably edible landscape.
You are beginning to eat the landscape. (2001: 96)

Although Aslanides' description of sunrise over the Limestone Plains recalls the staple food of settler culture, cultivated in much of south-eastern Australia at considerable cost to both Indigenous people and their land, we are now slowly beginning to recognise that native flora and fauna too are "demonstrably edible". The challenge that remains, though, is not only to regain a sense of Australia's varied landscapes as nourishing terrains, and to seek their continued, or, in many cases, restored flourishing for the benefit of a more-than-human community of life. If Canberra is to become a place where some common ground might be found, as promised by its name, the decisions that are made there amidst the unconformities of Capital Hill must be such as to enable more than just a privileged few to find a place at the feast. To this end, the ecopoetics of the erstwhile Limestone Plains will need to be supplemented by a postcolonial ecopolitics within, and beyond, the hill-bound houses of Parliament.

Notes

[1] On Aboriginal understandings of 'country' as a 'nourishing terrain' see Rose 1996. On the Canberra area specifically, see Flood 1996, Jackson-Nakano 2001, and Gammage 2002.
[2] I am grateful to Paul Carter for this observation in a conversation at the symposium on *Ecologies and Environments in an Expanded Field*, University of Adelaide, 4 July 2004.
[3] On nature as Trickster, see Haraway 1991: 199-201.
[4] One need only look at the determination of Lady Jane Franklin (1791-1875) wife of Sir John, Lieutenant-Governor of Van Diemen's Land. Though hugely sympathetic to the arts and sciences (she founded the first Royal Society for the Advancement of Science outside of Britain, and also Hobart's Botanical Gardens), she did not hesitate to place a one shilling bounty on snakes in Van Diemen's Land (Tasmania); 12,000 snakes later the idea was abandoned. See also Judith Wright's poem 'The Killer'.
[5] Selection referred to the choosing of land by 'selectors' for farming (generally between 40-640 acres). What began as an attempt to break the monopoly of the earlier arrivals, the squatters, whose land holdings were immense, became a land-class war between the selectors and the squattocracy. See 'Selection' in *The Oxford Companion to Australian Literature* (1994) for a discussion of the Selection Acts (1858-1872) and a discussion of literature concerned with selection as a theme.

[6] In conversation with Roderick Shaw in the early 1960s, Campbell also observed, "I think there's a lot of thinking in art — the kind of thinking that formed cells in Nature that built themselves into different animals, trees, shells". This evolutionary process, like that of artistic creativity, he insists does not follow a preconceived plan: "this is the thing which does away with God and makes evolution terribly exciting" (1981b: 27).

[7] In this, Campbell's view of the poet's calling draws close to the participatory theory of ecopoetics that I have proposed as a corrective to the overvaluation of the human voice, and human language, found in Martin Heidegger, whose work has been drawn upon by some ecocritics, most prominently Jonathan Bate (Rigby 2004a).

[8] On the ecopolitics of Griffin's Canberra design see also Wright 2001.

[9] The greening of Canberra was largely undertaken by T.C.G. Weston, who was appointed Officer-in-Charge, Afforestation (later, Parks and Gardens) for the ACT in 1913, and also made Director of City Planning by Sulman in 1926 (Gray 1999). Weston's tree-planting project was carried further by Lindsay Pryor, who was appointed Superintendent of Parks and Gardens in 1944, a position that he held until he retired in 1958 (Hince 1993).

Bibliography

Primary Sources

Aslanides, Timoshenko. 2001. *A Calendar of Flowers. Selected Poems 1975-2000*. Wollongong, NSW: Five Islands Press.

Boyd, Bertha. 1994. 'Australian Dewdrops' in Gillespie 1994: 55-56.

Campbell, David. 1970. *The Branch of Dodona and other Poems: 1969-1970*. Sydney: Angus and Robertson.

——. 1981a. 'Autobiographical Sketch' in *Poetry Australia* 80: 5-6.

——. 1981b. Conversation with Roderick Shaw in *Poetry Australia* 80: 26-32.

——. 1989. *Collected Poems*. North Ryde, NSW: Angus and Robertson.

Franklin, Miles. 1963. *Childhood at Brindabella. My first ten years*. Sydney: Angus and Robertson.

Gale, John. 1977. *History of and Legends Relating to the Federal Capital Territory of the Commonwealth of Australia* (Queanbeyan: A.M. Fallick and Sons, 1927). Facsimile reprint, North Sydney: Library of Australian History.

Gillespie, James ('The Wizard'). 1994. "Lake George" in Gillespie 1994: 124-25.

Gillespie, Lyall (ed.). 1994. *Early Verse of the Canberra Region. A Collection of Poetry, Verse and Doggerel from the Newspapers, Other Publications and Private Sources*. Canberra: Local History Series.

Halligan, Marion. 2003. *The Point*. Crows Nest, NSW: Allen and Unwin.

Hope, A.D. 1965. *The Cave and the Spring: Essays on Poetry*. Adelaide: Rigby, 1965.

Shumack, Samuel. 1967. *An Autobiography, or Tales and Legends of Canberra Pioneers* (ed. J.E. and S. Shumack). Canberra: Australian National University Press.

Smith, Charles Throsby. 1820. Journal entry for November 1820. National Library of Australia MS689.

Thwaites, Michael. 1993. *The Honey Man and other Poems*. Canberra: Trendsetting.

Wright, Judith. 1994. *Collected Poems 1942-1985*. Sydney: Angus and Robertson.

Secondary Sources

Abell, R. 1991. *The Geology of Canberra*. Bureau of Mineral Resources Bulletin 233. Canberra: AGPS.

Bate, Jonathan. 2000. *The Song of the Earth*. Cambridge, MA: Harvard University Press.

Brissenden, Robert F. 1987. 'Introduction' in Heseltine 1987: 1-6.

Cameron, John. 2003. 'Beneath Capital Hill: The Unconformities of Place and Self' in Tredinnick, Mark (ed.) *A Place on Earth: An Anthology of Nature Writing from Australia and North America*. Sydney: University of New South Wales Press: 55-64.

Flood, Josephine. 1996. *Moth Hunters of the Australian Capital Territory: Aboriginal Traditional Life in the Canberra Region*. Downer: J.M. Flood.

Gammage, Bill. 2002. *Australia under Aboriginal Land Management. 15th Barry Andrews Memorial Lecture*. Canberra: University College, ADFA.

Gillespie, Lyall. 1991. *Canberra 1820-1913*. Canberra: Australian Government Publishing Service.

Gray, J.E. 1999. *T.C.G. Weston (1866-1935), Horticulturalist and Arboriculturalist. A critical review of his contribution to the establishment of the landscape foundations of Australia's National Capital*. Unpublished PhD thesis. Canberra: University of Canberra.

Haraway, Donna. 1991. *Simians, Cyborgs, and Women: The Reinvention of Nature*. New York: Routledge.

Heseltine, Harry (ed.). 1987. *A Tribute to David Campbell*. Kensington, NSW: University of New South Wales Press.

Hince, Bernadette. 1993. *A Pryor Commitment. Canberra's Public Landscape 1944-1958*. Unpublished Msc. Thesis. Canberra: Australian National University.

Jackson-Nakano, Ann. 2001. *The Kamberri. A history from the records of Aboriginal families in the Canberra-Queanbeyan district and surrounds 1820-27, and historical overview 1928-2001*. Weereewaa History Series, vol. 1. Canberra: Aboriginal History.

Rigby, Kate. 2004a. 'Earth, World, Text: The (Im)possibility of Ecopoiesis' in *New Literary History* 35(3): 427-42.

———. 2004b. *Topographies of the Sacred: The Poetics of Place in European Romanticism*. Charlottesville: University of Virginia Press.

Rose, Deborah Bird. 1996. *Nourishing Terrains: Australian Aboriginal Views of Landscape and Wilderness*. Canberra: Australian Heritage Commission.

'Selection'. 1994. in *The Oxford Companion to Australian Literature*. Wilde, William H., Joy Hooton and Barry Andrews (eds). Melbourne: Oxford University Press.

Taylor, Ken. 1999. 'Picturesque Visions of a Nation: Capital City in the Garden' in *The New Federalist* 3: 74-80.

Wallace-Crabbe, Chris. 1987. 'Squatter Pastoral' in Heseltine: 87-99.

Walsh, Gerald. 1987. 'David Campbell's Family Background: The Blackman and Campbell Families in Australia, 1801-1917' in Heseltine 1987: 7-20.

Wright, David. 2001. 'Ecopolitics by Design: Walter Burley Griffin's Canberra' in *Ecopolitics* 1(2): 13-16.

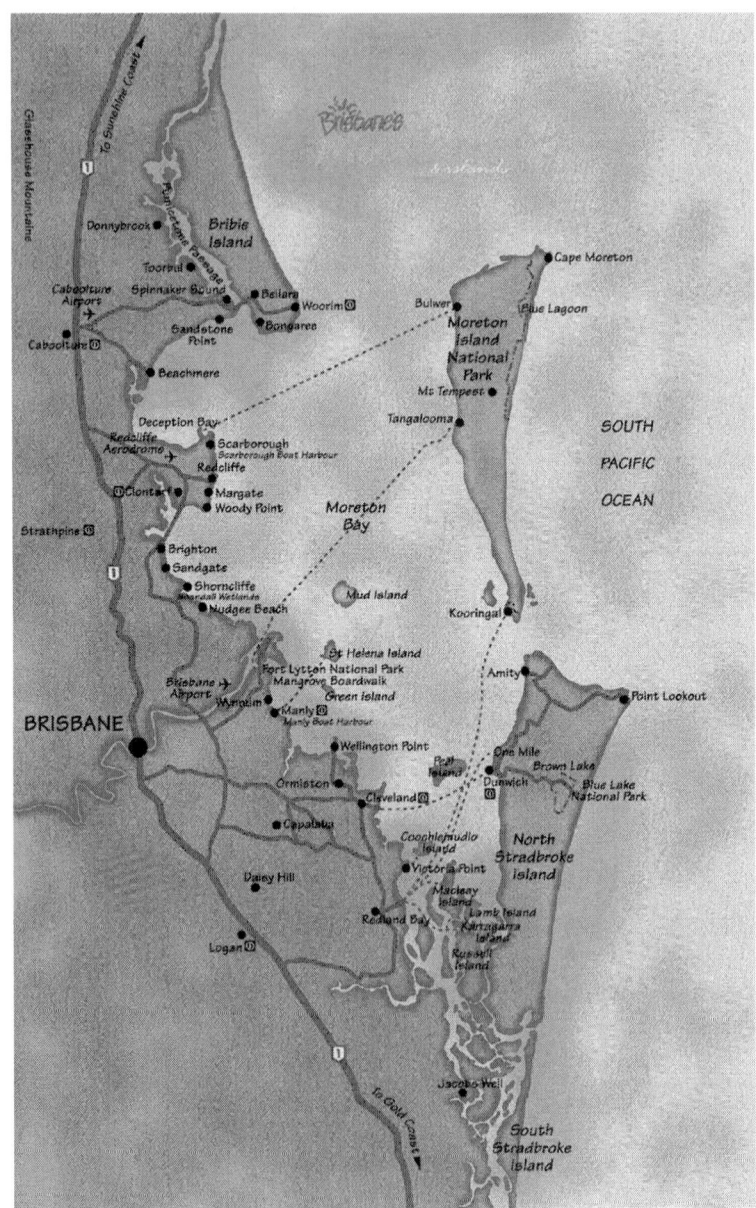

Figure 7

Hugging the Shore:
The Green Mountains of South-East Queensland

Ruth Blair

Abstract: Extrapolating from their observations of the relationship between the Blue Mountains and the New South Wales coastline, David Foster and Martin Thomas have concluded that the sea and the mountains represent a "fundamental divide in the mental geography of Australia" (Thomas 2004: 36). The south-east Queensland coast presents a different experience of the relationship between sea and mountains. Here, from northern New South Wales to Noosa, north of Brisbane, the mountains, clearly visible from ocean, bay, and shore, are an intrinsic part of the coastal experience. This chapter looks at some writing about two of the coastal mountains with substantial national park areas: Lamington and Tamborine. It considers how writing about these areas reflects on the process of engagement with the natural world, the process by which settlers become dwellers, and the particular understanding of our place in the world that can evolve out of the experience of "the frontiers between the wild and the cultivated" (Schama 1995: 574).

> Below the mountain the coast was still beautiful, with no more than a few patches of buildings, low and unpretentious. From the mountain the ocean was limitlessly blue. (Wright 1999: 248)

In south-east Queensland and the far north of New South Wales, the mountains come down to the sea — or close to it. The painter William Robinson captures this proximity in 'Creation Landscape — the dome of space and time', where the forests of the border ranges swirl with glimpses of sky and sea.[1] The coast, from just below the Queensland-New South Wales border to Noosa, north of Brisbane, has major off-shore islands[2] and a hilly, occasionally mountainous, hinterland that, for residents and visitors, is part of what 'the coast' means. To the north are the peaks of the Glasshouse Mountains, then the Blackall

Range. Further north, Noosa has its own hilly hinterland. To the south, the border ranges with their plateaus and spurs, and finally Mount Warning, form the coastal backdrop. Cook described them on his voyage up the east coast in 1770, beginning with Mount Warning:

> A high point of land, which I named Cape Byron, bore N.W. by W. at the distance of three miles. It […] may be known by a remarkable sharp peaked mountain, which lies inland, and bears from it N.W. by W. From this point, the land trends N.13 W.: inland it is high and hilly, but low and level near the shore; to the southward of the point it is also low and level. […] [A little further north, the location of dangerous breakers] may always be known by the peaked mountain which has just been mentioned, and which bears from them S.W. by W. for this reason I have named it MOUNT WARNING. […] The land about it is high and hilly, but it is of itself sufficiently conspicuous to be at once distinguished from every other object. (qtd. in Groom 1949: 12)

A century and a half later, Arthur Groom surveyed the coastal mountains from that "high and hilly" country:

> We sat on the point of Binna Burra. It was a clear summer day. Eighteen miles eastward the Pacific breakers rolled along the visible coastline from Southport to Cook's Point Lookout on Stradbroke Island. Northward on the horizon Cook's Glass House Mountains jutted up […] ninety-two miles by air line; and beyond [them] the Blackall Range joined the Conondale Range well over one hundred miles from Binna Burra. (p. 144)

Binna Burra, on the Lamington Plateau of the McPherson (border) range, was in the process of becoming a tourist site, with a 'guest house' like that established by the O'Reilly family on another part of the plateau. Most of these mountainous areas today include substantial areas of national parkland. They are an inseparable part of what 'the coast' means in this area, part of the tourist experience, where a holiday stay, even on the Gold Coast, along with trips to 'Sea World' or 'Movie World', includes a day trip to "the green behind the gold", as a study of land use in the Border Ranges puts it (Monroe and Stevens 1976: 52).[3] And all have been written about, painted, photographed, and, indeed, sung or had music made about them.

   These are not distant mountains, not the far horizon of the Blue Mountains, west of the Sydney coastline, that prompted David Foster in *The Glade Within the Grove* (1996) and, taking up his point, Martin Thomas in *The Artificial Horizon* (2004), to extrapolate that the sea and the mountains represent a "fundamental divide in the mental geography of Australia" (Thomas 2004: 36). The Blue Mountains, says Foster's narrator, are "the sea's antithesis" (Foster 1996: 33). That the coastal mountains of south-east Queensland and northern New South Wales are precisely not "the sea's antithesis" is the starting point for this chapter. They are visible from the littoral — indeed visible when one is bobbing about on the sea, visible from the offshore islands — and linked to the sea in a multitude of ways. Thomas Welsby, the chronicler of Moreton Bay[4] in the early twentieth century,[5] describes the Glasshouse Mountains as "useful guides to schnapper grounds from Cape Moreton to far north Caloundra" (1967: 41). The connections between mountain and bay are lyrical as well as useful:

> The windings of Pumice Stone Passage place the mountains in every changing position and at early morning, ere yet the sun has risen, if the tide permits an onward journey [...] these changing positions are most interesting to watch. Beerwah almost always comes foremost, now hiding Coonowrim under its heavy silent shelter, again letting it stand by its side as though in guardianship, and as the sun throws its light on the peaks and foliage of the mountains, the run up towards Mellum Creek is entrancing. (vol. 2, p. 41)

For reasons of scope, and because they have attracted the largest amount of writing, I will look at some representative writing about the Lamington Plateau and Tamborine mountain which is the Gold Coast's (and Brisbane's) hill station. Some of the accounts I will present are by well known writers; other writers are less well known. Some are or have been active conservationists; some are settlers; some residents; some just passing through. Some of the texts are in prose; some are poems. All of the writers have been moved to express the sense of what these mountains have told them. Apart from the mention already made of Cook, explorers' accounts will not be included. The journals of Logan and of other explorers, notably Alan Cunningham and Matthew Flinders who, in his circumnavigation of the continent, explored many points on shore, are a story in their own right.[6] My concern here is more with representations of a *relationship* with the land, looking at how occupiers become dwellers and how visitors become lovers.

The story I am telling is a story of white settlement, because the Aboriginal relationship with the land is, like that of the explorers, another story. Aboriginal stories are often connected to naming. Where the mountains are concerned, the larger groupings (e.g. ranges) tend to have settler names, while individual mountains often have Aboriginal names.[7] This is the case, for example, with the Glasshouse Mountains whose individual mountains have Aboriginal names. Sometimes Aboriginal stories involve accounts of origins but sometimes names, in particular, relate to activities in the landscape. 'Tamborine', for example, is said to be a version of an Aboriginal word meaning 'Place of Yams' (Groom 1949: 125). Mount Roberts was named 'Binna Burra', meaning the 'Place of Beech Trees' (*Gmelina leichardtii*, not the Antarctic Beech, *Nothofagus moorei*, also found in the area) (Groom 1949: 127).

1. Green Mountains

I begin with the Lamington Plateau, part of the McPherson Range, sitting on the Queensland-New South Wales border, and one of the first National Parks in Queensland. Arthur Groom came as a visitor to the area in 1925. *One Mountain After Another* (1949) is a history of settler relationships with the mountains, including his own experiences. It is also a story of motivations behind the establishment of the first National Parks in Queensland. One of the early settlers, Robert Martin Collins, inspired by Yellowstone National Park in the United States (created 1872; dedicated 1890), became a Member of the Legislative Assembly of Queensland in 1896 and planted the seeds of interest in his passion: a National Park along the McPherson Range (Groom 1949: 63-64). Neither Collins nor the man who carried on his work, Romeo Lahey, one of the founders of Binna Burra Guest House, was a writer, but their stories, compellingly told by Groom, show the passionate sense of belonging that settlers in this area could develop. Lahey, from the second generation of a timber-getting (mostly cedar) family, "could see and visualize the ultimate denudation of the hills" and the effect this would have on the "balance of nature" in the area. (Groom 1949: 77). In taking up Collins's campaign for a National Park, Lahey campaigned door-to-door in the area, held dances and public meetings, and gave illustrated lectures (Groom 1949: 80).[8]

Thanks to the efforts of many under Lahey's guidance, in 1915 the Lamington National Park of 47,000 acres came into being and was gradually added to between 1915 and 1935.

Collins and Lahey lived in valley settlements. In 1911, before the passing of the legislation for the Lamington National Park, eight members of the O'Reilly family took up blocks on what was then called Roberts Plateau. Groom describes the early days:

> They humped their packs to 3000 feet. [...] They tackled the standing wall of jungle; hundreds of acres of giant trees, entwined and held with a tangling mass of vines and creepers, some of them as thick as a man's body [...] they knew the art of felling scrub [...] the rain-forest must come down. It must dry and rot awhile, and then burn in a concentrated and planned inferno of smoke and flame. Then the grass seed must be sown and weeds kept low, and perhaps in due course cattle could be enticed up [the] track. (p. 86)

This is all happening at the same time that Lahey and others are campaigning for a National Park in the area. The way the story evolves might, as Groom says, be described by a businessman as a story of "goodwill with commercial value" (p. 89). Many wanted the O'Reillys re-located. Here is what happened. Not only lovers of the bush, but scientists began to take an interest in the temperate rainforest of the mountains, as it was gradually recognised that

> the McPherson Range was a meeting place of much of the plant life of north and south. It had types of plant life existing only elsewhere thousands of miles away, with no quick and obvious explanation of the gap in between. (p. 88)

Gradually transformed into conservers as well as farmers, through friendships forged with nature lovers and through their own sense, having previously lived in the Blue Mountains, of the special qualities of the area, the O'Reillys "cherished the friendships based on mutual appreciation and love of the wild life" (p. 88) and the Field Naturalists' Society had the good sense to nominate several of the O'Reillys as honorary rangers.

Arthur Groom tells this story with a keen dramatic sense, with fine perceptions, and with grace. *One Mountain After Another* (1949), with its mixture of history, polemic, personal experience and description, deserves to be in the pantheon of Australian nature writing. We talk a lot these days in Australian nature writing circles about filling some

perceived gap, about not having a nature writing tradition in the way
that America does. Yet we don't always see how books like this and
Welsby's works *are* our tradition. In early settlement — and we are
only now, in Australia, at the point where Thoreau *et al.* come in, 200
years down the track of the first permanent white settlement in the
eastern United States — the stories are of doing, more than they are of
reflecting. Groom makes this story of the Border Ranges not a separate history, but one connected to the wider social world. He ends with
a chapter called 'The Blood-Red March', which begins by telling of
his own experience of walking with friends on a day when strange
formations of small clouds began to march across the sky, turning
crimson far too early in the afternoon:

> The jungle was deathly still; and there is nothing more silent than a great forest in
> which all life has come to a standstill. Our footsteps in soft leaf-mould sounded
> loud by contrast. The temperature was cold enough to vaporize our breaths in long
> plumes. Instead of the usual grey of an overcast day, we felt and saw, coming
> down through the trees and overwhelming the depth of shadow, a cold, red infil-
> tration of light and atmosphere. [...] Its reflection was subtle and diffused, from
> every leaf and trunk and log, from every rock. (p. 186)

They return home to the news that Germany has invaded Russia, and
the strange phenomenon they have witnessed becomes a prophecy in
their own lives. Groom, writing in 1949, urges the connection between
these events and conservation values:

> We live now in the aftermath of war. Armies of occupation are in different coun-
> tries; starvation and misery, crime and distrust, are rife. A frightful bomb hangs as
> a sword of Damocles. There is disturbing restlessness in people, which can grow
> easily once again into frightful bloodshed and ruin. [...] [S]urely in the face of
> these facts [...] we must recognize the supreme importance of complete liaison
> between civilization and Nature. [...] The primitive places of the world, with the
> National Parks of the present and future, designed to hold in sanctuary the natural
> things that man has been fleeing from for so long, may yet go a long way towards
> making the world a peaceful place to live in, by providing the balance in health,
> peace of mind and inspiration, so essential to all men and women. (p. 190)[9]

What makes the Lamington story, as told by Groom, so compelling, so
full of lessons and ideas for us today, is what it tells of the complexity
of the route from settler to dweller. The Native American writer Leslie
Marmon Silko has a lovely expression in her novel *Ceremony*: "be-

longing with the land" (1997: 117). Deftly, through skewing the grammar, she erases the usual connotations of the word 'belonging'. It is an
expression of a piece with the Heideggerian term 'dwelling', much
used in the literature of place today. The picture Groom gives of
Collins and Lahey and the O'Reilly family is of settlers who become
dwellers, who learn to 'belong with' the land. There is, as Groom
encourages us to understand, something more in the O'Reilly story
than "goodwill with a commercial value" (p. 89).

And the O'Reilly family produces a writer — one of the youngest
of the pioneering brothers and sisters, Bernard. In 1937 a mail plane
was lost in the south-east corner of the state. Bernard O'Reilly believed it had gone down in the mountains. Requests for an account of
his impressive feat of tracking down the plane caused him to write
Green Mountains, which tells two stories — that of the crash and the
rescue, and that of the family settling on the plateau. He later ap-
pended *Cullenbenbong* — further stories of the family and the area.
Bernard was 12 when the family moved onto the mountain. He grew
up meeting naturalists and writers like Charles Barrett and Alec Chisholm, to whom he pays tribute in his Introduction.[10] The rescue story
is exciting. When all had given up on the plane, O'Reilly believed
they were looking in the wrong direction and set out on his own,
finding the plane and two survivors, only one of whom remained alive
by the time the rescue party got to them. Though O'Reilly says that
"[t]oo little of this book is devoted to my favourite themes, birds and
wildflowers" (1981: s.p.), the landscape is an integral part of the story
and in the telling even of the most dramatic moments, O'Reilly not
only describes the terrain but takes time to name plants. Looking at
the cliff of a waterfall where one of the party, Jim Westray, had died
trying to reach help, he reflects:

> Here he made his fatal mistake. The cliff to the right was completely covered with
> giant Helmholtzia lilies with sabrelike leaves, seven feet long. These gave appar-
> ently safe hand and foothold to the bottom of the cliff. Westray was not to know
> that there is nothing more brittle or treacherous than those safelooking footholds.
> (p. 38)

I am old enough to have had childhood visits to 'O'Reillys'' when
Rose, Tom, and Bernard were still alive, though Bernard no longer
lived at the Guest House. There were hearty three-course meals,

packed lunches for hiking, endless cups of tea, and slides and stories at night. *Green Mountains* was important because it storied the places we were delighting in discovering — one of the walks, for example, was to Westray's Grave. (I doubt the very upmarket ecotourist experience of today quite matches up, though that is perhaps unfair to the O'Reilly family who still run the enterprise, as descendents of the Laheys do Binna Burra ecotourist lodge.) As well as the stories, we would re-live the experience of the forest in the book:

> Down from the lush green of the trees hung ropes and festoons of leafy vines, away aloft were incredible tree gardens, tons of ferns and blooming orchids weighing down the huge boughs which supported the jungle roof. Great palm trees reared their umbrella tops aloft. The jungle floor was a delicate, intricate embroidery of contrasting greens which were countless varieties of fern; all the conservatories of the world rolled into one. (p. 132)

I had always thought *Green Mountains* a rather unimaginative title. It was the name the O'Reillys gave to their guest house and of course, being largely rainforest, the surroundings were definitely green. But in writing this essay I see another meaning in the title. These precisely are green, not blue mountains. From the coast they appear green, not the blue of distance — "the green behind the gold" (Monroe and Stevens 1976: 52).

2. White Witches

The Lamington National Park, like the Border Ranges in general, is an area of great beauty, and a debt is owed to those who early saw the desirability, on all kinds of grounds, of conserving it. There is not, however, anywhere near the body of writing about this park that we find about its near neighbour — a spur of the McPherson Range — Tamborine Mountain. I believe the reason for this disparity is that, being National Park, the Lamington plateau attracts visitors but has few dwellers. There are poems and some pieces of music inspired by the forests, especially the ancient Antarctic Beech trees, but there is no substantial body of work, either poetry or prose, about the area. It seems that genuine dwelling is a requirement for more than passing reflections. Tamborine Mountain, with its broad, flat top (seven miles long and, at its broadest, three miles wide) and views of the Gold

Coast, is a settled area, to the point of concern today about continuing sub-division of farming properties.

The word 'magical' is neither clichéd nor hyperbolic in relation to Tamborine Mountain. Judith Wright, certainly the most famous writer to live on the mountain (continuously from 1946 to 1966), captures the magic in her autobiography, *Half a Lifetime*:

> We would spend an afternoon walking down into the rainforest that covered the mountain slopes, marveling at the wealth and variety of life there, or an evening walking down the track into the parks, finding dead logs illuminated with a pale light from rotting wood and rows of blue phosphorescent fungi. Below the mountain the coast was still beautiful, with no more than a few patches of buildings, low and unpretentious. From the mountain the ocean was limitlessly blue. (1999: 248)

Tamborine Mountain was worked by timber-getters and settled in the last decades of the nineteenth century. The first settlers were the Curtis and Geissman families. A descendant of the former, Raymond Curtis, lives on the mountain today. He is an accomplished musician, composer, and poet. His wife Eve has written a history of the mountain, *The Turning Years* (1990). In 1908, thanks to the efforts of the early Curtises and others, Queensland's first National Park was created on Tamborine Mountain — an area called Witch's Falls. From the beginning, Tamborine, like Lamington, was seen as a potential place of retreat. In 1896 John Cameron opened a small boarding house (Groom 1949: 126), and through the early decades of the twentieth century, Brisbane folk made the somewhat arduous journey to the mountain top. Among them was a highly successful novelist and poet, columnist for the *Bulletin* magazine,[11] and founding member of the Queensland Press Club, Mabel Forrest.[12] In 1929 Mabel Forrest built a house on the mountain. The house still stands and she has descendants still living nearby. Forrest called the house 'White Witches' after the white-trunked local Eucalypt and her novel of that name. There is a story to be told about witches and Tamborine. The idea is part of a larger story about European mythologies inhabiting the Australian landscape, but the term also reflects the slumbering gothic qualities of this now largely rural landscape.[13] Here is a poem of Forrest's that also continues the witch metaphor and that expresses the intimate connection between ocean and mountain:

'Mountain Rain'

All the grey witches came up from the sea
And they trailed their cloaks of ragged grey
Over the wet mountain ways to me.

O wet and wild was the mountain way!
They dropped wet streamers across the hedge
And spattered pools at the red road's edge.

Burned through the rain in the garden place
The rose of fuchsia's drooping head,
Crimson of canna and cyclamen,
Snapdragon tall, in their close-set bed,
While the branches, etched with a stormy pen,
Of mountain trees lay against the sky
To trip the witches as they flew by. (1985: 126)

I like this poem for the way it captures a particular quality of this area: settlement and forest living beside each other. The history of Tamborine is, not surprisingly, a conflicted one in terms of the forests. Judith Wright describes how the forest remained the enemy for many of the long-term residents. She and Jack McKinney found that "the beauty of the mountain had endless fascination as we tried to identify trees, ferns, palms, birds and insects" (1999: 248), yet they found "a kind of hostility still to those deep forests — since most of the descendants of the few early arrivals had spent much of their childhood and youth battling the forest for a niche on which to farm and live" (p. 248). The Antarctic beeches (often referred to locally as "the bitch trees" [p. 263]) and the cedar were all gone and what rainforest remained was largely in areas difficult of access for timber-getting. Hilda Curtis, who had recorded flora and fauna with "an old black-and-white camera", was, Wright says, an exception in her passion for the forests (p. 248).

To return to Mabel Forrest's poem, Tamborine folk were then and are still committed growers of introduced species, and Tamborine is a haven for sub-tropical dwellers who yearn for temperate gardening. (The possibility of growing canna lilies and cyclamen together is many a gardener's dream!) But the forest in her poem is not in some kind of opposition to the settler garden — not the enemy. Tamborine today is a place beloved of gardeners who are also (often first and foremost) conservationists.

3. Wild Garden

Raymond Curtis grew up on a farm beside a national park on Tamborine Mountain (Curtis 2003: 74). During 1980 he worked for the National Parks and Wildlife Service on the mountain and kept a daily journal. In the manner of Gilbert White and Henry David Thoreau, he made a book out of it, which he eventually published in 2003 as *Rainforest Journal*. That the book was published locally and has had a fairly local audience does not diminish its significance, for it is of and for this place, but at the same time is an exemplar of the value of expressions of committed, reflective writing about specific localities that we have not nearly enough of in Australia. As Curtis and his fellow worker clear tracks and tend the wild gardens of the national park areas on the mountain, they observe the life of the forests, and Curtis records their observations:

> Walking back up the track through the rainforest in the late afternoon, we saw a lyrebird about nine metres up in a tree. It is unusual to see one in a tree at all, but to be able to watch it for five minutes is quite remarkable. (p. 30)

> So many plants here are new to me, who have lived my life on the eastern rainforest side of Tamborine Mountain, that I am surrounded by surprises every day. (p. 34)

> Today in grading the track, I needed to cut through a few greenhood orchids. I hated doing so, but it was necessary — and there are plenty of them all over the mountainside. Anyway, in the process I discovered how they multiply. (p. 41)

> As we work, we are constantly in the company of great hoop pines. (p. 47)

> Everywhere in this thickly wooded valley between the Knoll and the Beacon there is the sound of life. (p. 52)

> Beside the track I saw a black and gold wasp flying around a large huntsman spider which was running rather unsteadily over the leaves on the scrub floor. (p. 70)

The book of the journal contains some of Raymond Curtis's poems, which express his deep love of this mountainous area. The poems are

more extensively collected in *Double Rainbow* (1989). He is also, as I
have mentioned, an accomplished composer. In conversations I have
had with him, it has become clear that he made a deliberate choice to
remain on the mountain, when he might have developed his musical
and poetic talents elsewhere. He began a youth orchestra on the mountain, as well as a choir. With his wife Eve, he has worked hard to
preserve the integrity of the relationship between Tamborine's wild
and settled places. I mention all these things because Raymond Curtis
so broadly demonstrates the congruence of life and art, and the value
of creative expression as a way of being in the world.

4. Flame Tree

Judith Wright lived on Tamborine Mountain for 20 years, from 1946,
when she bought a small cottage that she and Jack McKinney called
'Quantum'. After the birth of their daughter Meredith, they moved to
a larger property, 'Calanthe'. McKinney died in 1966, and Wright
later moved to Braidwood, near Canberra. Wright is without question
one of the handful we might name the greatest Australian poets. She
has been, also, one of the foremost environmental activists in Australia. The mountain was not some lofty retreat. It was her dwelling place
while she developed as a poet and activist. "I was", she says in *Half a
Lifetime*, "lucky to live in a quiet, beautiful place with a man whose
jokes and conversation kept me happy as well as in love and too busy
to be tempted far into the controversies of the time" (1999: 277). And
she remarks: "Fortunately I loved gardening and looking after fowls"
(p. 277). It is a daunting task to comment on Wright's poetry in this
short space. I hope to demonstrate her affection for the Tamborine
landscape and its creatures, but also to show how she draws our attention to something special about the nature of poetry in the very broad
spectrum of writing about nature.

Let's begin with Wright's collection of poems called *Birds*, first
published in 1962, dedicated to her daughter (then 12 years old), and
beautifully illustrated in the original edition by Annette Macarthur-
Onslow. The birds in this collection are mostly mountain birds. The
poem 'Brush Turkey' attempts to consider from the bird's perspective
what the loss of forest habitat can mean, as the bird has learned to
scavenge from tourists:

He learns the scavenger's habits
with scrap and crumb —
his forests shrunk, he lives
on what the moment gives:
pretends, in mockery,
to beg our charity. (1971: 180)

And he has learned to manipulate the gardener, "[aping] the backyard bird":

Ash-black, wattles of scarlet,
and careful eye,
he hoaxes the ape, the ogre,
with mimicry. (p. 180)

The poems have a delightful particularity in the quality of their observations. Of thornbills:

Their tiny torrent of flight
sounds in the trees like rain,
flicking the leaves to the light —
a scattered handful of grain,
the thornbills little as bees. (p. 167)

But in every poem, too, Wright does the further work of the poet, which is to record the interactions between the individual and the world outside the self and to draw meaning from experience. In *Birds*, Wright, sometimes on a light note, sometimes on a more serious, uses a variety of metaphorical tools, including anthropomorphism, to achieve this end. Of satin bower-birds (rainforest birds that collect blue objects for their mating bowers):

In summer they can afford their independence,
down in the gullies, in the folds of forest;
but with the early frosts they're here again —
hopping like big toy birds, as round as pullets,
handsomely green and speckled, but somehow comic —
begging their bread. A domestic,
quarrelling, amateur troupe. (p. 179)

These aren't frivolous associations and the poem continues to seek, through metaphor, a way to express the meaning of the non-human world:

> Look — the young male bird —
> see his eye's perfect mineral blaze of blue.
> The winter sea's not purer
> than that blue flash set in a bird's head. (p. 179)

The great poems about the Tamborine forests are an early poem about an ancient plant form, 'The Cycads', and three poems about the flame tree (*Brachychiton acerifolia*). All of these poems drink deeply of the knowledge and wisdom that the forests can offer. I am not using this metaphor lightly, as these intense poems give a sense almost of feeding on — drawing life from — the natural world. The cycads, whose "smooth dark flames flicker at time's own root," seem "[a]mong the complicated birds and flowers / [...]a generation carved in stone." (1971: 41-42). They are the lesson of time:

> Take their cold seed and set it in the mind,
> and its slow root will lengthen deep and deep
> till, following, you cling on the last ledge
> over the unthinkable, unfathomed edge
> beyond which man remembers only sleep. (p. 42)

The flame tree is the lesson of life. These deciduous trees are one of the glories of the south-east Queensland temperate rainforest — flashes of scarlet on dark green hillsides in spring. In three poems in different collections,[14] Wright reflects on the dramatic bursting forth of the masses of small, coral-like flowers.

In the first poem, 'Flame-tree in a Quarry', the tree is the very stuff of life, protesting the human desecration of the landscape — "the old cry of praise" coming out of "the torn earth's mouth":

> Out of the very wound
> springs up this scarlet breath —
> this fountain of hot joy,
> the living ghost of death. (1971: 62)

In 'The Flame Tree', the poet asks:

How to live, I said, as the flame tree lives?
— to know what the flame-tree knows; to be
prodigal of my life as that wild tree
and wear my passion so? (p. 97)

'The Flame-tree Blooms', written after the death of Jack McKinney, is
not about a forest tree. A true Tamborine poem, it is about a domestic
flame tree, grown in Wright's and McKinney's own garden:

It was you planted it;
and it grew high and put on crops of leaves,
extravagant fans; sheltered in it the spider weaves
and birds move through it. (p. 291)

Flame trees can take a long time to 'perform' — to flower at all, and
then to flower before leaf growth:

For all it grew so well,
it never bloomed, though we watched patiently,
having chosen its place where we could see
it from our window sill. (p. 291)

The poem continues:

Now, in its eighteenth spring,
suddenly, wholly, ceremoniously
it puts off every leaf and stands up nakedly,
calling and gathering

every capacity in it, every power,
drawing up from the very roots of being
this pulse of total red that shocks my seeing
into an agony of flower.

It was you planted it;
and I lean on the sill to see it stand
in its dry shuffle of leaves, just as we planned,
these past years feeding it. (p. 291)

Wright became an environmental campaigner while living on Tamborine Mountain. In 1963, she and others formed the Wildlife
Preservation Society of Queensland. A major concern was the Great

Barrier Reef, threatened by oil drilling and by mineral and limestone mining. Without this thirteen-year campaign, the reef would not exist today in all its extent as a great natural wonder.[15] Apart from a poem like 'Rainforest' (*Phantom Dwelling*, 1985), Wright's later poems are not specifically about Tamborine. They are, however, deeply influenced by her developing understanding of the environmental crisis produced by the industrial world. Her astute essays, such as 'The Individual in a New Environmental Age', collected in *Because I Was Invited* (1975), present her ecological perspective. Shirley Walker sees this perspective reflected in her later poems that show, says Walker, a suspicion of the romantic imagination "as both narcissistic and egotistical" and the poet as one among other conquerors, using nature "to express human concerns rather than a concern for nature" (Walker 1996: 32).[16] While there is an undoubted shift in Wright's poetry, I do not find this watershed view of it entirely convincing. There are obvious Romantic elements and strong Pastoral elements in Wright's writing. Tamborine has been for a long time more Pastoral landscape than wilderness, but, as I said above, its inhabitants experience, and Wright explores, the presence of the border between forest and cultivation. One of the cycad groves sits today on the edge of a road; another is deep in the National Park. Mabel Forrest's witches hint at the wild 'other' that lurks beyond the edge and that becomes for Wright a channel to a sense of the human as part of something overwhelmingly larger than our activities. But with her poem 'The Cycads', something more than the Romantic sublime is going on — or rather, the sublime becomes a way of learning the message of humility and responsibility that underpins any serious environmental awareness today. The seeds of a keener sense of where the lines are drawn (akin to A.R. Ammons's advice to the philosopher of nature in 'Gravelly Run': "hoist your burdens, get on down the road" [1986: 11]) are already, I believe, well planted.

Wright had a sense of responsibility in spades, and no small part of that was her sense of indebtedness to and responsibility towards Aboriginal peoples — from those whom her family, settling on the New England Tableland of New South Wales, had displaced,[17] to the Aboriginal people of Tamborine Mountain, also long displaced. Here, too, Tamborine played a part, for it was from her Tamborine base that she developed her friendship with the Aboriginal poet from Stradbroke Island, visible from Tamborine, Oodgeroo Noonuccal (yet another conversation between sea and mountain).[18] Wright ends *Half a Lifetime* by recalling dispossession of Aborigines by her family and other European settlers on the New England tableland, her sense of it in her childhood, and her deepening sense of it on Tamborine. Since her childhood, she says, she has travelled "over many stolen lands", and lived in some, particularly the country of Yugambeh, or Tamborine, to whose people she must "apologise even more deeply". She ends:

> To all of the peoples of the old and true Australia on whose land I have trespassed and whom, by being part of my own people, I have wronged, I plead forgiveness. To all of them I owe that overweighing debt of life itself, and to all of them I now bend my head and say Sorry. Sorry, above all, that I can make nothing right. (1999: 296)

5. "The necessary intimacy of wildness" (Schama, after Thoreau [1995: 578])

Foster and Thomas are right, of course. The sea and the mountains do mean different things. What I have tried to show in this essay is that their meanings, in Australia, are not necessarily remote from each other. In the coastal area of south-east Queensland that I am discussing, the deep space and time of the sea and the deep time of the forest almost connect, as they do in William Robinson's painting. Settlement and tourism domesticate, to a degree, both wildernesses. But both wildernesses talk, and occasionally fight, back. At the end of *Landscape and Memory*, Simon Schama teases out of Thoreau's writing his profound insights into the concept of the wild and its role in Western social life, with the concomitant perception that "neither the frontiers between the wild and the cultivated, nor those that lie between the past and the present, are so easily fixed" (1995: 574). The settlers who have become dwellers in the areas discussed in this essay work on those fluid borderlines.

So too do the visitors, for whom the coastal mountains of south-east Queensland are now well-exploited tourism resources. Those of us who live in the area tend to take the mountains for granted: feel like an afternoon drive to Tamborine? a day trip and a bit of a walk at Lamington? a hike up one of the Glasshouse mountains? From the metropolis of the area, Brisbane, or from the coastal resorts, it's not far to go. At Springbrook (another tourist destination on the edge of the Lamington Plateau) the delighted young friends I took along for an afternoon break from intensive 'World' experiences on the Gold Coast spotted a satin bower-bird's nest just behind the wall of the car park, and saw magpies making an aerial attack on a giant lace monitor (the goanna *Varanus varius*) in the picnic ground. At Binna Burra you don't have to go far along a well-graded walking track to come to a grove of Antarctic Beech. Raymond Curtis describes such a grove on a walk from O'Reilly's:

> They are exceptionally old trees — thousands of years — which, though apparently too old to seed, continue to grow and sucker out from the original trunk in a sprawling circle. They are so ancient that one can see the original ground level — perhaps two metres up the knotted twisted root-system about one's head. (2003: 19)

Among these ancient trees "whose hearts were old when Solomon was young" (Raymond Curtis, "Antarctic Beech Forest" in *Double Rainbow* 8), or dwarfed by a Strangler Fig (*Ficus watkinsiana*), one has, however fleetingly, the experience of Wright's 'The Cycads', brushing the edge of time.

Notes

[1] The vista in this painting stretches from Springbrook, over the top of Mount Warning, to the coast. Reproduced in Lynne Seear (2005: 10-12).
[2] Stradbroke and Moreton Islands, which form Moreton Bay, offshore from the mouth of the Brisbane River, and Bribie Island, offshore from the Glasshouse Mountains area and the beach town of Caloundra, forming Deception Bay. Because the bays and the Pumicestone Passage (between north Bribie Island and the mainland) offer more opportunities for off-shore sailing than the ocean, there are a number of works describing the mountains from the bay areas or the off-shore islands. Thomas Welsby is quoted below on the Glasshouse Mountains. David Malouf has a touching poem about seeing these mountains across water: "Seen always across / a bay called Deception — abandoned pier, bait-kiosk, the prawnfleet swinging at anchor with the moon — five gables of glass" (1970: 15-16). In Vance Palmer's novel *The Passage*, the narrator describes the view from the Pumicestone Passage to the Blackall Range behind Caloundra: "Beyond [the Passage] rose the mountains in a wall, purple in the clear sky, yet so near that you could almost pick out the threads of road running up their sides" (1944: 16).

[3] *The Border Ranges: A Land Use Conflict in Regional Perspective*, commissioned by the Royal Society of Queensland in 1976, addresses the importance of the Ranges as a tourist resource linked to the Gold Coast: "The Ranges provide a scenic back-drop to the coastal tourist resorts. One only needs to see the scars on the Adelaide Hills caused by quarrying to appreciate how critical is the need to conserve an escarpment backdrop" (Monroe and Stevens 1976: 51). The ranges are said to add "variety" to the general holiday experience (p. 52), with some holidaymakers seeking "a much deeper experience of the rainforest environment", motivated "by either a desire to escape from the pressures of urban life or a special interest in nature" (52).

[4] See above note 2.

[5] Thomas Welsby (1858-1941) awaits re-discovery as a great writer of Australian nature and place. A distinguished Brisbane businessman, his various enterprises included part-ownership of a shipping company. He wrote seven books about the history and his own experiences of Moreton Bay. In 1967, A.K. Thomson edited the works as a collected edition. His best known book, included in the collection, *Schnappering and Fishing in the Brisbane River and Moreton Bay Waters;[with] a Wandering Discourse on Fishing Generally* was published in 1905.

[6] There is a vast literature on the explorers. For a general approach to the rhetoric of explorers in Australia see Paul Carter, *The Road to Botany Bay* (1988), and Robert Dixon, *The Course of Empire* (1986). See also Tom Lynch's discussion of explorers in chapter 4.

[7] This concept of naming (the act of insisting on particulars rather than generalizing) demonstrates traditional recognition of bioregional differences. See 'Aboregional', chapter 11.

[8] Tim Bonyhady (1993) has written on the significance of the slide shows of Olegas Truchanas and Ralph Hope-Johnstone in the campaign to save Lake Pedder in Tasmania in the 1970s.

[9] Groom is of his time in writing about the 'primitive' places of the world. His chapter on Aborigines, too, while showing a will to include them in his story, is embarrassing today for, if not an overall patronizing tone, certainly patronizing moments.

[10] Charles Barrett (1879-1959), a well-known naturalist and journalist, edited the journal *The Victorian Naturalist* from 1925 to 1940. His many books include *In Australia's Wilds: The Gleanings of a Naturalist* (1919). Alec H. Chisholm (1890-1977), the editor-in-chief of *The Australian Encyclopedia* (1958), was a literary scholar with a strong interest in the natural world. He published a landmark collection of Australian natural history writing, *Land of Wonder: The Best of Australian Nature Writing* (1964).

[11] *The Bulletin*, first published in 1880, has an important role in Australian literature as the major vehicle for publishing poetry, short stories, and essays.

[12] Mabel Forrest (1872-1935) was a prolific writer. Besides poetry and short stories, she wrote six successful novels. In 1926 her novel *The White Moth* (1924) was made into a film, *The Moth of Moonbi*, directed by one of the most successful film makers of the early Australian film industry, Australian Charles Chauvel.

[13] On Mabel Forrest and witches, see Marie-Louise Ayres (1996).

[14] 'Flame-tree in a Quarry' is from *Woman to Man* (1949); 'The Flame-tree' is from *The Gateway* (1953); 'The Flame-tree Blooms' is from *Shadow* (1970).
[15] See her account in her book *The Coral Battleground*. The Great Barrier Reef is again under threat, this time by more insidious enemies — global warming, exacerbated by the damage done by run-off from coastal cane farming.
[16] See also Shirley Walker's earlier essay in *Vanishing Edens* (1992).
[17] Judith Wright was born in 1915 at Thalgarrah Station, near Armidale, New South Wales. Her ancestors arrived in Australia during the 1820s and 1830s and established several large properties in the Hunter Valley and New England regions.
[18] For a discussion of Oodgeroo Noonuccal's work, see chapter 11.

Bibliography

Primary Sources

Ammons, A.R. 1986. *The Selected Poems*. New York: W.W. Norton.
Curtis, Raymond. 1989. *Double Rainbow: Poems*. N. Tamborine, Qld.: Raymond Curtis.
Forrest, Mabel. 1985. 'Mountain Rain' in Curtis, Eve (1988): 51.
Foster, David. 1996. *The Glade Within the Grove*. Milson's Point, NSW: Random House.
Malouf, David. 1970. *Bicycle and other Poems*. St Lucia, Qld.: University of Queensland Press.
O'Reilly, Bernard. 1981. *Green Mountains and Cullenbenbong*. Fortitude Valley, Qld.: Kemp Place Investments.
Palmer, Vance. 1944. *The Passage*. Melbourne: Robertson and Mullins.
Silko, Leslie Marmon. 1997. *Ceremony*. New York: Viking.
Welsby, Thomas. 1967. *The Collected Works* (ed. A.K. Thompson). 2 vols. Brisbane: Jacaranda Press.
Wright, Judith. 1962. *Birds*. Sydney: Angus and Roberston.
——. 1971. *Collected Poems 1942-1970*. Sydney: Angus and Robertson.
——. 1977. *The Coral Battleground*. Melbourne: Thomas Nelson.
——. 1999. *Half a Lifetime* (ed. Patricia Clarke). Melbourne: Text Publishing.

Secondary Sources

Ayres, Marie-Louise. 1996. 'Mabel Forrest and the Witch' in Pearce, Sharyn, and Philip Neilsen (eds) *Current Tensions: Proceedings of the 18th Annual Conference of the Association for the Study of Australian Literature*. Brisbane: Queensland University of Technology: 76-84.
Bonyhady, Tim. 1993. 'Lake Pedder' in *Island* 65: 29-34.
Carter, Paul. 1988. *The Road to Botany Bay: An Exploration of Landscape and History*. New York: Knopf.

Chisholm, Alec H. (ed.). 1964. *Land of Wonder: The Best Australian Nature Writing.* Sydney: Angus and Robertson.

Curtis, Eve. 1988. *The Turning Years: A Tamborine Mountain History.* N. Tamborine, Qld.: Eve Curtis.

Curtis, Raymond. 2003. *Rainforest Journal: Tamborine Mountain National Parks 1980.* N. Tamborine, Qld.: Raymond Curtis.

Dixon, Robert. 1986. *The Course of Empire: Neo-classical Culture in New South Wales 1788-1860.* Melbourne: Oxford University Press.

Groom, Arthur. 1949. *One Mountain After Another.* Sydney: Angus and Robertson.

Monroe, Ronald, and N.C. Stevens. 1976. *The Border Ranges: A Land Use Conflict in Regional Perspective.* Brisbane: Royal Society of Queensland.

Robinson, William. 2001. *Darkness and Light: The Art of William Robinson* (ed. Lynne Seear). S. Brisbane, Qld.: Queensland Art Gallery.

Schama, Simon. 1995. *Landscape and Memory.* London: HarperCollins.

Seear, Lynne. 2005. *William Robinson: Paintings and Sculptures 2003-2005.* Collingwood, Vic.: Australian Galleries.

Thomas, Martin. 2004. *The Artificial Horizon: Imagining the Blue Mountains.* Carlton, Vic.: Melbourne University Press.

Walker, Shirley. 1996. *Flame and Shadow: A Study of Judith Wright's Poetry.* St Lucia, Qld.: University of Queensland Press.

——. 1992. *Vanishing Edens: Responses to Australia in the Works of Mary Gilmore, Judith Wright and Dorothy Hewett.* [Townsville, Qld.]: James Cook University and Foundation for Australian Literary Studies.

Tales of the Austral Tropics:
North Queensland in Australian Literature

Robert Zeller

Abstract: From the late nineteenth century to the present, writers' conceptions of tropical North Queensland have undergone a gradual development. In the work of Ernest Favenc, the North was a kind of hell, a testing ground for Imperial heroes. In that of E.J. Banfield, it was a paradise and land of opportunity. For Jean Devanny, the region was an arena for human action and a potential land of redemption. The satirist Thea Astley used North Queensland locales as a crucible in which human failings were distilled. More recent works by David Malouf and Alex Miller try to come to terms with the region's history of exploitation and dispossession, and suggest how white Australians might come to be at home there.

> Perhaps no more desolate, depressing scenery can be found anywhere in the world than on the mangrove-flats of North Queensland. As you row slowly up some saltwater creek, nothing is visible on either side of low banks of oozy mud, awash at high-tide, covered with writhing and distorted trees [...]. [O]ne expects to meet at every turn a crew of skeletons gliding along with Satan at the helm. Now and again a branch creek breaks the monotony of the scrub, for the shore here is a perfect labyrinth [...] of watercourses, whilst the only living occupants visible are armies of hideous crabs, or an occasional evil-looking alligator [...] .
>
> By day it is dismal enough; by night it is worse. The venomous mosquitoes buzz about you in myriads, strange sounds and cries resound through the twisted roots of trees [...] and, as the night wears on, a white mist, cold and dank, breathes deathly clamminess over all. (Favenc 1997: 15)

Thus begins Ernest Favenc's 'The Last of Six', first published in the Sydney *Bulletin* in 1890 and later collected in a volume of his stories. Favenc's tropical romances are the starting point for my discussion of how tropical North Queensland has been written into Australia's literary consciousness over the last century or so. It has been seen as both hell and paradise, but in neither case has the mythical construction done much good for the natural environment, which has suffered tremendously as a result of resource extraction, pastoralism, agriculture, and population growth. The literature produced about the region, usually by writers who came from elsewhere, developed from an uncertainty about what might be made of this apparently inhospitable place through a period when it was seen as a possible paradise and land of economic opportunity to a time in the late twentieth century when writers began to explore what it might mean for white Australians to be at home there.

This region lies north of about 21 degrees south latitude, roughly from Mackay to the tip of Cape York Peninsula. There is a fairly narrow coastal plain, much of it devoted to the growing of sugar cane. Beyond the Dividing Range is an agricultural and pastoral area that includes the Atherton Tableland. The landscapes are not those of the stereotypical Australian bush, and they have not usually loomed large in either the national imagination or the canon of Australian literature. Sometimes the region is subdivided into the Wet and Dry Tropics — north and south of Townsville, respectively. Offshore is the Great Barrier Reef as well as many islands, of both continental and coral origins. Of course, on the local level, environments are much more diverse — mangrove estuaries, dune systems, sclerophyll forests, swamps, grasslands, etc.

To say that the Reef and the islands are offshore, though, is not to make them separate from the continental area. In describing the Aboriginal patterns of settlement and land use on the Cape York Peninsula, Chase and Sutton note,

> The Nesbit River area consists of seven patrilineal territories which divide the coastal lowlands into roughly parallel segments, each forming a strip from the ocean back to the mountains. [...] To such landbased calculations, however, must be added the marine environments extending eastwards beyond the beachline to include reefs, bars and the small off-shore islands. All of these are seen as being equally part of the 'country' along with the landmass, and contain mythological sites. (1981: 1830)

Islands and, to a lesser extent, reefs figure in some of the writing I will cover. They have figured much more prominently, however, in scientific writing about the region, both professional and popular (see Bowen and Bowen 2002), which I will not touch on here.

White settlement came relatively late to the tropical North. In the early days minerals and timber were heavily exploited. The first major agricultural product was bananas, produced through the labour of Chinese (Reynolds 2003: 65-66). Then in the late nineteenth and early twentieth century came the development of the sugar cane industry, supported at first by the importation of indentured labour obtained from the islands of the South Seas, often by less-than-scrupulous means. After that, the fortunes of the area tended to rise and fall with the price of sugar. Now tourism is a major component of the economy.

The region has suffered its share of environmental problems, including the importation of the infamous cane toad in addition to the effects of extensive logging, grazing, and cane growing. The Reef and some of the rainforest remnants enjoy World Heritage status, though both remain under threat. The region is also seeing population growth because of its attraction for retirees, the influx of whom may well put a strain on the infrastructure and further tax the natural environment.

For a long time, the attitude of European Australians towards their tropics was ambivalent. As historian David Walker has shown, there was widespread concern that British stock might degenerate in the tropical climate. At the same time there was a concern that if the North (the Northern Territory as well as North Queensland) were left underpopulated, it would eventually be occupied by 'Asiatic hordes'. The region's history has had an unsavoury racial aspect, in terms of both the dispossession of the indigenous inhabitants and the racism directed at the Chinese and the South Sea Islanders (often called Kanakas) who went there to labour. These issues recur in writing about the region.

Another aspect of writing about North Queensland involves environmental disputes. Such disputes range from E.J. Banfield's protests to the Queensland government about its enforcement of laws protecting birds to Judith Wright's *Coral Battleground*, which recounts the fight to protect the Barrier Reef from oil drilling, to Thea Astley's *It's Raining in Mango*, which begins and ends with references to the protest against building a road into the Daintree.

1. Favenc and Banfield: Hell and Paradise

The work of Ernest Favenc (1845-1908) and E.J. Banfield (1852-1923) appeared originally in newspapers — Favenc's in the *Bulletin* and Banfield's in the *North Queensland Register* and the *Townsville Daily Bulletin*. Favenc, writer of sensational stories in the tradition of Rider Haggard, explored much of the inland of North Queensland; he also worked as a miner and a drover. According to North Queensland scholar Cheryl Taylor, he "understood his task as author as aiding in the construction of the new nation's vision of itself, and in asserting the uniqueness of that vision" (Favenc 1997: xxvi). That vision was decidedly white and heroic in its upholding of the ideals of the British Empire. The tropical landscape in his stories tends to be malevolent, as the passage quoted above suggests. Taylor says of these stories that "human agency in evil and terror is often secondary to the agency of particular landscapes, most often the desert, but also the reefs, mangroves and caves" (p. xxviii). Here is a strain that will return in different forms in later writing about the region: nature as antagonist, and as an obstacle that must be overcome rather than accommodated or adapted to.

This is in line with a literature of Empire where unsettled lands were testing grounds for intrepid male adventurers. But as Lawrence Buell has noted, writers in newly settled lands also made use of European models of the pastoral. The pastoral could be used to normalise the appropriation of land from indigenous people; at the same time, though, it could also serve as

> a bridge [...] from anthropocentric to more ecocentric concerns. For the pastoralization of new worlds, in spite of some of its original motives, also created a space for the eventual advancement of nature's claims on human society. (Buell 1995: 52)

E.J. Banfield serves as an excellent example of Buell's point.

Banfield is best known for his stay on Dunk Island (1897-1923), a move that enacted the European fantasy of retiring to one's own desert island. While there, he produced three books: *Confessions of a Beachcomber* (1908), *My Tropic Isle* (1911), and *Tropic Days* (1918). A fourth collection, *Last Leaves from Dunk Island*, appeared posthumously in 1925. In addition to those collections of essays, though, he also wrote travel books, such as *Within the Barrier: Tourists' Guide to the North Queensland Coast* (1906; also published in 1907 as *Queensland: The Winter Paradise of Australia*). Before that he was among those advocating the separation of the North into a separate colony, and in many of his newspaper columns he argued for the agricultural development of the region (he was particularly enthusiastic about bananas). Banfield, so to speak, first put North Queensland on the literary map:

> If I am successful in convincing that North Queensland is neither a burning fiery furnace nor yet a sweltering steamy swamp; that the country is not completely saturated with malaria; that there are vast areas which no drought can tinge with grey or brown, where there are never-failing streams, and where cool fresh water trickles among the shale and shattered coral on the beaches, where sweet-voiced birds sport and resplendent butterflies flicker, then these writings will have been to some purpose. (Banfield 1994: 87)

Banfield's fellow Townsville journalists referred to him as "our man in Eden" (Noonan 1983: 124). And in *Confessions of a Beachcomber*, he refers to Dunk as "This isle of dreams, of quietude and happiness; this fretless scene; this plot of the Garden of Eden" (Banfield 1994: 41). (Before the Beachcomber could take possession of this Eden, though, the original inhabitants of Coonanglebah, some of whom figure in the 'Stone Age Folks' section of *Confessions*, had been dispossessed.) Significantly, Banfield's Eden reference introduces his "interference" with the natural world as he found it: "there should be no rude and violent upsetting of the old order of things; but just a gentle restraint upon an extravagant expression here and there, a little orderliness, and ever so slight a touch of practicality" (p. 41). At the same time, Banfield was publishing his 'Rural Homilies' advocating the development of North Queensland as a fruit-growing region.

Popular in the first half of the twentieth century, Banfield is not as much remembered now. However, I believe he merits study as one of the first significant Australian nature writers, in part because he serves to illustrate Buell's point about the pastoral being used to "advance nature's claims". From his youth he had an interest in the natural world, but Banfield was a journalist rather than a scientist. As biographer Michael Noonan says, "Banfield never saw himself as a methodical or skilled scientific investigator, but as an observer 'eager to know how Nature, not under the microscope, behaved; what were her maiden fancies, what the art with which she allures'" (Noonan 1983: 105). I would add that he was also an accomplished naturalist.

I am not the first to note this quality in Banfield. Harry Heseltine has commented that "Banfield was [...] capable of recording natural data with real accuracy and thoroughness", also suggesting that he was "the inheritor of the tradition of natural observation which produced men such as John Burroughs in America and Henri Fabre in France" (1986: 66). Banfield thus is not an isolated case nor an oddity, but an Australian manifestation of an international movement in the second half of the nineteenth century. If that century was the age of the naturalist, in its later stages it also saw the growth of natural history writing for a popular audience, both by professional naturalists and by journalists.

Banfield is often compared to Henry David Thoreau. Like Thoreau, in his move to Dunk Island to recover his health he practiced what Buell has characterised as an "aesthetics of relinquishment" (1995: 143-79). And like Thoreau in Concord, Banfield on Dunk based his natural history writing on detailed observations of a limited area over a long period of time. According to Buell,

> What distinguishes *Walden* and other epics of voluntary simplicity [...] is that the arrangement of its environmental furniture into linear corridors through which the protagonist strides becomes less important than what Thoreau calls deliberateness: the intensely pondered contemplation of characteristic images and events and gestures that take on a magical resonance beyond their normal importance now that the conditions of life have been simplified and the protagonist freed to appreciate how much more matters than what normally seems to matter. (pp. 152-53)

Evidence of Banfield's abilities as a careful and informed observer, beyond that provided in his writing, is that he was credited with the discovery of a new species (a rat, *Uromys banfieldi*). He also had a great fondness for birds and curiosity about their habits and migrations.

Banfield characterised himself as a "cheerful disciple" of Thoreau (Banfield 1994: 44), and for the epigraph of *Confessions of a Beachcomber*, he chose a passage from *Walden* (it is also on the plaque above his grave, making it both epigraph and epitaph): "If a man does not keep pace with his companions, perhaps it is because he hears a different drummer. Let him step to the music which he hears" (Thoreau 1971: 326). He was quite familiar with Thoreau's writings, especially *Walden*, but also *A Week on the Concord and Merrimack Rivers*. And part of *My Tropic Isle* has structural similarities to *Walden* (Zeller 2002: 135-45).

One major aspect of Banfield's Dunk experience was his concern about birds, in particular campaigns for bird protection. He devotes the third chapter of *Confessions* to the bird life of Dunk. In the opening section of that chapter, entitled 'Birds and Their Rights', Banfield states that a desire to protect wildlife was one of his motivations for moving to Dunk. "[I]t was resolved", he says, "as other phases of island life matured, that one of the first ordinances to be proclaimed would be that forbidding interference with birds" (1994: 93), though he was somewhat inconsistent in that he did not hesitate to shoot falcons he found preying upon other birds. His ordinance received official status by an act of the Queensland government, and Banfield became the honorary warden of the sanctuary. Probably most readers of this book (which was originally published in Britain and only later in Australia) would have found astonishing the notion that any non-human species could possess rights; at the same time, they may well have sympathised with Banfield's concern for the birds' treatment.

By the 'rights' of birds, Banfield apparently means their being able to feed and breed free from the molestations of humans. He notes that moral suasion has done little good in protecting native flora and fauna. In fact, he says, "The printed law of the land says in ponderous paragraphs all duly numbered and subdivided, that it is unlawful to kill many Queensland birds; and the pains and penalties thereof, are they not set out in terrifying array? But who cares?" (pp. 93-94). People go on shooting and collecting anyway. But Dunk and "two neighbouring groups of islands" (p. 128) were decreed to be off limits to shooting, and Noonan gives instances of the ire of the normally even-tempered Beachcomber when someone dared to flout his clearly posted notices.

Banfield was among the first writers to bring the Barrier Reef to international popular attention, relying on accounts of the species he observed and descriptions such as the following, from 'Garden of Coral':

On the rocks rest stalkless mushrooms, gills uppermost, which blossom as pom-pom chrysanthemums; rough nodules, boat- and canoe-shaped dishes of coral.

Adhering to the rocks are thin, flaky, brittle growths resembling vine-leaves,
brown and golden-yellow; goblets and cups, tiered epergnes, distorted saucers,
eccentric vases, crazily-shaped dishes'. (p. 130)

The field of natural history encompasses the disciplines we know as
systematics and ecology, and *Confessions* contains examples of both.
Examples of systematics would include Banfield's descriptions of the
island's birds and trees. Directly following 'Birds and Their Rights'
he enumerates a bird census, listing 129 species, including the common and scientific names (pp. 94-98). In his discussions of both birds
and trees we often get the Aboriginal name as well. For the birds, he
discusses their appearance and habits. With the trees, we get the
physical characteristics and often the interrelationships between the
tree and other living things.

In the section devoted to the Torresian imperial-pigeon (*Ducula
spilorrhoa*), we also learn about its appearance, its former numbers,
the threat from hunting, its food, its breeding habits, its place in the
island's ecology, and even its qualities as food — "the flesh being
dark, tough, and of an earthy flavour" (p. 119). Clearly, Banfield feels
that these are wonderful birds, deserving of protection, especially so
since

The whole of the tribes […] though scattered for feeding over an immense area of
the coast congregate on four or five islands — miles apart — to rest and breed.
The assemblages are indeed prodigious; but they represent the gathering together
of clans which have a very wide dispersal. Crowded together the host appears in-
numerable, but on the mainland during the day […] the pigeons seem scarce. […]
Any other species of native bird which took to gregarious habits might seem as
numerous as this […] . [B]ecause the poor pigeon, conspicuous and heedless, has
the instinct or habit of association, it is argued that they outnumber all the other
birds, that their legions are infinite, and that that fact is sufficient license for destruction of thousands during the breeding season […]. To preserve them
effectually certain islands should be proclaimed sanctuaries, and genuine sports-
men will never indulge their propensities when haunted by the thoughts of the
consequent cruelty. (pp. 116-17)

Banfield's point is that even though the birds seem numerous, they
really aren't when their entire range is considered; also, hunters are
taking them at their most vulnerable point — when they are concen-
trated during the breeding season. His observations serve rhetorically

to identify us with the sympathetic observer as well as with the threatened bird.

He devotes eight pages ('The Conquering Tree', pp. 197-205) to a discussion of mangroves. This section is noteworthy because Banfield takes an ecological point of view. He describes the mangroves not in isolation, but in relation to the other plants and animals with which they coexist. I find this one of the more fascinating sections of the book. We learn the process by which mangroves colonise new areas; the physical properties of the plants and the ways in which humans use the wood; the fish, molluscs, and crustaceans that inhabit mangrove swamps; and the "birds of cheerful and pleasing character" that can be found there (p. 204). "In most of its aspects", Banfield tells us,

> a mangrove swamp is not only the scene of one of nature's most vigorous and determined processes, but to those who look aright, a theatre of many wonders, a museum teeming with objects of interest, a natural aviary of gladsome birds. (pp. 204-05)

This contrasts significantly with Favenc's view quoted above.

Nature as theatre, as museum, as aviary — all three suggest Banfield's approach to nature writing. All three are human constructs in which nature is displayed or allowed to perform. It is both interesting and wonderful, instructive and moving.

2. Jean Devanny: "There are things to do here that I'll like"

For Jean Devanny (1894-1962), there was also no contradiction between studying and chronicling the natural environment of the region and espousing development which might be harmful to that environment. For her, nature is important as an arena for human action, which would include mining and logging as well as fishing, grazing, agriculture, and the study of natural history. She goes well beyond Banfield, whose agricultural suggestions seem modest in comparison, and her view reflects the growth of the North in the early twentieth century. Devanny moved there for good in 1939, after a period of activity in support of the Communist Party, the move coming as something of a personal escape. According to Carole Ferrier,

Devanny made an immense contribution, through her novels and activism, to the workers' movement and the women's movement in Australia. The historical conjuncture, and the Party within which she found herself, partly built and then largely paralysed her, and diverted her into writing on natural history and about aboriginal customs and life. (1980: 30)

It is arguable, however, that rather than being a diversion, her natural history writing was more significant than her novels.

The works of fiction set in the region include *Sugar Heaven* (1936), *Paradise Flow* (1938), *Roll Back the Night* (1945), and *Cindie: A Chronicle of the Canefields* (1949). The non-fiction includes *By Tropic Sea and Jungle* (1944) and *Travels in North Queensland* (1951). She could wax as lyrically descriptive as Banfield about the beauty of the natural world; at the same time she admired those who were able to make a living by exploiting what she called "Australia's living wealth" (Devanny 1944: 125) — the fishermen, loggers, miners, and pastoralists.

She sees nothing wrong with logging (though she does lament the waste in the early timber industry). The big trees need to be cut, she says: "To fell these forest giants in the heyday of their glory seems to strike old Mother Nature in the face but, like humans, they fall into senile decay and, if not taken down in their prime, are useless" (p. 130) — useless, of course, to humans; she does not consider the function of the trees in the ecosystem. She also advocates developing the Gulf country, including damming rivers and bringing in cattle. Like Banfield, she made herself into an accomplished naturalist, describing some of the same species he did, and travelling and working with professional biologists.

In her fiction, there is a contrast between the conflicts created by human activity and the "gorgeous flaming background of the tropics" (Devanny 1936: n.p.). Also, human appreciation of the climate and landscapes of the North is something of a touchstone of a character's worth. In *Sugar Heaven*, we find Dulcie "enchanted" by the beauty of the butterflies: "She was opening up to the marvels of nature as a flower unfolds to the sun" (p. 225). This parallels the awakening of Dulcie's political consciousness. And in *Cindie*, Blanche Biddow hates the place, while Cindie takes to it right off, and indeed it is Cindie, brought north as a domestic servant, who turns out to be cane grower Randolph Biddow's greatest help in running his operation. She also treats the indentured Kanakas well. One of Devanny's concerns in the novel is the use, and the phasing out, of Kanaka labour in the canefields, and the racism of the European population.

Devanny also uses nature as a correlative for characters' libidinal impulses. Repressed Southerners find in the fecundity of nature a way of getting in touch with their true sexual selves. In *Paradise Flow*, Laurel, the wife of the planter Big Mac, with whom she has not had sex in years, "wandered through the plantations; her desire to know man linked with her awakened awareness of the earth and growing things" (1938: 168). David Walker notes that in 1899, William Z. Ripley, author of *The Races of Europe*, asserted that tropical heat caused "surexcitation of the sexual organs" (1999: 144), an effect that some of Devanny's characters seem to suffer from.

3. Thea Astley: "this degrading love for landscape"

To move from Favenc and Banfield to Devanny to Thea Astley is to move from the Romantic view to that of the social realist to that of the satirist. And I would contend that this shift is due at least partly to the growth of the North and to the social and environmental problems that growth has caused. Landscape figures importantly in most of her works, a number of which are set in North Queensland (see Perkins 1993). A full exploration of Astley's North Queensland works would be far longer than this chapter, so I will touch on just two that deal with the coastal area of the tropical North: the short story collection *Hunting the Wild Pineapple* (1981) and the novel *It's Raining in Mango* (1989). Bruce Bennett has said of the former, "There is no stronger example in short fiction of the Australian landscape as protagonist" (2002: 210). The collection depicts a world where the oppressiveness and threat of the tropical North are palpable. The narrator, Keith Leverson, who has come here to escape the rigors of regular work and colder weather, describes nature in terms of its extremes, and the human inhabitants partake of its extremes. He calls the place a "second-rate Eden" (Astley 1981: 3). Heseltine notes that

All around [Astley's] descriptions of North Queensland and its denizens [...] there hovers a fictional ambience as close as anything we have to parts of Graham Greene — a sense of how tropical lushness and climatic extreme can combine to heighten the human capacity for wrongdoing and corruption. (1992: 12)

The three stories in the collection I find most interesting in terms of the depiction of nature are 'The Curate Breaker', 'A Northern Belle', and 'Ladies Need Only Apply'. The first tells of the conflict between Catholic Father Rassini, whose spirituality seems all but absent and who administers his parish in a coldly calculated way, and the Anglican Canon Morrow, of whom we learn that

> His profiled dignity ignored landscape orisons, loops of summer wind, the peculiar dispensations of green and pungent trees. He was immune to the nostalgia of horizons that slid past his office-jobbing for the Lord and only once or twice in his boyhood years, triggered by some special combination of sounds or the tantalising perspectives of avenues, had he ever imagined departures of the spirit. (Astley 1981: 49)

This passage (where "horizons" echoes "orisons") describes the capacity of the land to appeal to the spirit — a capacity the man of the cloth ironically ignores. In contrast, at the story's end Father Rassini finds himself touched by a spiritual reawakening triggered by the heavy wet-season rain:

> He set the bike in the garage under the water-logged mango trees. They were shifting their branches uneasily under the weight and in a sudden unshackled moment, Father Rassini, who hadn't done such a boyish thing in years, turned his face up to them, opened his mouth and took communion. Unexpectedly he felt vigorous, alive. An inexplicable joy took hold of him as he gazed about the spongy garden, exotically beautiful with the dampened flames of hibiscus and poinsettia, limp now but still burning. (pp. 58-59)

The "departures of the spirit" come to him not through his priestly offices but as a gift from the fecund nature of the tropics in all its exotic glory (though the plants mentioned are introduced, like his religion). The images here are an apparently paradoxical combination of sodden earth and burning fertile possibility. The way to joyous awakening is mediated by the natural world rather than by its anointed priest, whom we find elsewhere in the story taking advantage of his aged father. So we cannot take the epiphany straight.

The theme of excessive fertility takes a different turn in 'A Northern Belle', a somewhat Faulknerian tale about a woman named Clarice, born to wealth and social position in "one of those exhausted, fleetingly timbered places that sprang up around the tin mines of the north" (p. 79) — the exhaustion stemming from the extraction of both minerals and timber. After a life spent rejecting suitor after suitor, she expends her reproductive energy on her garden: "It was as if all her restrained fertility poured out into the welter of trees and shrubs" (p. 87). Yet, as can happen in the North, the reproductive energy of the earth itself finally defeats her, setting at naught her efforts to create an orderly garden. Carolyn Bliss states that "Astley is interested in the dialectics of power and oppression" (1992: 202); I would add that the oppression need not be of or by humans. The dialectics are played out subtly in this story as the landscape yields and then regains the upper hand over the gardener.

The dialectics are played out much more obviously, however, in 'Ladies Need Only Apply', in which Sadie, a schoolteacher on leave, takes a position as a housekeeper and gardener with Leo, a macrobiotic music teacher living up in the hills, where an "intransigent fecundity dominated two shacks which were cringing beneath banana clumps, passion-vines, granadillas" (Astley 1981: 121). In this story, as in Astley's other fiction, nature gets the violent verbs. The sun "shouted at the sea" (p. 116) and "was clouting the room with light" (p. 124); "flowers and leaves exploded in tropic swagger" (p. 122); at one point Sadie "looked down at the garden and the barbaric leaf shape and sheen with its succulent pulpy cannibal gobbling of heat and moisture" (p. 126). The two wage constant war against nature in order to keep a garden going.

When the wet season finally arrives, it overwhelms everything: "Monsoon clouds kept hauling their freight from the north as the sticky heat of the day glued the landscape into a ripening circle that sprouted more trees, more fruit" (pp. 138-39). "The whole sky was rioting [...]. Every surface absorbed and sucked the sky down into it" (p. 141). Sadie is finally beaten into submission; the creek floods; she makes her way naked across the bridge between the two huts, and hauls herself toward Leo's veranda, where "A blown passion vine caught her before she reached his stairs and plunged her [...] on her face into slush" (p. 144). She ends the story totally debased.

In these stories, nature seems to have shaped the people of the North into something different from their southern counterparts. They have come because they don't fit in elsewhere or because they want to escape or because they are tourists, temporary or semi-permanent. But they have just brought their problems and faults with them, the point seeming to be that the tropical environment makes them, or enables them to be, more fully what they already are.

In *It's Raining in Mango*, Astley uses landscape in similar ways — as overwhelming fertility that bests human attempts to tame it and as a sometimes appealing but ultimately degrading object of love — but the spiritual element is absent. This land, however, is also home. The novel is a history of the Laffey family, told retrospectively through the consciousness of Connie, one of the next-to-last generation of Laffeys. This change in narrative perspective from detached and ironic observer to family member (and maybe also the change from male to female narrator) changes somewhat the way the landscape is presented. Human connection to the land is the novel's central concern, and the pattern of development is the family's becoming at home in the landscape over the course of several generations.

From the mid nineteenth century, when Cornelius Laffey arrives to take up his journalistic career in North Queensland, to the late twentieth, when Connie's son (Cornelius's great grandson) Reever participates in an environmental protest against road building through the rainforest, the family members in various ways are absorbed back into nature: when George dies, his wife retrieves his body and buries it on their land; Nadine and her fellow prostitutes are swept out to sea, in their house, by a flood ("the river, lusting for the sea, gave a final rabid thrust, and she felt the house surge and lift like a boat and then begin its slow-turning waltz out to the waters of the bay" [p. 64]); Will gives up his inhibitions and rolls in the hay with his hippie tenants; and at the end of the novel Reever departs on foot for further north.

Another important aspect of the novel is that, in parallel with its telling the story of Cornelius Laffey and his descendants, it tells the story of the Aboriginal Bidiggi and *his* descendants. The rest of Bidiggi's family is killed in one of the 'dispersals' condoned by the colonial government, and he is later befriended by Cornelius's young son George, who was traumatised as a child when he came across the rotting corpses of massacred Aboriginal people. Cornelius is sacked from the newspaper for writing an article protesting the killing. In the twentieth century, Harry and his wife Clytie hide the child of Nelly when the police come to take that child away. Still later, Billy Mumbler is jailed for non-payment of taxes he knows nothing about, and when he returns to Mango, he is beaten up by a group of hoons. The title of the novel and of one of its chapters comes from a letter Billy receives from his mother while he is in jail: "Not much fish in river till las week, plenty then you should see. Water come up real high. Them white folks other side was cut off. You come soon, you homes hear, its rainin in Mango" (Astley 1989: 191). By this point in the story we know that this is the home not only of Billy and his family but also of the Laffeys.

The process of human degradation that a love for the land can entail is seen throughout the Laffeys' family history, from the arrival of Cornelius to the departure of Reever in the novel's concluding scene. The narrator Connie is most perceptive about the family's relationship to place — it is she who inverts the cliché and coins the phrase "heart is where the home is". Ironically, the only family member to leave the North and not return is the one who took them there — Cornelius. His wife Jessica Olive proceeds to go into business and put down roots. When she visits her son's homestead near Mango, she reflects on the relationship between gender and perception of the land:

> Cut off, Jessica Olive thought, peering critically about, sniffing at woodsmoke. But when were we anything but that, she mused, in this dangerously new country? Her pursed lips wanted to scorn the romanticising of settler drudgery, the sort of rubbish that those southern jingoistic papers printed, mush doggerel by scribblers who'd barely come to terms with the day-to-day and failed to understand the tension between landscape and flesh. Only men would write it. A woman wouldn't waste the time, couldn't find time to waste. (p. 72)

Both of these books have to do with the "tension between landscape and flesh", whether that tension is created by the enervating heat of the 'build up' to the wet season, the hard labour of clearing land for settlement, or the threats of cyclone and flood.

Astley has stated in an interview, "I think the notion of the whole world as a Garden of Eden is as good a way to approach the Creator as any way is. But man has messed up the Garden" (p. 36). This Eden is definitely a post-lapsarian one, for despite the outward appearance of paradise, it demands of its inhabitants that they must labour and suffer and die. When Connie is able to resuscitate a drowning victim, the first words out of his mouth are "Thanks for nothing" (p. 165).

In the episode that opens and closes the book, a protest is going on over the building of a logging road into the rainforest. Based on the Daintree controversy of the 1980s, the confrontation pits the logging interests, with the backing of the Queensland government, against the conservationists. In the century and a half that the Laffeys have been in the North, large tracts of forest have been cleared for agricultural and pastoral use.

In the protest, for the first time, this backwater has become the centre of attention for outsiders on both sides of the dispute. For many of the protestors, the stakes are political as well as environmental, for despite their apparent concern for the land, they do not belong here, are not at home. Reever's protest is that of someone protecting his home place. "*My source is here,*" he says, "*in the north, inextricably*" (p. 238). He proposes to walk north, taking Billy Mumbler along. "What will you do when you get there?" Connie asks.

> "I'll leave my footprints, that first," Reever says. "And I'll stand and see and be satisfied."
> "That won't be enough," Connie says. "You'll want to stay and start the whole cycle all over again."
> "Maybe," Reever says. "I don't think so. Who knows? Keep a light burning."
> (p. 240)

The 'cycle' Connie refers to encompasses both the history of exploitation of the natural world and the process of learning to come to terms with the new place as home. Reever leaves open the possibility of return. He offers his uncle Will the chance to go along, but is turned down, in part, perhaps, because his uncle's vision of remaking the landscape in English terms is played out. Reever "finds he is close to weeping and the morning is too beautiful for that" (p. 240). Then he "shakes his head free of everything" (p. 240) and begins walking north.

Whether we are to read this as a hopeful ending depends on whether we believe that anything has been learned in the last century and a half of white settlement in North Queensland. Astley has amply demonstrated the human capacity to respond to the land as a place of deeply moving beauty and as one of seemingly malevolent anti-human violence. Both the black and white inhabitants have been degraded over the time the novel covers — the former mainly as a result of the invasion of the latter, the latter partly as a result of their pioneering efforts. Astley's usual cast of drifters, losers, and self-centred louts is counterbalanced against the Laffey inability to fit in with the racist and exploitative mainstream.

4. Malouf and Miller: North Queensland as Home

The idea of how white Australians might be at home in this region has been taken up by other writers, such as David Malouf in *Remembering Babylon* (1993) and Alex Miller in *Journey to the Stone Country* (2002). Landscape figures prominently in both novels: both deal with the issue of dispossession of the original inhabitants, and in both white inhabitation is mediated by other characters. In Malouf's novel, Gemmy Fairly, a white man who has lived many years with the local indigenous people, engages some of the white characters in seeing their adopted home as natives. In Miller's, a white woman returns to a place where she grew up and becomes at home there through the guidance of an indigenous man with whom she becomes involved.

The *eco* of *ecology* and *economy* derives from the Greek *oikos*, or *house*. The trajectory of writing about tropical North Queensland has been from a mythical view of the place to one where it can be conceived of as home, and to some extent that trajectory has been affected by a growing awareness of the ecological realities of the place. While Astley moves in that direction, Malouf and Miller seem to explore ways for white Australians to come to terms both with the place itself and the history of relations with its indigenous people.

The world of *Remembering Babylon* is that of the coastal area near Bowen in the late nineteenth century; it is a liminal place, with the pioneering families on the boundary between civilisation and the unknown region beyond. To them the unfamiliar natural world is a threat. Reverend Frazer, however, sees in Gemmy a potential way of learning about the natural world in indigenous terms:

> *This is what is intended by our coming here: to make this place too part of the world's garden, but by changing ourselves rather than it and adding thus to the richness and variety of things. Our poor friend Gemmy is a forerunner. He is no longer a white man, or a European, whatever his birth, but a child of the place as it will one day be.* (Malouf 1993: 132)

But Frazer's vision is rejected in favour of the usual practice of importing familiar plants and animals in an effort to remake the land in European terms. Still, by the end of the novel, there is a suggestion that Janet McIvor and Lachlan Beattie have begun to realise that learning about Australian nature is a multidimensional project — one that involves coming to terms with a sometimes shameful past. In this, Malouf is at least tentatively more optimistic than Astley.

Journey to the Stone Country takes place mainly in the pastoral country beyond the Dividing Range, and the narrator distinguishes between the degraded landscape created by some of the graziers and the potentially fruitful land in its undisturbed state. The novel is full of descriptions of trees and various landscape features. The Stone Country of the title is the sacred ground of Bo Rennie's ancestors. The plot brings him together with Annabelle Beck — who has returned to the country of her childhood. As they travel through the landscape of the North, they experience firsthand the failures of previous attempts at white inhabitation as well as those of government policy toward the indigenous population. Bo's intercession, it is implied, is necessary for Annabelle's fully coming to terms with her family's history, and they look forward to living together in the land they had left as children.

In these two novels, the landscape is still fraught with danger, but unlike the physical threats presented in earlier fiction, it is the danger of cultural appropriation and misunderstanding. In order to find a way to inhabit the land, the characters have to understand that it was already inhabited before they arrived.

Over the past century-plus of white writing about North Queensland, the garden image has persisted, whether it is Banfield's coral gardens of the Reef, Astley's vision of a "second-rate Eden", or Malouf's conception of the region as a garden whose virtues and possibilities are still awaiting discovery.

5. Conclusion

My own interest in the literature of North Queensland was prompted mainly by my visits to the region, including several to Dunk Island. As Buell says, "to connect the literature of place with the actual place that gave rise to the literature can deepen not only one's sense of the book itself but one's sense of what it means to be in communion with place" (1995: 337). At the same time, it can make the reader aware of how the place has changed since the book was written. Visiting present-day Bowen, it is difficult to imagine the world of *Remembering Babylon*, but not that of Devanny's canefield fictions or Astley's contemporary satires. Where the Beachcomber once lived on Dunk is now an expensive resort, complete with airstrip; admittedly, the rest of the island is protected as a park. But otherwise, little remains from Banfield's day, save the cairn above the graves of him and his wife. Even two decades after the Beachcomber's death, Devanny was noting the vulgarisation of the island (Devanny 1944: 29).

Walking the trails, though, paying attention to the flora and fauna, and looking out over the neighbouring islands and coastline, one can get a sense of the qualities of the place that Banfield was writing about. At the same time, the presence of a feral pig or the arrival of a plane from the mainland can interrupt one's sense of communion and dispel the idea that this is a 'pristine' natural environment. This complicates the experience of communion that Buell talks about, but the experience can serve as a reminder of the power of literature to draw us to these special places and our responsibilities as people who care about them.

Bibliography

Primary Sources

Astley, Thea. 1981. *Hunting the Wild Pineapple*. Ringwood, Vic.: Penguin.
———. 1989. *It's Raining in Mango*. Ringwood, Vic.: Penguin.
Banfield, E.J. 1994. *Confessions of a Beachcomber*. St Lucia, Qld.: University of Queensland Press.
———. 1911. *My Tropic Isle*. London: T. Fisher Unwin.
Devanny, Jean. 1944. *By Tropic Sea and Jungle*. Sydney: Angus and Robertson.
———. 1986. *Cindie: A Chronicle of the Canefields*. New York: Viking Penguin.
———. 1938. *Paradise Flow*. London: Duckworth.
———. 1936. *Sugar Heaven*. Sydney: Modern Publishers.
———. 1951. *Travels in North Queensland*. London: Jarrolds.
Favenc, Ernest. 1997. *Tales of the Austral Tropics* (ed. Cheryl Taylor). Sydney: University of New South Wales Press.
Malouf, David. 1993. *Remembering Babylon*. New York: Pantheon.
Miller, Alex. 2002. *Journey to the Stone Country*. Crows Nest, NSW: Allen and Unwin.
Thoreau, Henry David. 1971. *Walden*. Princeton, NJ: Princeton University Press.

Secondary Sources

Astley, Thea. 1991. Interview in Willbanks, Ray (ed.) *Australian Voices: Writers and Their Work*. Austin: University of Texas Press: 26-42.

Bennett, Bruce. 2002. *Australian Short Fiction: A History*. St Lucia, Qld.: University of Queensland Press.

Bliss, Carolyn. 1992. Review of Astley (1981) in *World Literature Today* 66: 202.

Bowen, James, and Margarita Bowen. 2002. *The Great Barrier Reef: History, Science, Heritage*. Cambridge: Cambridge University Press.

Buell, Lawrence. 1995. *The Environmental Imagination: Thoreau, Nature Writing, and the Formation of American Culture*. Cambridge, MA: Harvard University Press.

Chase, A., and P. Sutton. 1981. 'Hunter-Gatherers in a Rich Environment: Aboriginal Coastal Exploitation in Cape York Peninsula' in Keast, Allen (ed.) *Ecological Biogeography of Australia*, vol. 3 (Monographiae Biolocicae 41). The Hague: W. Junk: 1817-52.

Ferrier, Carole. 1980. 'Jean Devanny's Queensland Novels' in *Ariel* 8(3): 20-30.

Heseltine, Harry. 1986. 'The Confessions of a Beachcomber' in *The Uncertain Self: Essays in Australian Literature and Criticism*. Melbourne: Oxford University Press.

——. 1992. 'A Space of Her Own' in *Australian Book Review* 144: 12-14.

Noonan, Michael. 1983. *A Different Drummer: The Story of E.J. Banfield, the Beachcomber of Dunk Island*. St Lucia, Qld: University of Queensland Press.

Perkins, Elizabeth. 1993. 'Hacking at Tropical Undergrowth: Exploration in Thea Astley's North Queensland Novels' in *Outrider* 10: 377-86.

Reynolds, Henry. 2003. *North of Capricorn: The Untold Story of Australia's North*. Crows Nest, NSW: Allen and Unwin.

Walker, David. 1999. *Anxious Nation: Australia and the Rise of Asia 1850-1939*. St Lucia, Qld.: University of Queensland Press.

Zeller, Robert. 2002. 'A Thoreau in Paradise: E.J. Banfield's *My Tropic Isle*' in *The Concord Saunterer* 10: 135-45.

Islands

CA. Cranston

Abstract: This chapter investigates the impact of literary tropes on island topography. The survey approach of island literature is abandoned in favour of ecocritical praxis, examining instead the literature of selected temperate islands (with populations varying from 2 to 20,000). Cattle farming, ideological disjunction, and mortality are explored in two settler autobiographies set in 'paradise' (Three Hummock Island); "descent with modification" is traced in the text and the farming practices (sealing, Soldier Settlement pastoral, and salvage) in a work of fiction based in 'Eden' (King Island); and in the final work (indigenous autobiography and myth set on North Stradbroke Island), the politics of the 'land ethic' and land rights confront a sea country pastoral.

1. Introduction: Islands and Islanders: Marginal and Monocultural?

It is the 16th September 2006, Civic Square, Launceston, Tasmania. It is noon; the blue coat of a well-groomed Schnauzer reads "Pulp Fiction"; a woman in a white tee shirt distributes bumper stickers that read "Tasmania: Your Corrupt State". This, a counter-point text to Tourism Tasmania's slogan "Tasmania: Your Natural State", is reinforced by the offering of white facemasks by another woman; a further *gestural* text, denoting extinction, is embodied by two short people who pass by dressed as wedge-tailed eagles; TV's gardening personality Peter Cundall is on the Public Address system, his anaphoric refrain "The reason why..." is a litany of reasons why the proposed Long Reach pulp mill should not go ahead. Ten days earlier David Suzuki, visiting Launceston to promote his autobiography, set the tune by referring to wood chipping and pulping of old growth trees as "the dumbest thing I've ever heard" (Andrews 2006: 10).

The scene, reminiscent of protests against the establishment of the North Broken Hill/Noranda Wesley Vale pulp mill in the 1990s, demonstrates that Tasmania is an island divided: mere consonants signal chasmic divisions between conservation and conservative groups, between Green and Greed. Gunns Limited, the company underwriting the Long Reach pulp project, is at litigious "logger-heads" with The Wilderness Society and with Greens Senator, Bob Brown. It was division of this sort that, in 1972, brought the United Tasmania Group into being. The UTG was the forerunner of the Australian Greens (Brown and Singer 1996: 67). As such, the global impact of the former UTG highlights the first point concerning the reading of islands: it warns against any reading of them as mere marginalia to mainland activities.

The second challenge to the received reading of islands that the above scene demonstrates is the notion of islander-sameness or human 'monoculture' (which at its most damning translates as 'incestuous'). Diversity in political, cultural, sociological, and bioregional concerns (as demonstrated in the Greens versus Gunns scenario) defies such notions, which are derived from images of closed communities bound by the restrictive geography of an encompassing body of water — images perhaps produced by what Joel Bonnemaison calls *insularophobes,* interpreted as "fearer[s] of islands" by Grant McCall, Centre for South Pacific Studies, UNSW (1997: 1). The term, though, engages in geographical determinism by conflating ideas about islands (as remote) with ideas about islanders (making them insular). This view is expressed by island-escapee (and possible *insularophobe*) Peter Conrad in *Down Home* (1988). The island and its inhabitants are satirised as textbook examples of misplaced independence and insularity: "When I was back, the state resounded with a series of agrarian dramas fomented by indigenous Crusoes or scions of the Swiss Family Robinson, fighting for their right to live on their own desert island" (1988: 112).

Down Home is a psychological geography of Tasmania. The physical geography created by its encompassing body of water is a reminder that 'islands' (a word derived from two primary elements [OE. *ae*; L. *aqua*] and 'land') are also marine environments and that, unlike inland mainlanders, islanders are keenly aware of more than their footprints on thin topsoil. They cannot afford to be land-centric. Thus, what is at issue for those gathered in Civic Square is not just deforestation, or the fact that plantation trees being young and eager to grow consume large amounts of (increasingly) scarce water; or that thousands of tonnes of particulates would be released into the air, but also that thousands of tonnes of organochlorines would be pumped into the Bass Strait and (apart from the effect on marine habitat) filter into the food chain. Islanders cannot escape their own effluent. Additionally, while the scene above demonstrates *political* dividedness and diversity of the islanders, the "island" of Tasmania is geographically divided and diverse; the island state is in fact an archipelago state, composed of 334 islands (Brothers *et al.*, 2001, vii; though The Australian Government Geoscience website lists 1,000 islands for Tasmania).[1] And while it is true that not all of these islands are peopled, most are inhabited. Which raises the question:

1.1.   What are Islands? Inclusions and Omissions

What is an island — beyond the fact that the islands under discussion are oceanic islands, the type ringed by a continuous littoral zone? This chapter is concerned with the biogeographical reality of islands as contexts and with the construction of islands in texts. On that latter concern, we saw Bonnemaison's conflation of context and text through the use of the term *insularophobes* (above); the conflation is a continuation of a trend that has been 'Donne' to death. Donne's oft-cited "No man is an Iland intire of it selfe; every man is a peece of the continent, a part of the maine" continues evolutionary "descent with modification" (to quote Darwin on Evolution). Peter Conrad writes "Insularity is a Tasmanian Creed. On the island, everyman is — or wants to be — an island" (1988: 112). Donne's and Conrad's sentiment is taken up by Tasmanian artist Patrick Hall in a print titled "No, Man is an Island" (Wood 2003: 153). In the above examples, consideration and valorisation of islands appears to be related to human numbers. Thus a third challenge to the reading of islands is that they are reductively constructed as escape from the human population into self-sufficiency and Romantic solitude (see Alliston's *Escape to an Island* [1966]) but also, when populated, as parochial cultural prisons (Shimmins' *Eden Observed* [1999]). Such views engage in a variety of perceptions, from island use-value, to island-essentialism.

Enter nissology, "[t]he study of islands on their own terms" (McCall 1997: 1). Nissology is shored by its own association (International Small Islands Studies Association [ISISA]), its ideas are as broad in scope as the ecology/economy foci that opened this chapter. The Association continues to debate the nature of islands in terms of geo-physiology (such as size), and geo-psychology (such as insularity and isolation). Iain Orr for instance states that, for an island to be an island, one must be able to walk around it in 24 hours; conversely, ISISA president Godfrey Baldocchino posits that size doesn't matter. For the purpose of this chapter the islands chosen contain the word *island* as part of their nomenclature, and all are temperate zone islands. These include Three Hummock Island, King Island (with a brief reference to Bruny Island), and, lying just south of the Tropic of Capricorn, North Stradbroke Island, which presents a temperate zone with a difference. By cleaving to the word 'islands', I avoid embroilment in discourses surrounding matters of size whilst simultaneously declaring my allegiance to a text that incontrovertibly designates islands as "islands".

Tasmania then, is not up for discussion. Many have already dedicated time and energy to the literature of place concerning this, the largest offshore island, lying south of the world's largest inhabited island continent. It is not necessary to repeat that work, though this means omitting some of that island's most visible landscape writers (and it seems almost impossible for mainland Tasmanians not to mention landscape in their work). Omissions include contemporary writers such as Chris Koch's re-imagining of Tasmania as an ersatz England (*Boys in the Island*, 1958; *Across the Sea Wall*, 1965); the *topophobia* in the verse of Graeme Hetherington; the pastoral of Kathleen Graves, and in the prose and verse of fellow-farmer, Barney Roberts, and the non-fiction by Michael Sharland (*Birds of the Sun*, 1967). Little wonder then, that Robert Cox in a review (*Island*, 2000) writes,

> Tasmania is full of stories. Perhaps only Ireland and Iceland, among the world's myriad islands, surpass it as storytelling places, and both of those have a much longer surviving history then Tasmania. I know of no other place in Australia where stories so abound. (p. 106)

But as well as texts, significant contexts have been omitted: islands such as Flinders, Cape Barren, Maria, as well as the offshore islands of other states (Western Australian has 3,747 islands) and the Northern Territory. Depending on one's mental orientation (water or land), the Coral *Sea*, or Queens*land*, islands of Dunk Island and Fraser Island have been passed over in favour of North Stradbroke. (See Chapter 10 for a discussion of Dunk Island and E.J. Banfield.) Similarly Fraser Island, the nineteenth century setting for Patrick White's historical fiction *A Fringe of Leaves* (1972), has already received a generous allocation of words on woodchips.

1.2. Challenging Marginalia: Moonscapes and Island Time

The sheer magnitude of the topic and the potential to misjudge the impact of an island as a literary context is demonstrated in this chapter's omission of any in-depth discussion of Bruny Island, one of Tasmania's offshore islands. Adventure Bay, Bruny Island (42° 37'S; 147° 21'E) is the site of Captain James Cook's landing on 26 January 1777. The landing signalled processes of human and land colonisation that became an all too familiar pattern on the mainland. Lunawanna-alonnah (Palawah name) was also the home of the Nuenonne tribe and of Truganini, the last Tasmanian full blood. Bruny is also where, in 1788, Captain William Bligh planted European crops — and began the little England that fills the minds of Chris Koch's characters. The sowing of seed signalled the transformation of land and eating habits. Previously attuned to the nomadic culture of its human and non-human inhabitants, the land is set to the bite of the plough, the implanting of immigrant seed, and the weight of the cloven hoof. So to return to the first point concerning island marginalisation: the case of Bruny Island demonstrates once again that islands can not be assumed to be peripheral to their mainlands; indeed, islands are the nexus as in the first law of ecology that "everything is related to everything else" (Commoner 1980: 16).

Along with received readings of islander sameness (second point) comes the third point that has to do with the notion of island/er isolation and insularity touched on earlier in reference to Bonnemaison, Donne, Conrad, and Hall. Some challenges to the idea of island (as opposed to islander) isolation are expressed in Danielle Wood's novel, *The Alphabet of Light and Dark* (2003), set primarily on Bruny Island. Along with the historical connections that make the island hum with centricity, the major character, Essie Westwood, considers the element that connects all islands:

> She watches the ocean, the Great Southern Ocean. There are more than a thousand unbroken kilometres of it between herself and the Antarctic ice shelf. The bright blue water that fills up the windows of her apartment in Perth, they call the Indian Ocean. But Essie thinks it's odd to name oceans. Since water finds its own level, there must be only one, a single enormous ocean cupping the jutting continents and filling up the bays and bights of the globe; one and the same body of water lapping, aqua-clear and warm, on equatorial beaches, and beating against the coasts and the hemispheres' extremes. (pp. 36-37)

The extract confirms an idea of the connectedness of islands as expressed by nissologist Epeli Hau'ofa (McCall 1994: 2). He writes,

> There is a world of difference between viewing the Pacific as "islands in a far sea" and as "a sea of islands". The first emphasises dry surfaces in a vast ocean far away from the centres of power. Focussing in this way stresses the smallness and remoteness of the islands. The second is a more holistic perspective in which things are seen in the totality of their relationships. (Hau'ofa 1993: 152-53)

Placing islands within a single marine space in order to signify "the totality of their relationships" helps to reconfigure the projection of (perceived) island isolation on its inhabitants. But it is limited by its Earth-boundedness. For in fact the seas that surround islands share a relationship with territory that is 238,857 miles away (mean distance): the moon.[2] In Wood's novel, a conversation between Essie and her discarded lover David articulates the ecology of an earth-moon relationship: "*There is a theory that the moon was calved from the earth,* he had told her":

> *At some time in prehistory, he had said, when the surface of the earth was molten, the entire outer layer of the world rose and fell in waves with the magnetic force of the sun. These waves, made up of soupy stuff which would one day be metal and earth and stone, grew larger and larger, threatening to unbalance the world. Until a colossal wave let go of the earth altogether, lurching off into space, spinning itself into a globe. It became the moon, a satellite child caught in the orbit of its parent. (p. 153)*

Wood's source is Rachel Carson's *The Sea Around Us* (1951: 336). The idea that the Pacific basin is a kind of parturition scar caused by the birth of the moon has since been abandoned in favour of the giant impact theory (that an impact to the Earth blew out the material that is now the moon) (Bryson 2004: 63). Either way, the expressed wish to extend the ecology of interconnectedness beyond earth's boundaries is, however, tangible and apt. For the moon binds all islands. And it does so in at least two ways, one poetic, the other geophysical.

First, from a poetic or textual perspective, the moon is, for many islands, their closest neighbour inasmuch as it is the unwavering 'mainland' visible to all islands. (The Australian mainland, for instance, is beyond the regard of its island state.) The full moon 'floating' in a sea of space — its landscape pitted with the ironic nomenclature of (waterless) seas — is a potently visual reflection of island 'isolation'; but the poetics of isolation are undermined by the second point, the geophysical, which is that the moon creates the gravitational phenomenon of tidal ebbs and flows along the earth's littoral zones, exerting approximately double the force of its solar counterpart. As distinct from the popular geo-psychological reading of islanders as inwardly turned, the physical entities that are the islands themselves are naturally bound to a far bigger, indeed *cosmic*, range of reference. Islanders, consciously or otherwise, are daily affected by the moon's presence through tidal influence, and in turn, through its 'flow on' impact on shipping, flooding, and erosion. The following extract reveals the influence of the moon on the landscape. Set on the first island context under discussion, Three Hummock Island, it is from Eleanor Alliston's *Island Affair* (IA):

> It was on that 'voyage' that I noticed, in my favourite group of granite sculpting 'Mother with Child at Knee', that somehow, sometime, the child, (ten tons of it) had disappeared [...] slipped away into the sea forever. Since then I have observed that on two places the upper 'storey' in a group of devils' marbles, near the high water line on that wild coast, are there no more. (1984: 60)

The erosion and disappearance of the granite is of course a result of the combined effects of physical forces over time. Configured as a mother and child, it suggests, however, universal human anxiety concerning the unobserved unrecorded mortal life. The "passing" of the granite figures is recorded only because of Alliston's gaze. Which brings us to the fourth challenge concerning the reading of islands — that, by extension, perhaps *insularophobes* at their darkest, fear that for individuals, the 'island time' of island living is ahistorical, perhaps even nihilistic.

2. The Empirical Response: "The Price (and Economics) of Paradise". Three Hummock Island. Palawah Name: Noepartrick 40°24'S, 144°57'E Population: 2

> "Now Mrs Alliston, you say that you
> intend to stay on this island all your life.
> Tell me, you have a cemetery, I trust?"
> "No. But we have a *lovely* compost
> heap." (IA 78)

On the monochromic cover of *Island Affair* an elderly couple stands on the littoral zone of an island to the northwest of Tasmania. The male, warmly dressed in dark slacks, jumper, and shoes, his gaze following the straight line of his arm, points beyond the pages of the book. Next to him is the partially clad figure of his wind-swept wife, Eleanor Alliston (1913-2003); she too gazes into the grey distance. What captures the attention of this frail couple remains unstated; what captures the attention of this reader is the woman's vulnerability: the weather appears cold, yet her still-firm legs are naked, her bare feet curl around the sharp edges of the conglomerate rock on which the couple stand. It is a pictorial rending of Wordsworthian ambivalence as expressed in the lines "Nature never did betray / The heart that loved her" ('Lines', ll. 122-23). Shot against a background of sea and beach, forever renewing, the wintry scene foregrounds a couple on the edge, tipping into the winter years of life. *Island Affair*, Eleanor Alliston's sequel to the autobiographic *Escape to an Island* (1966) presents a startling image of human temporality and a gentle return to the image of the compost heap where life is food, food is life:

Thirty years of an unfinished concerto and now we are locked in forever on exasperating, delicious, Three Hummock Island. Our recipe for paradise was: one island (it must be on the fortieth parallel); one growing family; marinade the two together in the heady wine of individual freedom for a few score years or more. The outcome is a dish of eternal fascination, somewhere to be, to stay forever. (IA 1)

The extract describes *eu-topia* (place): paradise; tribe-making; self-reliance; island time that is "eternal" and "forever". The writer's "*eu-tropisms*" (text), reflect a mental landscape projected on Australia (as an island) as "the Eldorado of old dreamers", as Eutopia, as Hy-Brasil (Ikin 1988: 255). Alliston's next comment, however, that "[n]ow John and I make up the entire population" confirms an altered state and impending annihilation of these "old dreamers". The tribe has flown the island nest, and the erosion of the granite "Mother with Child at Knee" plays itself out on a human scale.

On the other hand, the written word momentarily hedges the temporality by which Nature (being without feeling) can care not a whit for her lovers. *Island Affair* provides closure to the breathless enthusiasm of raising a family on an island (from their arrival in 1951), as explored in *Escape to an Island* (ETI). The illusion of compressed time, as wrought by the 'sudden' disappearance of the granite sculptures, has its flesh and frond counterpart in which infancy also 'disappears'. Islander-time with its associated nihilism (the nothing-ever-happens-here lament that is simultaneously capitalised on by 'time-capsule' tourism) is time recorded by the slow-time physical cycles of natural history. Alliston's gaze reveals that 'change' is more observable in others; the self, caught up in day to day living, accommodates a process of 'erosion' which differs markedly in the degree of consciousness from that attributed to the charted 'time' of historical events:

> We hardly ever know which day of the week it is. There are reminders, though, that months have gone past. The peacock's tail, only tiny (was it yesterday?), is in no time undulating like an Arabian carpet, two metres long [...]. Or, on going to answer the mother brushtail possum's knock on our back door [...]. [This] surely cannot be that baby, whose head, walnut size, used to peep out bright eyed in the mink-soft slit of mother's pouch, for tonight the mother possum wears that half-grown offspring proudly round her neck, stole-wise. (IA 48-49)

When Alliston's mother-in-law visits and is invited to join the tribe on the island, the *Ausländer*'s response is that isolation is premature 'death': "if you two dears are ready to leave the world [...] well, I'm not!" (p. 40). The written word on the other hand suggests an island's importance as an eventful place; the word implicates it in human history, or linear time, and it records the transference of ideas. In the following extract (which demonstrates island interconnectedness), Alliston notes that the exiled Giuseppe Garibaldi visited the island in 1852 while captaining the *Carmen*. His Romantic description constructs the island as a site imbued with healing powers:

> How often has that lonely island in Bass Strait deliciously excited my imagination, when, sick of this civilized society so well supplied with priests and police agents, I have returned in thought to that pleasant bay, where my first landing startled a covey of partridges, and where amidst lofty trees of a century's growth, murmured the clearest and most poetical of brooks […]. (qtd. in IA 125)

It was Three Hummock (both as an island of imagination and, in Wordsworthian terms, as the object of "emotion recollected in tranquillity") that purportedly led to Garibaldi's settling on the island of Caprera, off Sardinia. As imaginative node and hub of activity, Alliston's "paradise" (IA 1) is articulated within the maritime inscriptions of latitude and longitude. Part of the Hunter Island Group, covering an area of 6966.56 hectares (Brothers 2001: 77), its native fauna includes Little Penguins, Short-tailed Shearwaters, Hooded Plovers, and tiger snakes. It is also one of a number of islands used for grazing livestock, where the littoral zone provides practical benefits of reduced fencing. As a 'paradise' then, it is hardly untrammelled. But settlement on the island by the Allistons suggests that, contextually, untrammelled post-war paradise was any place where a high concentration of humans were not. John Alliston was ex-Royal Navy, decorated by King George VI (IA 1); the end of the Second World War brought numerous ex-servicemen escapees to islands, with the help of the Government Soldier Settlement Scheme.

The Allistons and Three Hummock Island, however, were not part of that scheme. They asserted their independence early: "We were establishing a private kingdom, where we must provide the finance for every one of the essential services" (IA 22). In the early days, with the wherewithal of cattle-management in place, the Allistons address the business of tribe-making. Four children, three born on the island, complete the idea of island paradise informed by twentieth-century post-war Romantic Primitivism and pragmatism. Beyond the civilised gaze, daughter Ingrid is shown paddling naked in the water (ETI facing p. 89), followed by a caption on the same page, "We chose the island to give our children this". It is an antipodean appropriation of

Rousseauan ideology (noted in the Garibaldi quote) in search of a life uncorrupted by civilisation:

> It was largely for the sake of our children (born and unborn) that we elected to come to this remote, inaccessible island; we wanted to create a little world of our own moulding. And it seemed that we were able to provide the three younger ones with an early childhood of near perfection. (IA 63)

"Remote, inaccessible" idealism comes up hard against reality shortly after arriving. There's a bushfire; seven-month old Warwick takes ill; there's no working radio; SOS smoke signals catch the attention of a passing boat. Once transported to the mainland, Alliston is rebuked by the doctor: "These islands are no place for kiddies" (ETI 17). The scene reveals the conflict between the idea of paradise as a treasure-island of self-reliance, and the realisation that staying on the island without seeking help from 'civilisation' would have meant certain death for the child. As the granite sculpture 'Mother with Child at Knee' confirms, all matter is implicated in a web of ecology; self-reliance is a delusion (or, to reinvoke Donne, "No man is an Iland intire of it selfe"). Seen through the lens of parental responsibility, the double bind of islands is revealed as both life-affirming and risky. The hidden subject of mortality raises additional ethical issues: Alliston's island experience is a living dialogue with Malthusian and *laissez-faire* doctrines. While "standing on the beach at low water", she finds herself questioning the ethics of human intervention in the non-human world:

> we beheld a dozen flotillas of those tiny sapphire-blue sea creatures, Portuguese Men o' War, balloonsails filled, floating dreamily around the end of the wharf, towards us. Does one try to save them, to shoot them out to sea again, so that stranded, the 'wings' may never lose that lovely iridescence or their soft bodies turn to hardened leathery nothingness? And I pick up a great black shiny lumbering beetle which I found crawling dazedly up the long, long beach towards the sandhills. Is it kind to take it up? Or kinder to leave it? With stick feet it tries to cling as I gently put it down, above the tideline. As with animals, so with people, it is so hard to decide the part we ought to play in their lives. (IA 60)

The human parallels — direct, and anthropomorphic — demonstrate conscious awareness of another double bind: rescuing-intervention can impact on the mortality of other populations:

It is the same dilemma as we feel when the leopard-spotted Arctic seal[3] is apparently stranded on the dry top of the beach, seemingly left behind by the tide. It barks, showing a mouthful of dreadful teeth, and squirms round hysterically when we try to move it. The best way seems to be to tickle its nose, then run towards the sea with the seal in feeble pursuit. Then, once it is in the shallows, it can either strand itself again, by choice or swim out to sea, 'smiling', its Edwardian drooping moustaches shedding the sparkling waters joyfully. I wish, though, it would not decimate our fairy penguins. (IA 61)

So too the Allistons' presence constitutes intervention, with resulting anthropogenic impact. For instance, the Allistons' primary income is from cattle farming, but to ship cattle to Woolnorth for auction requires a ferry; the purchase of the *Eleanor* necessitates the building of a wharf which in turn results in "a new industry ... that of servicing a Commonwealth department" (IA 94). The PMG (telecommunications) sets up a tower on Sugarloaf Mountain; the four-year project results in "a giant pylon with an equally giant 'dish' on top of 'our' mountain"; as well, Telecom builds overnight labourer's quarters "nestling plumb in the middle of that secluded lotus-eaters' dell which we had vowed to preserve unspoilt" (IA 94). Telecom also builds an airstrip "ten times the size of ours, right beneath the shadow of the Mountain" (IA 108). The Western Geophysics Company (USA) undertakes mineral exploration, facilitated by the *Eleanor*, the Allistons' farming equipment, and with Alliston as tracker.

"Linking up once again with civilisation was profitable" (IA 94) Alliston muses. Her new anti-Romantic sentiment demonstrates transformation; cattle farming is an *anti*-pastoral industry where idealism bows to use-value. She voices this early: "[w]e hated the cruelty of castrating and ear marking" (IA 23). It takes time for the Allistons to compare the price of their original idealism with the economics of raising cattle, though cattle farming does provide the income necessary to send Warwick and Robert to Geelong Grammar School (IA 33)[4]. It's an act which challenges perceptions of island-backwardness, as this was the same school Prince Charles attended in 1966. Hindsight, however, spurs recognition of yet another double bind in the founding of the Alliston clan on Three Hummock Island:

[…] the experiment of cutting ourselves off from our past in complete isolation has shown up one great weakness. From the age of eleven our children have had to battle their ways through boarding school and university as well as though all the social intricacies, completely without parental support. (IA 63)

The publication of *Escape to an Island* provides the funds for Ingrid's schooling (IA 58). And just as the *Eleanor* impacted on context, so too Eleanor Alliston's text. *Escape to an Island* becomes counterproductive to notions of isolation:

> And it was also because of the book that one Saturday afternoon we looked across the bay to see a flotilla of speedboats approaching the wharf.
>   Among the twenty complete strangers there were thirteen copies of my book which they asked me to autograph. Tourists were taboo, here, but to me they justified their presence if they came brandishing a copy of one of my books! (IA 80-81)

The comment belies Alliston's pragmatic streak. Film crews come, and Alliston's "private kingdom" becomes a proving ground against which development — agricultural and technological — challenges original notions concerning island living. Cattle raising is found to be neither economic nor bucolic; ideas concerning self-reliance and tribal togetherness are partially undermined by the medical and educational needs of the children — who are the very catalyst for the escape to the island in the first place. The politics between Alliston's entrepreneurial spirit and any foibles regarding intervention in the non-human world are further played out when, after reading the winds and the falling tide, she encounters a haunting scene of Nautilus beaching:

> From a distance I stood and watched a delegation of pacific gulls, pied Oyster catchers, two great Albatross, and some Fairy Terns. Like a welcoming committee, they were gazing intently into the sunset. One of the yellow masked gulls rose and cruised lazily across the shallows, until, 'clonk', it would drop like a stone upon something beneath the water's surface. But it brought nothing up for me to see. (1A 143)

The scene is rendered idyllic, but in this instance the gaze of the gulls is more penetrating than the writer's:

> But now, something much closer froze my footsteps. Stock-still, awed, unbelieving, I saw that the foamy frou frou of lace at the water's edge had become an animated, restless wave of nautilus shells. Everywhere they were three or four deep. And here and there, as the tide ran away, it was as though a bucketful of those fragile rarities had been heedlessly dumped. The writhing squids animated that

seething mass of porcelain white with the coal black of the spinal markings and the flesh tones of their own tentacles. (pp. 143-44)

Alliston intervenes, herself robbing the "bandit birds" of their feast, only to discover that the nautilus "seemed to have lost all instinct except to return as quickly as possible to certain destruction on the sands" (p. 144). For several nights, the family patrols the beach under a low moon, beside fast-receding tides "harvesting this windfall" (p. 146). The financial return of the "suicidal influx" (p. 148) on the littoral zone is converted into the "largest model of a slow combustion stove from England" (p. 148). Alliston's modified Romantic Primitivism is revealed towards the end of *Island Affair*. Prefaced by the modifier 'if' (a Wordsworthian favourite, also), it suggests encroaching mortality, and a gentle dissonance between island idealism and the phenomenology of island living:

> If we were starting off again from scratch, two young and in-love people, with one or two trusting children, and say, a small independent income, we would get our priorities right. First the power unit, *then* an undeveloped wilderness site, an empty canvas to which one takes tents, utensils, tools, seeds for a kitchen garden (naturally this must be on the magical 40th parallel). With your own supply of heating, lighting and power the creation of your own paradise must be helped and hastened immeasurably. (IA 158)

It's paradise with technology. And although the idea of islander 'isolation' was more of a possibility when the Allistons took up residency in 1951, the coming of phone technology on the island broadened communication possibilities and placed Alliston in the public gaze. Today, mobile wireless broadband availability demands a rethink of stock constructions about island paradises in relation to islander isolation.

3. The Imaginative Response: "Pastoral Catastrophe"[5]
King Island (Tatham's Lagoon: 39°47'S, 143°53'E)
Population: 2,500

Fifty-eight by twenty-one kilometres, part of Tasmania but oriented towards Victoria, King Island is bisected by a longitudinal line that (using the Universal Transverse Mercator [UTM] system) places the Eastern half in zone 55, the western half in zone 54, creating "The King Island Problem" and cartographic grid wars. (What the critically endangered orange-bellied parrot [*Neophema chrysogaster*] makes of this imaginary line during its annual migration stop-over [to zone 54] is not recorded.)

This site has produced a work of adult fiction, *Eden Observed* (1999) by Anne Shimmins. The title points the direction by which to read text and context; biblical Eden, Adam's garden, was created and settled after unnamed Creation was in place. King Island (the name is never mentioned in the text) is a parallel text; at the turn of the nineteenth century it was, ignoring the presence of other animate life forms, uninhabited, lacking a history of human-effect on the environment. Today, King Island farming land is recognised Australia-wide for its dairy products; its littoral zone is the graveyard of ships. The novel microscopes the anthropogenic impact on the island into a fictional account of invasion and contagion on a microbial and viral level. Patterned on Dante Alighieri's *La Divina Commedia*, it likewise has a three-part structure: Inferno; Purgatorio; Paradiso; it engages in textual latitude, portraying the hell and purgatory that pave the way for a pastoral paradise.

Dante's guide through the three regions is farmer-poet Virgil. In geological terms, *Eden Observed* is the most recent stratum in a process of textual sedimentation, or intertextuality, with texts layered upon texts. Similarly, I needed a guide to situate the context of *Eden Observed*. As I wandered the coastline looking for clues that 'Eden' was set on King Island, my guide Christian Robertson ("The only Christian on the island", he tells me) pointed out the hull remnants of the American *Whistler* embedded in the littoral zone since 1855.

3.1.   Farming Hell: Phase 1 — Striking Oil

The physical *Whistler* is fast disappearing though its story remains in the naming of Whistler's Point, located along Phoques Bay. 'Phoques', a word planted by the French in 1802, means 'seals'; but to the French, British and Americans, it signified oil. The word *phoques* provides the first of what I see as three stages, or layers, of farming the island. 'Farm' (from O.E. *feorm*) indicates food, provision; economics and settlement; or taking the Latin form, *firmare*, meaning 'to settle'; 'a preserve'; it also means 'to cleanse', 'to empty'. This first phase of farming of the island was sealing. After word got out about the seals, sealers and whalers from Britain, France, and America were on King Island farming the wilderness for its oil deposits.

American whaler Captain Amasa Delano (1763-1823) was among them. He writes of this time in *A Narrative of voyages and travels in the Northern and Southern Hemispheres* (1819). The French too kept journals of their sealing experiences on King Island. François Péron (1775-1810) a zoologist, observed that

> Rarely do the female seals offer violence [...] their looks bear an expression of despair; they dissolve into tears. I myself have seen one of these young females shedding abundant tears, whilst one of our sailors, a mean, cruel man, amused himself by breaking its teeth with the broad end of one of the oars of our longboat every time it tried to open its mouth. (qtd. in Micco 1971: 30)

This is not hunting; it is harrowing; it is harvesting; it is free-range farming. Within a decade the Southern elephant seal (*Mirounga leonina*) had been exterminated from King Island (Donaghey 2003: 4). It is a woeful enactment of the word 'farming': to cleanse, to empty.

So ended the first phase of farming. But all it would take to transform King Island into a material, Australian version of the pastoral would be a shipwreck and a mattress.

3.2.   Farming Purgatory: Phase 2 — The Central Character Is the Tomato

For it happened that, in one of many shipwrecks, an immigrant did survive — melilot (*Melilotus indicus*), a type of clover — its seeds apparently carried in straw mattresses that floated ashore (Donaghey

2003: 51). (Previously published references concerning melilot's origin are couched in caution; time, however, has enabled supposition to solidify into fact.) Early attempts at creating an island pastoral failed partly due to copper deficiency in the soil which caused anaemia in the animals, but the attempts failed primarily (Gillham 2000: 449) because of the widespread presence of poisonous pea (or tare: *Swainsonia lasertifolia*) which blinded cattle (Finzel 2004: 22). The melilot, however, took hold, strangled the poisonous pea (p. 23) and opened up the possibility of two narrative interpretations: one would be that of salvage and renewal. Another might see the melilot as the catalyst, transforming the island pastoral[6] into a site of catastrophe in which the literary meaning of 'catastrophe'— from the Gk 'overturning' — indicates the tragic dénouement of a story.

One of the ironies in this interdisciplinary coupling is that the natural sciences lead the literary academic back to the language of the epic poets. 'Dead' Latin lives and multiplies in the roots and stems of the organic world (as in *Melilotus indicus*), and it is the language of Virgil. His *Eclogues* (Gr. 'selections'; written between 42 and 39 BC) is also known as the *Bucolics*. Bucolics refers both to herd farmers (domestic 'nature') and to the literary form of the pastoral. One hundred years after the naming of Phoques Bay and the hunting of seal cows and bulls, the changed vegetation recreated an island-pastoral potential, which enabled the establishment of a pastoral industry. In 1902, King Island Dairy was established. The Dairy is the forerunner of a niche market for conspicuous consumption; road signs inform readers that it caters for "the famous", it promises "purity", and it is partly this branding of place that allows *Eden Observed* to be situated within that context. From seal cows and bulls to dairy factory farming: the second major phase of farming the island.

There are multiple textual footprints in Shimmins's novel, but canonical texts form its web of ideas. Set in the late 1980s, Bea Blake, a soldier-settler widow tends tomato beds on her farm, 'Eden'. Later, it is revealed that Bea(trice) — having lost her three-year old son, Will, while she was away trysting — performs life-long contrition by copying illuminations and text by name-sake William Blake (1757-1827, the last epic poet who, incidentally, died while working on Dante's text).

The problem with the above synopsis, of course, is that it violates the earlier comment that ecocriticism aims to be biocentric, reassessing anthropocentric assumptions by shifting focus away from the character-centred approach. In which case, given that ecocriticism "considers the relationship between human and non-human life as represented in literary texts" (Coupe 2000: 302), the central character is the tomato situated in a landscape of contagion. In the now of the novel (set 1989-1990, with flashbacks and two female narrators) the elderly Bea raises macrobiotic Harbinger tomatoes for mainland export. Tomatoes — *le fruit pomme d'amour* — presage what is to come, as its name 'Harbinger' signifies. The type of tomato grown at Eden also harbours a contextual nuance that gives the lie to the novel's setting: King Island was named for Governor King, in 1801, by Captain John Black, commander of the *Harbinger*.

The difficulty of living in 'Eden' challenges the pre-lapsarian pastoral as articulated in magazines "written for the loony alternative fringe-dwellers" (p. 180). Organic crops produce "potatoes with the rotten heart, fly-blown broccoli, sour turnips, but all good for us, all grown within forty kilometres of Eden, in season, without spray" (p. 180). Native fauna is poached and despatched by both Bea and her friend, Brody: muttonbirds (p. 30); crays (pp. 35; 169); undersized abalone (p. 49); possum shoots (p. 57); road-kill wallaby, and the joey found later in its pouch:

> With rotten unconcern [Brody] rips out the mewing joey, tiny blind face turned hopelessly to the light, paws scrabbling, frantic to be held. And tosses it out over the rocks where the sea, the only decent actor in this drama, gathers it in with a passing sigh. (p. 54)

While native animals get short shrift, introduced species fare better in the squalor of Eden: a goat, camellias, lilacs, hydrangeas, blackberries (p. 18), vegetables, chickens, and nine cats. The carnal Beatrice lives in a cathouse — an epithet in which species and sexism coalesce. The primary colours of the tomato, red and green, provide culturally specific indicators of Bea's past and present professions.

Bea attempts an act of salvaging when she takes in a human wreck, HIV-positive Francie (Francesca) Cain, a vagrant species from the mainland. Naming bears the burden of mythic accretion: with its Old Testament allusions and with its Dantesque Christian namesake in the second circle of Hell, where Francesca resides with her brother-in-law lover. Their guilt is in succumbing to the power of the text: Francesca tells Dante "the primal root / From whence our love gat being" was the reading of Lancelot's love for Guinevere: "The book and writer both / Were love's purveyors" (Canto V). Deconstruction theory argues for a multiplicity of meanings in a text, and that's certainly reflected in the novel's textual layering process; but deconstruction also argues that a text's meaning cannot be construed by reference to externalities. The fate of Francie's namesake indicates, however, that the reverse cannot be said to be true: text can impact, adversely or otherwise, on external realities. Furthermore the idea that "there is nothing but the text" is unsupportable in ecocriticism, which instead insists on the existence of the material environment that informs the writing mind, as con-text.

In the earthly realities of Francie's world, she, like Dante, can only ever observe Eden, and never belong. Though she's HIV-positive, Francie takes on the local kelper population one afternoon in the boathouse and, later, contaminates — but this time unknowingly — Bea's tomato crop. Contamination occurs because Francie, a heavy smoker, is a vector; her nicotine-stained hands cause the crop to be lost to mosaic virus (p. 213). (Tomato mosaic virus [ToMV], which is closely related to the Tobacco mosaic virus [TMV], was first reported in 1899, in Connecticut, and is one of the first plant viruses to be described.)

The invasive virus (ToMV and HIV) recalls the historic accident in which an invasive species, ostensibly secreted away in shipboard mattresses (a matter that is not without irony in this instance) gave rise to an island-image that markets purity. Francie's sojourn results in the apparent corruption of Eden, though as we've seen 'Eden' (any landscape that is constructed as inviolable) is not isolated from invasion, contagion, pilfering, and poaching and is anti-pastoral in its response to images of desirability. The ToMV causes economic ruin. The erasure of the tomatoes invites the *sous nature* ('under erasure') of playful deconstruction: tomatoes, the love fruit, Eden — a continuance of historical erasure in the name of purity.

If we extend the politics of place in which the island is itself a farm on a larger scale, then it too has been built upon a process of *sous nature*. I said Bea was the widow of a soldier settler. In those two words the novel extends its "warring forces of signification" in its literature/environment concerns from the battler's farm (p. 105) to include attitudes towards farming on a state level. The War Service Land Settlement Soldier Settler schemes of the two World Wars encouraged returned servicemen to take up farming with low investment loans (Hooper 1973: 148). A grid map of King Island divides areas into Soldier Settler selections, or if we were to be mischievous in our connective play (as the text is in its casual reference to "on our selection" [p. 39]), then what we have here are ecologues — Greek for 'selection'[7]— where soldiers engage in the dominating idea of the pastoral: "the search for the simple life [...] away from corruption, war, strife" (Cuddon 1999: 647). One of the later soldier settlers, Jim Paterson, author of *A King Island Settler's Tale* (2001), comments on the communal farming scheme:

> Each settler was expected to work on the Scheme for one to two years [...] — driving a bulldozer, driving tracked or wheeled tractors, clearing, ploughing, harrowing, seeding, draining, welding, engine reconditioning, fencing. [...] It was a bit like the Army — you were allotted a job and told to get on with it as best you could. (p. 16)

Where, in 1802, François Péron had described almost impenetrable forests on King Island, the clearing and harrowing — or ecocide — of land was accomplished with military precision:

Figure 8:

'Planning work for soldier settlement blocks at Pegarah'.

Photo: King Island Museum.

Figure 9: 'Heavy machinery at Reekara, brought to the island to clear the land, 1962'.

Photo: Judith Payne.

Greenpeace has its Rainbow Warriors, George Sessions his Eco-warriors, but these farmers were *bona fide* military, and the word Digger reinvents itself. The political ecology reveals itself in the language of dominance, as military language colonised the settlement. Biodiversity was successfully combated, as reflected in housing of regimented uniformity, constructed of fibro sheeting and iron roofing.

As recipients of funding from the Closer Settlement Board, the Blakes take up the scheme on the island, along with their two children. Bea expresses ambivalence towards the scheme — such as the compelling pastoral-romance of the wounded, healed by the age-old confluence of man and earth, as uttered in her sentence: "A new world, a fresh start. Give him strength [Bea] prayed, there on the tarmac [...]". Then there are the farmers, sacrificial fodder squeezed between bureaucratic machinery and an unforgiving earth — says Bea: "our brave new world as recruits in the army of the doomed, the next wave of soldier settlers" (p. 95). The Huxley "brave new world" allusion solidifies the irony implicit in the good idea.[8] As with the anti-pastoral rebuff to alternative life stylers figured in Bea's tribulations as a widow in Eden, so the anti-pastoral rebuff to the physical and psychical 'curing' of the wounded through land grants from the Soldier Settler scheme. Bea experiences her husband's derangement in the Hell of the family circle, and *The Divine Comedy*, the text that gave him hope in the POW camp, is reinterpreted as a blueprint for cruelty. She reflects on how it amuses her to observe the deluded ramblings of the faithful thinking that there is this desirable condition called self-sufficiency that comes through a love of the natural and an ability to do without. Thoreau is wonderful in theory but the reality of debt and deprivation is sobering. (p. 122)

In the world beyond the text — the world of King Island — those soldier settlers who had prior farming experience, who could exchange mobility for settlement, who were able to meet loan repayments, and who engaged in land consolidation by adding soldier settler properties abandoned by those beaten by farming or post-war fatigue are primarily the graziers of today.

But in the novel, Bea and her dead husband's friend, Brody, are losers in the system. Their farms are lost to consolidation. Bea can reflect wryly on "those newcomers with romantic ideas about the settlers and their achieving lives" (p. 119). The images are as inappropriate to experience as her attempt to cure Francie of AIDS with advice from *Vis Medicatrix Naturae: Hippocrates and the healing power of nature* (p. 151). Her macrobiotic farming at Eden, her attempted self-sufficiency, her relative poverty, and her infamy set her and her organic produce apart from the respectable image of pure goodness of the Primary Industries of the island.

The Island is the Ur-text that gave rise to the narrative pens of Delano, Péron, Baudin; it is the Ur-text which inspired Shimmins to engage in textual "descent with modification" (to quote Darwin on evolution) by invoking Dante's epic narrative and, consequently, Virgil's, whose rendering of the pastoral becomes ironic within the context of the Soldier Settler scheme. As Francie says, when finding Bea distraught over a quote from Shakespeare that affects her personally, "Books can be pretty dangerous territory, the ideas they make you have" (p. 205). And as noted, Dante's *The Divine Comedy* contains accounts of the unforeseeable power of texts to alter behaviour, such as the killing of Francesca, for reading and then acting upon a passage in the Romance of Arthur. Nature and text — the double helix of human makeup, where one strand is made up of what E.O. Wilson calls biophilia (the innate capacity of humans to love life) embracing biobehaviouralist Ellen Dissanayake's notion of *Homo aestheticus* (the aesthetic as a natural part of being human) (Love 2003: 77). Together nature and aesthetics constitute the matter of ecocriticism, which "considers the relationship between human and non-human life as represented in literary texts" and also "theorises about the place of literature in the environment" (Coupe 2000: 302).

3.3. Farming: Phase 3 — Salvage and Renewal

Shimmins's text, anti-pastoral yet coloured green, issued out from Dante's and from out of King Island. It necessitated a critical journey not just into text but into context. So I set about situating scenes, like the boathouse scene, where Francie takes on the kelpers, and found that though the building had been condemned, it had been salvaged, and reinvented as a "restaurant without food" by the local potter, Caroline Kininmonth, where consumers must satisfy their own desires with BYOF.

Unlike King Island Dairy, this wasn't high-end consumerism. This was when I became aware of what I see as an evolving, third phase of farming the island. My being in place as opposed to simply writing about place enabled what Glen Love calls "a productive 'consilience', a joining of the fields of knowledge" (2003: 88). Physicality had forced recognition of the consilience of histories: literary, natural, and now civil. Bea's attempt to live self-sufficiently while recognising that farming reflects a practical dependence on the environment is today reflected on a larger scale; and it's more promising because it is farming without the use of immigrant materials. The Roaring 40s for instance are harvested as a renewable energy source at the happily named, linguistic "consilience" of Huxley Wind Farm. King Island gets about twenty percent of its energy needs from the Wind Farm (begun in 1998) and CO_2 emissions are down by 2000 tonnes per annum (Australian Bureau of Statistics).

Tapping into the image of purity, local music teacher Duncan McPhee also harvests the sky by farming the nimbostratus: capturing 'Cloud Juice' from iron roofs for a global market. From a twenty-first-century perspective, it's possible to look back and read an apocalyptic version of the island; or instead, choose to see the wind, the storms, the sea, as being re-valued while still being mindful of the island's bioecology. The marine environment still offers up salvage after storms with the littoral zone promising a good harvest of Bull Kelp (*Durvillea potatorum*). Again the consilience of naming ("bull" kelp) recalls a non-invasive pastoral industry where kelpers collect the cast kelp and transport an annual harvest to the Kelp Industries plant in Currie — some of which ends up in the 'consilience' of ice-cream as an emulsifier.

This third phase of farming (farming without the use of immigrant materials) is also in place on the *land*. Roadside wallaby corpses undergo salvage and "renewal" at the hands of soldier settler descendent Robyn Eades, who skins and cures wallabies and possums for blankets and rugs, makes delicately-wrought purses and spectacle cases out of scrotums, and knits fingerless gloves for working hands out of possum fur.

The day I was to leave the island was the day when the first shipment of 500 wallabies was due to be exported for the gourmet meat market. But word had got out, and this time instead of seals under threat, it was the good name of King Island, contaminated by news that 1080[9] had been laid by some cattle farmers to protect grazing pasture. Consumers boycotted all King Island produce due to concerns about food web contamination and the random nature of the bait. Boycotting thereby also affected those who were farming alternative produce (Kempton 2005: 13). I photographed 1080 victims — wallabies and pademelons with no hit-and-run wounds lying well away from the road and without bullet holes; and I photographed an untargeted victim of 1080, and mused on the reading of this image:

Figure 10 : 1080 victim, Cape Wickham, King Island. Photo: CA. Cranston

Would mainlanders read this as a kitten, or as a feral cat? Was this a pet? Or a predator? It is as fraught with difficulties as is a reading — fact or fiction — of the pros and cons of melilot's introduction to the island by means of a shipwrecked mattress, as is the deranged reading of Dante's *The Divine Comedy* by a heart-sickened POW.

Though I had found salvage and renewal in some of the farming practices of the island, the novel ends with very little salvage or renewal. Francie's body is a landscape of disease. She notes earlier: "Possums, wallabies, people, even people, they all fertilise in the end, and this is the only certain meaning of life. I tell this to Dante, but it is hard to tell myself" (p. 57). Dante in this context is her kitten. Putrefaction will ensure regeneration, though Dante's reputation will ever issue "green from out the earth". Francie, however, dies unnamed, like the text that brought her to life, her copy of Dante burned in the squat where she is found and her cat, Dante, killed. Francie's bioecology — her impact on other organisms and her environment — is less final. Bodies, like texts, are not closed systems; they too impact on the world around them.

**4. Empirical *and* Imaginative Response: *Stradbroke Dreamtime*.
North Stradbroke Island. Murri Name: Minjerriba 27°35'S,
153°23'E. Population: 3,000. With Tourists: 20,000**

Shift the latitude, and imaginative constructions of island-living shift
with the changes in temperature. In the place that is the eye-land of the
mind, 'tropical islands' lend themselves to charges of 'exoticism'.
Islands are reduced to linguistic constructions and Aboriginal islanders to the quick-sand of mythic frameworks. The island under discussion here, however, is just south of the imaginary line that is the
Tropic of Capricorn; accordingly it doesn't qualify as 'tropical'. But
islands, at the very least, are polyphonic. Their utterances bespeak
use-value multiplicity, winds (whether temperate or tropical) articulate
the changing shorelines, severing land from land, depositing and
displacing human cargo.

North Stradbroke is such an island. Depending on one's point of
view, this 38 by 12 kilometre island is either a 'new' or a displaced
island. Separated from its southern counterpart in 1896, it was geographically once part of a group linked to the mainland (Durbridge
and Covacevich 2004: 48). Now part of the Moreton Bay Marine Park
(Murri name, Quandamooka), it was also once an "institutionalised
island" (2004: 86) utilised as a convict and military depot by Com-
mandant Patrick Logan (1827), as a quarantine station (1850), and as a
missionary station (1892-1942). During World War II it was home to
the Sixth Platoon US Army; wartime demand for ilmenite, rutile (for
titanium) and zircon resulted in the establishment of sand mining on
the (predominantly sand) island (2004: 106). It was, in 1970, the
unwitting player in an Australian 'first' when the government rejected
a mining venture at Cooloola Sands in favour of national park status.
Stradbroke served the unenviable function of worst-case scenario:
"tours contrasting Cooloola with the mining-devastated Stradbroke
Island turned public opinion against mining [at Cooloola]" (Lines
2006: 96). Consolidated Rutile sand mining, tourism (which author-
ises stretches of the littoral zone to be reconfigured as an SUV high-
way), and natural foreshore erosion at Amity Point make the very
foundations of Stradbroke Island a contested site.

It is also culturally contested, as in its name. Though contemporary
maps of the island bear the name Minjerriba ('place of the mosquito'),

that name originally applied to South Stradbroke Island. Furthermore 'Minjerriba' is a construction of mainlander Aboriginals and is not derived from the resident Noonukul tribe (Steele 1994: 30). Why this concern for nomenclature? Steele's conclusion is that local inhabitants named small localities but not the island as a whole (p. 31). If this is so, then the act of insisting on particulars rather than generalising is one that demonstrates traditional recognition of bioregional (let us say for the moment, Aboregional) differences; it is therefore a refusal to essentialise the island. Synergistically, this idea (the refusal to essentialise based on the cultural practice of naming) applies therefore to its indigenous inhabitants. The notion of geographical determinism was taken to task in the opening of this chapter. However, the text under consideration here, Kath Walker's *Stradbroke Dreamtime* (1972), depicts island figuration as human figuration, or to put it another way, it insists on an ecological interrelationship, a 'land ethic', between human and non-human worlds.

The term 'the land ethic' was proposed by Aldo Leopold (1887-1948) in *A Sand County Almanac* (1949; rpt. 1989). Leopold's work (set on his "sand farm" family refuge in Wisconsin in 1935 [xviii]) is not exactly contemporaneous with the setting of the first section of *Stradbroke Dreamtime* (the 1920s and 1930s), but it is close enough to provide a (con)textual challenge to his statement (under 'The Ethical Sequence') that

> [t]here is as yet no ethic dealing with man's relation to land and to the animals and plants which grow upon it. Land, like Odysseus' slave-girls, is still property. The land-relation is still strictly economic, entailing privileges but not obligations. (p. 203)

(In the case of islands and the later discussion on dugongs, we need to extend 'the land ethic' to include the oceanic space that makes up the Exclusive Economic Zones [EEZ] girdling each island.) Leopold suggests that a land ethic had to evolve sequentially, beginning with "the relation between individuals", then moving to "the individual and society" (pp. 202-203), so that finally "[t]he land ethic simply enlarges the boundaries of the community to include soils, waters, plants and animals, or collectively: the land" (p. 204).

4.1. Aboriginalism, and Aboregionalism

This is the world described in *Stradbroke Dreamtime* (1972) the first prose work by Oodgeroo Noonuccal (1920-1993). Better known as the Aboriginal poet whose (if I may indulge) "landmark" publication *We are Going* (1964) ushered in black words on white pages. Whereas Bob Hodge notes, "the majority of her poems address white readers directly and polemically" (1994: 74), the framework for reading this prose text with its shift in intended readership (it is dedicated to her grandchildren) dictates a focus on green poetics, rather than on the black politics of its author. That is to say, the reading strategy will favour an ecocentric rather than anthropocentric approach. A contemporary common appeal to future-oriented thinking about environmental impact is to refer to "our children's children"; *Stradbroke Dreamtime*, dedicated "For my grandchildren", is a voice in that chorus. Partly about growing up as a sand-island indigene, *Stradbroke Dreamtime* describes the experiences of a single Aboriginal family. These experiences therefore should not be 'Aboriginalised' or taken as representing the mythic ecological indigene (discussed later). Written while staying at Tamborine Mountain with friend, activist, and writer Judith Wright (Walker 1987: 4), the work was authored by the then named Kath (Jean Mary Ruska) Walker. The book's title, the author's former name, and the name of the island she writes about all bear the marks of colonisation. ('Kath' will be used in this essay in keeping with the historical structure and mythical progression implicated in the prose work.) Dedicated to her grandchildren, the book is both revenant and, paradoxically, forward-thinking myth making. Consequently, the book as artefact confirms the comment by Mudrooroo Narogin (Colin Johnson) that an Aboriginal writer is "a Janus-type figure with one face turned to the past and the other to the future while existing in a postmodern, multicultural Australia in which he or she must fight for cultural space" (qtd. in Smith 1994: 84). The book is divided into two sections, 'Stories from Stradbroke' (autobiographical, contextual) and 'Stories from the Old and New Dreamtime' (mythological, textual).

'Stories from Stradbroke' is a type of *Bildungs*-sketch without a hero; situated in the experiential world, it portrays a diversity of personalities, human and non-human communities, and nature contexts which together refute notions of Aboriginal essentialism, or

'Aboriginalism' (a neologism engendered by Hodge and Mishra in 1990 (Knudsen 1994: 107)). According to critic Eva Rask Knudsen, Aboriginalism

> situates the *real* Aborigines within the mystical domain of the Dreaming and constructs the Aboriginal person from there as an otherwordly and much desired 'other' to the white imagination that controls the image. (107)

Conversely, *Stradbroke Dreamtime* sets the first part of its "mystical domain of the Dreaming" in the physical reality of Stradbroke Island; furthermore, the transformation of flesh and blood into (legendary) image — in figures such as "Sammy of Myora" (p. 40) — is controlled by black imagination and black experience. And unlike the four works discussed previously, this collection names the island that gave birth to the Dreamtime stories: the emphasis therefore is on stories *from* place, rather than *about* place. In *Stradbroke Dreamtime* (as we'll see in 'Oodgeroo' [p. 56]) culture is portrayed as inextricably bound to, and arising out of, nature. Nature, then, is primary.

In addition, the book's title signifies recognition of local island/er individuation while (by evoking 'Dreamtime' myths that are specific to place) simultaneously engaging with, and complexifying, stereotypical constructions of Aboriginalism. Everyday events deconstruct essentialist notions. 'Family Council' (p. 28), for instance, concerns the poor hunting skills of young Kath. This not only places her outside of white constructions of gendered-Aboriginalism (i.e., only males hunt, and all are good hunters), but temporarily, it challenges constructions of harmonious Aboriginalism by placing her outside of the family circle of her own accusatory siblings, whose views concerning the hunting of animals differ from Kath Walker's.

Previously it was pointed out that the received reading of islands is one that reflects on the inhabitants; the idea is one of islander-sameness or human 'monoculture'. Island-dwelling indigenes and immigrant settlers put the lie to such a statement. As Eve Fesl notes, in a curious double-bind situation in 'The Road Ahead', as a child Oodgeroo and her family were "among a fortunate few not part of the 'settlement' system. She and her family were known as 'outsiders' by the Murri community" (1994: 142). In *Stradbroke Dreamtime*, family incidents continue to confront essentialism, as in 'The Left-hander' (p. 23) and 'Repeat Exercise' (pp. 31-32). Here, the social opprobrium attached to Kath's left-handedness at school extends beyond skin colour relations and into a stigmatised body-zone familiar to *all* lefties raised in a right-handed society.

The foregoing analysis appears to have abandoned an ecocritical approach and to perpetuate literature's concern with character. But to return to my earlier neologism, the collection is Aboregional; the local (family and community) and the bioregion are portrayed as inextricable. As such the collection lends itself absolutely to ecocriticism's concerns, which are to examine the "relationship between human and non-human life as represented in literary texts" (Coupe 2000: 302). Whereas previous analyses of this writer's work have tended to focus on human (racial) relationships, the first story under consideration, 'Carpet Snake' (pp. 26-27), broadens the critical boundaries by enlarging "the boundaries of community", as suggested by Leopold. 'Carpet Snake' introduces totemic connections to the land, and to its human and non-human inhabitants. It also introduces the difficulties accompanying this ecological perspective.

4.2.   Human–Nonhuman Relationships, and 'Traditional' Recycling

Kabool (the Carpet Snake) is the island's totem (Steele 1994: 29). Writes Walker, "[m]y father belonged to the Noo-muccle tribe of Stradbroke Island, and the carpet snake was his totem. He made sure he looked after his blood-brother" (p. 26). The difficulty with espousing interconnectedness of land, human, and non-human life (and here, Kabool is the nexus) is of course that humans turn to the land and to non-humans for their food. The narrator tells us that while tribal members are forbidden to eat their totem (their "blood-brother"), they may, however, eat the totems of other tribes. Speciesism (a value-hierarchy of species, which places humans as the pinnacle animal and works its way 'downward') is condoned inasmuch as animals are valued differently (protected as spiritual material or hunted as food) according to tribal differences, i.e., according to *human* cultures. The conservation flow-on effect of animal protection through totemic-relativism is at its base, utilitarian: "In this way there was food for all" (p. 45).

Despite its protected status as a totem, the "ten-foot carpet snake we had as a pet" (p. 26) is implicated in an ecology of cooperation and competition which threatens to feed marital discord and disrupt the domestic economy, even as it serves to demonstrate diversity of opinion in the indigenous community: "My mother belonged to a different tribe. The carpet snake was not her totem. She hated old Carpie, because of his thieving ways" (p. 26). The "thieving ways" of 'Carpie' (Kabool) extend to his appropriation of Mother's fowl and their eggs. Even totems, it seems, have material needs, and a farmyard drama of power relations between indigenous and introduced (colonial) species is played out under sufferance. Metaphysical totemic powers are gently earthed in the scatological: the toilet shed doubles as a confessional booth where Kath "used to sit in the lavatory for hours and tell him [her] innermost secrets" (p. 27).

Like his "blood-brother", Kath's father also shares Kabool's "thieving ways". In 'The Tank' (p. 14) low-waged "Dad" salvages a leaky water tank from "the white man's rubbish dumps" (p. 14). It is a story about transforming junk into capital; Dad recycles and renovates the inside of the tank with cement "borrowed" (p. 14) from the government. An agent of change, his "borrowing" is, in a sense, an early withdrawal from a scheme now in place, seventy years later, in which the government offers rebates on water tanks in an attempt to redress critical water shortages (Courtney 2004: ABC-TV). Earlier, a point was made warning against the reading of islands as mere marginalia to mainland activities; currently, North Stradbroke Island is in the 'geophagous' business of selling water pumped from Eighteen Mile Swamp (53ML/day) to the mainland (Durbridge and Covacevich 2004: 8, 19). 'The Tank' — its real-life counterpart an iconic image of rural white Australia — celebrates self-sufficiency and adaptability. Dad's proactive 'conservation' ethos, driven by family and financial need, today finds acceptability in green-lifestyle circles. This same method of tank repair, along with how-to instructions, can be found in the alternative publication *The Earth Garden Water Book* (2004: 6).

The water tank, along with the farming of chickens, demonstrates an evolving relationship between an indigenous family, the harvesting of water and food, and 'resource development' using immigrant materials. As well as the practical issue of food-gathering, the ethical issues raised in espousing interconnectedness of land, human, and non-human life are made explicit in 'Kill to Eat' (p. 8), where "Dad taught us how to catch our food Aboriginal-style, using discarded materials from the white man's rubbish dumps". The comment raises questions to do with culture (Aboriginal and "white man's"), with the transformation of junk into 'new'-tradition hunting materials, and with nature (killing ethically). It also presents an opportunity to position the narrator within a particular green discourse which, as I hope to show, conflicts, or at least, runs 'widdershins' to some of the black discourse of current Quandamooka Elders.

4.3.   Human-Nonhuman Relationships and Traditional Hunting

'Kill to Eat' is a 'pecking order' moral fable. A young boy's vanity turns to anger when he misses his mark; he deliberately retaliates by taking the life of a kookaburra, "a bird we were forbidden to destroy" (p. 10). The "Aboriginal law" that forbids killing "for the sake of killing" (p. 10) has its Western counterpart in an 'eight-point plat- form', originating in 1973 (a year after the publication of *Stradbroke Dreamtime*). Devised by eco-philosophers Arne Naess and George Sessions, and revised in 1984, the third rule states: "Humans have no right to reduce this richness and diversity [of life] except to satisfy *vital* needs" (qtd. in Hay 2002: 43). The platform "has come to be seen as the definitive principles of deep ecology" (p. 43). The deep ecology platform — built upon Aldo Leopold's 'The Land Ethic', and with a social philosophy oriented toward bioregionalism —provides a framework in which to focus on the interrelationship of the human and non-human world.

In other words, I want to read *Stradbroke Dreamtime* ecocritically rather than as a text solely about *humans* in the natural world (for as noted, the production and Aboriginal content of *Stradbroke Dream- time* make it a polyvalent 'text'). And I do this, first, to recover the bedrock realities of environmental thinking and practice in literature (the concern of ecocriticism), and second, to identify *Kath Walker's* green politics as expressed through the *Stradbroke Dreamtime* narra- tive, rather than read 'Kath Walker' as the exemplar Aboriginal, an embodiment of "the myth of the 'Ecological Aboriginal'" (Lines 2006: 165). Deep ecology is eco-centric, that is, it is anti-anthro- pocentric — human culture is human chauvinism (speciesist) when it assumes *a priori* rights over other biota. In other words, in this collection of moral and mythic fables addressed to her grandchildren, to what degree does the 'land ethic' of the deep ecologists (where all species have equal and intrinsic value) resonate in Walker's work? And if it is indeed in operation, how are the green ecocentric politics of the 'land ethic' reconciled with the black anthropocentric politics of 'land rights' (where the traditional "owners" of the land assert hunting privileges in accordance with tribal law)?

In the family setting, we've already seen disagreement concerning hunting and totemic sanctuary. It would seem reasonable, then, that beyond the domestic community, Aboriginal consensus regarding nature/culture clashes might not always be achievable. Two points stated earlier confirm: (1) the idea of islander-sameness or human 'monoculture' as unsustainable, and (2) the idea that islands cannot afford to be land-centric owing to the existence of food resources beyond the terrestrial. Because an island's size is greatly enhanced by the waters beyond the littoral zone (the EEZ area), an island's traditional hunting practices are apt to come into conflict with governmental (white man's) policy. The question of whether one upholds Aboriginal 'land rights' in the matter of hunting vulnerable species is one that engages the politics of race, culture, and species. Currently, North Stradbroke Island is part of the Moreton Bay Marine Park Island where the Amity Banks Turtle and Dugong are protected. Protected status wasn't the case at the time at which 'Dugong Coming!' (p. 40) is set (in the 1920s, 1930s). But the story, published in 1972 (shortly after dugongs were granted protected status in 1967), shows Kath the child and Kath the adult articulating a shift in position regarding human culture and the well-being of another species. And that position differs on two counts from that held by the current Quandamooka Elders.

The first disjunction has to do with gender. 'Dugong Coming!' introduces a figure, heroic in his time, "Old Sammy of Myora" (Sammy Rollands), "the catcher of dugong" (p. 40). With dugong capture comes proportional sharing of the meat — a carnivalesque communion — as families gather at the foot of Gaphembah Hill, "the sharing-out place" (p. 40). While (according to Durbridge and Covacevich) present-day Quandamooka Elders hold that "[t]he women were not allowed to look upon the captured animal before it was cut

up" (2004: 67), the scene in 'Dugong Coming!' shows no such segre-
gation. Men, women, and children gather together for the cutting up
and distribution of the dugong meat. Whatever tradition the Quandamooka Elders are evoking is not shared by Walker's lived, community
experience. Similarly, her familial experience of men's and women's
business as stated in 'Going Crabbing' is such that "Dad believed in
equality of the sexes, especially where work was concerned. If there
was a job Dad wanted done, it didn't matter which of his children was
closest — that one could do it" (p. 20).

The second disjunction between the author's position and that of
the Elders concerns her attitude toward non-human species and extends beyond cultural anthropology into sea country pastoral:

> The dugong is a mammal. It has two hearts which are joined together, and it is
> able to stay alive in the sea as well as on land. It is a large creature, very much like
> a seal. It has, too, another name: it is often called the sea-cow. The flesh is a great
> delicacy, and was part of the staple diet of the Aborigines. (p. 40)

The past tense ("was part of the staple diet") suggests a change in
traditional habits. Unlike the Carpet Snake, the Dugong is not under
the Noonukuls' totemic protection; if it is to survive, it must rely on
'institutional' laws (including monitoring of its seagrass meadows),
and recreational 'Go Slow' boat legislation. (Both the Amity Banks
Turtle and the Dugong are shallow-water species.) "Today" (writes
Walker in 1972), "when the white man's food is eaten so widely by
Aborigines, the tribe no longer hunts the dugong. They believe that to
hunt dugong when their bellies are full would be to act against the
natural law of 'kill to eat'" (p. 42). In choosing to place the protection
of the dugong above traditional cultural practices Walker's position
predates the 1991 Queensland land rights bill that "allowed Aborigines to claim land rights over all the State's national parks" (Lines
2006: 293). Those "land rights" extend beyond the littoral zone into
the Moreton Bay Marine Park, also known as Quandamooka. Consequently the dugong is sacrificed in an intra-species trade off, where
"with protective legislation, on Stradbroke, only traditional owners
can hunt dugong and turtle for traditional use. The Quandamooka
Dugong and Turtle Group make decisions on the number that may be
taken" (Durbridge and Covacevich 2004: 67). The legislation carries
the presumption that the Group will naturally do the right thing. And

it's possible that the Group might choose not to take the lives of any dugong. But they have been accorded the right to act. In this case the 'land-relation' of the Quandamooka Group is (to return to Leopold's land ethic comment, above) one that appears to entail "privileges but not obligations" (Leopold 1949; rpt. 1989: 203). The southern Great Barrier Reef dugong, now listed as vulnerable under the Nature Conservation Act 1992, numbers about 4,220 of the 72,000 projected to have been present in the early 1960s (Marsh 2005: 484). Clearly, the views of at least one of Minjerriba's most outspoken indigenous activists and writers are not the views of the Quandamooka Dugong and Turtle Group. Walker's biocentric position in 'Dugong Coming!' warns against old ways and nostalgia associated with anthropocentrism — as expressed in the figuration of "the black man" as the enemy of the dugong:

> The dugong still feed in Moreton Bay, and I am sure they must wonder what has become of their enemy, the black man. Sometimes, in July, when I see the chewed weed floating ashore on the high tide, my mouth waters for the taste of dugong. But the law of the tribe is good, and no one intends to break it just because of a longing for what used to be. (p. 42)

This, the last paragraph of 'Dugong Coming!', ends the first section and prepares for what comes in 'Stories from the Old and New Dreamtime'. The final sentence above suggests a need to adapt to current conditions rather than "longing for what used to be". "Old" Dreamtime refers to deep time, the time before and after creation, in which creation undergoes sequential transformation. It is, to return to an earlier image, a type of pre-Moon time (in which the moon calved from the earth as a result of impact. See section 1.2). So, in 'The Midden' the Rainbow Serpent is "the Mother of Life" who created the land, the totems, and from these, the tribes (p. 49). These cultural constructs are familiar figures in an oral literature that predates Greek and Roman creation literature — a literature of a people who colonised the land 40-60,000 years prior to European colonisation (estimates differ). "Old Dreamtime" is history and geography combined; it is slow motion 'Island time', the singing into being of evolving landscapes through myths of transformation.

Of course, "Dreamtime" is yet another anglicised version of an Aboriginal concept, that of 'Altjeringa'. Roland Robinson (1912-

1992), an atypical Jindyworobak contributor, nature poet, and author of verse including *Language of the Sand* (1949) and *The Shift of Sands* (1976), summarises 'Altjeringa' as the pre-creation time (1966: 215). So the idea of a *"New* Dreamtime" appears paradoxical. What *Stradbroke Dreamtime* is, is autochthonous writing about Aboriginality; it reclaims traditional Aboriginal myths and retells them from an indigenous perspective. But, as critic Anne Brewster points out, its author also *makes myth*: "she devises her own stories and myths about her tribal homeland" (1994: 97). Along with cosmos, land, and animal creation myths, the New Dreamtime includes creation myths that concentrate specifically on plant life. In other words this is literature mindful of the "land ethic" in that "[t]he land ethic simply enlarges the boundaries of the community to include soils, waters, plants and animals, or collectively: the land" (Leopold 1949; rpt. 1989: 204). Humans are depicted as the nexus in human/animal/plant relationships: according to the Old Dreamtime, the literary genesis of human/animal relationships had to do with keeping the Law (those animals that did, evolved "human form" and were given a totem "of the animal, bird or reptile [from] whence they came" [p. 45]). As a continuation of the human/animal/plant cycle, Walker's New Dreamtime stories depict plant life originating from humans. These include 'Tuggan-Tuggan' (Silky Oak), 'Talwalpin and Kowinka' (Cotton-tree and Red Mangrove), 'Pomera' (Banksia), 'Boonah' (Bloodwood Gum), 'Tia-Gam' (Lawyer Vine), and 'Mai' (Black Bean).

The pivotal story is 'Oodgeroo: Paperbark-tree' (p. 56). Seldom if ever are myth origins traceable, but 'Oodgeroo' of course is also the name that Walker took in 1987. In the story, a detribalised woman writes herself and the stories of the lost tribes back into existence. This is done by gathering sticks from the dead fires of the lost tribes. Using the charred wood ('the old') to make black marks on the living (paper) bark tree ('the new'), and with a little inspiration in the form of Biami, she inscribes the stories of the Noonuccal tribe until all the charred sticks are gone. Through the act of writing, "she recalled the stories of the old Dreamtime, and through them entered into the old life of the tribes" (p. 56). The myth describes the inventing of stories that invent landscapes that invent the storyteller. Symbolically this is the woman's return to the inseparability of human history and natural history. The nihilism referred to in the Three Hummock Island discussion, where a sense of erasure results from the unregarded body, is here irrelevant. In the New Dreamtime, the old woman is not 'self' conscious; she is guided by Biami, who "put into her mind a new way in which she might find those stories and her tribe" (p. 56). Geosophical links to place and dreamtime create a narrative of continuity whereby Island time is no longer ahistorical or nihilistic.

As allegory, 'Oodgeroo' describes the relationship of trees to the act of writing. It describes the relationship between storyteller and resources. As mentioned above, Walker's New Dreamtime stories depict plant life originating from humans. In 'Oodgeroo' the Paperbark-tree and the tribal woman, both indigenes, participate in a co-operative economy. She is permitted to take the bark to write on because "[t]hey knew she was not greedy" (p. 56). In return, when the old woman's stories are complete and the Paperbark-trees are in bloom and at their most energy-intensive stage of production, "they took her into their tribe as one of their own" (p. 56). The cyclical process of life, death, and regeneration is also stated in Eleanor Alliston's comment regarding the "compost heap" (IA 78); it is also to be found in *Eden Observed* in Francie's comment that "Possums, wallabies, people, even people, they all fertilise in the end, and this is the only certain meaning of life" (Shimmins 1999: 57). In plain terms the 'Oodgeroo' story describes a reciprocity of resources, the exchange of carbon banks that will enable two forms of creativity. It will assist in the perpetuation of the physical world of the *Melaleuca quinquenervia* as well as the symbolic world of Oodgeroo.

Today that relationship would more aptly describe the relationship between the writer, the paper, and the plantation. To return to the opening scenes of this chapter: should the Long Reach pulp mill go ahead (and with the managing director of Forestry Tasmania also the head of the Pulp Mill Task Force[10], the government and industry are 'on the same page' and charges of islander 'monoculture' or incestuousness begin to seem less outrageous), there will be no reciprocity of resources. Indigenous forests will burn into tree crops of immigrant species that will shelter little more than tax investments. Being young and eager to grow, plantations consume ground water resources at an astonishing rate, affecting water catchment areas and food crops. But there will be paper. Paper for businesses, for academics, and for authors, who might wonder at the bioecology — the impact on other

organisms and the environment — that writing the world into existence has on the very thing itself.

Notes

[1] The Australian Government Geoscience website lists 1,000 islands for Tasmania, 1955 for Queensland, and 3,747 for Western Australia.

[2] The part that the sun, and therefore global warming, plays in sea-level rise in threatening the vulnerability of islands is unquestionable; but unlike the moon, its landscape is not textualised, and it exerts lesser gravitational force in influencing tides.

[3] Range and diet suggest that the 'leopard-spotted Arctic seal' (perhaps a reference to the Arctic Spotted Seal [*Phoca largha*]) is more likely to be the Antarctic Leopard Seal (*Hydrurga leptonyx*), a known predator of penguins.

[4] Alliston's editor, nissologist Stephen Murray-Smith (1922-1988; co-author of *Bass Strait Bibliography* [1981]; editor of *Mission to the Islands: The Missionary Voyages in Bass Strait of Canon Marcus Brownrigg, 1872-1885* [1987]) was also educated at Geelong Grammar School. His daughter Joanna Murray-Smith is the author of *Judgement Rock* (2002) a novel about a woman's search for a rare orchid, set on Tasmania's Deal Island (Kent Group).

[5] An earlier video version of this paper, titled 'Cutting Corners', was delivered at the conference of the Association for the Study of Literature and the Environment (ASLE), Eugene, Oregon, 2005.

[6] There are at least two additional pastoral texts that concern us here: the material world of ecology in which pastoral refers to pasture, "land covered with grass or other small plants, used by farmers as a feeding place for animals" ('Pasture' 1995); and the literary construction of the pastoral, in which "The dominating idea and theme of most pastoral is the search for the simple life away from the court and town, away from corruption, war, strife, the love of gain, away from 'getting and spending'". (Cuddon 1999: 647). Readers are advised to consult Love's chapter 'Et in Arcadia Ego: Pastoral Meets Ecocriticism' (2003: 65-88) for a survey of the pastoral in the work of other scholars such as Lawrence Buell.

[7] In Australian literature the word *selection* is most closely associated with Steele Rudd (Arthur Hoey Davis) as in *On Our Selection* (1899), *Our New Selection* (1903), *Sandy's Selection* (1904), and *Back at Our Selection* (1906). Though Rudd was part of the bush realism era of Henry Lawson and Barbara Baynton, the Dad and Dave characters resurfaced in World War II, when "they caused the official Defence Department stamp on wartime supplies (D↑D) to be known, wherever there was an Australian Army Q-store, as 'Dad and Dave'" (Rudd 1969: cover flap).

[8] There is also an allusion to Shakespeare's *The Tempest*, another island drama. Miranda is taken with the visitors to their island; but Prospero, who has experienced the outside world, knows that they could mean trouble.

[9] "Compound 1080, or sodium monofluoroacetate, is a naturally occurring compound produced by many species of Australian plant. Sodium monofluoroacetate occurs

naturally in about 40 native plant species in Australia, primarily of the genus, Gastralobium [sic], which grow in Western Australia, across northern Australia in the Northern Territory and in central Queensland. No fluoroacetate bearing plants are known to occur in Tasmania or the other southern States" ('1080 Poison' 2006). In Tasmania, the government subsidises farmers and the woodchip industry to poison possums and wallabies with 1080. 1080 has been banned in Brazil since 1982 because of its danger to humans. 1080 is also banned in most States of the USA. In 2002-03, 23% was used by Forestry Tasmania; 47% by farmers, and 30% by private forestry ('1080 Poison Ban' 2004). 1080 has since been banned on public land in Tasmania (December 2005) but is still legal on private land.
[10] Robert Lindsay Gordon takes up the Forestry Tasmania position effective 1 January 2007.

Bibliography

Primary Sources

Alliston, Eleanor. 1966. *Escape to an Island.* London and Melbourne: William Heinemann. [ETI]

——. 1984. *Island Affair.* Elwood, Vic.: Greenhouse Publications. [IA]

Carson, Rachel. 1951. *The Sea Around Us.* New York: Oxford University Press.

Conrad, Peter. 1988. *Down Home: Revisiting Tasmania.* London: Chatto and Windus.

'Dante's *The Divine Comedy'*. Henry Wadsworth Longfellow (trans.). On line at: http://www.everypoet.com/archive/poetry/dante/dante_contents.htm (consulted: 27.10.2006).

Delano, Amaso. 1817. *Delano's Voyages of Commerce and Discovery: Amasa Delano in China, the Pacific Islands, Australia and South America, 1789-1807.* The original 1817 edition was published as *Master Mariner* by James B. Connolly in 1943. On line at: http://www.delanoye.org/Primary/amasaXVI.html (consulted: 27.10.2006).

Gillham, Mary E. 2000. *Island Hopping in Tasmania's Roaring Forties.* Devon: Arthur H. Stockwell.

Murray-Smith, Joanna. 2002. *Judgement Rock.* Camberwell, Vic.: Penguin.

Paterson, Jim. 2001. *A King Island Settler's Tale.* West Hobart, Tas.: J. Paterson.

Péron, François. 1971. *Voyage of Discovery to the Southern Lands (1800-1804).* (tr. Helen Mary Micco) (*King Island and the Sealing Trade 1802*). Canberra: Roebuck.

Shimmins, Anne. 1999. *Eden Observed.* Hobart, Tas: Bumble-bee Books.

Walker, Kath. 1972 rpt. 1987. *Stradbroke Dreamtime.* North Ryde, NSW: Angus and Robertson.

Wood, Danielle. 2003. *The Alphabet of Light and Dark.* Crows Nest, NSW: Allen and Unwin.

Secondary Sources

'1080 Poison'. 2006. Food and Agriculture, Dept of Primary Industries, Water and Environment, Number 14 Agdex 685. On line at: http://www.dpiwe.tas.gov.au/ inter.nsf/WebPages/RPIO-4ZM7CX?open (consulted 25.10.2006).

'1080 Poison Ban Welcomed'. 2004. On line at http://www.wilderness.org.au/ campaigns/policy/elections/federal/2004/1080 (consulted 25.10.2006).

'1384.6 Statistics Tasmania'. Australian Bureau of Statistics. On line at: http://www.abs.gov.au/Ausstats/abs@.nsf/0/417f8537cb527e15ca256c320024164 9 (consulted: 27.10.2006).

Andrews, Alison. 2006. 'Eco-warrior has plenty of fight left' in *The Examiner* (7 September 2006).

Bonnemaison, J. 1990. 'Vivre dans l'ile. Une approche de l'îléité océanienne'. *L'Espace Geographique* 2: 119-25. Cited in McCall, Grant. 'Nissology A Debate and Discourse from Below'. On line at: http://southpacific.arts.unsw.edu.au/ resourcenissology.htm (consulted: 18.08.2006).

Brewster, Anne. 1994. 'Oodgeroo: Orator, Poet, Storyteller' in Shoemaker, Adam (ed.) *Oodgeroo: A Tribute. Australian Literary Studies* 16(4): 92-104.

Brothers, Nigel, David Pemberton, Helen Pryor and Vanessa Halley (eds). 2001. *Tasmania's Offshore Islands' Seabirds and Other Natural Features.* Hobart: Tasmanian Museum and Art Gallery.

Brown, Bob, and Peter Singer. 1996. *The Greens.* Melbourne: Text Publishing.

Bryson, Bill. 2004. *A Short History of Nearly Everything.* Sydney: Black Swan.

Carroll, Joseph. 1995. *Evolution and Literary Theory.* Columbia and London: University of Missouri Press.

Commoner, Barry. 1980. *The Closing Circle: Man, Nature and Technology.* New York: Alfred A. Knopf.

Coupe, Laurence (ed.). 2000. *The Green Studies Reader: From Romanticism to Ecocriticism.* London: Routledge.

Courtney, Pip. 2004. 'Landline: "Water Tanks Make Urban Comeback"'. On line at http://www.abc.net.au/landline/content/2004/s1096547.htm (consulted 23.2. 2006).

Cox, Robert. 2000. Review of *Along These Lines: From Trowenna to Tasmania* by CA. Cranston (Launceston: Cornford Press, 2000) in *Island* (83): 106-08.

Cuddon, J.A. 1998. *The Penguin Dictionary of Literary Terms and Literary Theory.* Ringwood, Vic.: Penguin.

Donaghey, Richard (ed.). 2003. *The Fauna of King Island: A Guide to Identification and Conservation Management.* King Island: King Island Natural Resource Management Group.

Durbridge, Ellie, and Jeanette Covacevich. 2004. *North Stradbroke Island.* North Stradbroke Island: Stradbroke Island Management Organisation.

Earle, Sylvia A. 1995. *Sea Change: A Message of the Oceans.* New York: Random House.

Fesl, Eve. 1994. 'The Road Ahead' in Shoemaker, Adam (ed.) *Oodgeroo: A Tribute. Australian Literary Studies* 16(4): 141-146.

Finzel, Eva. (ed.) 2004. *From Gentle Giants to Green Pastures: A History of Environmental Change on King Island*. King Island: King Island Natural Resource Management Group Inc.

'Fishing and Aquaculture'. 2006. Department of Primary Industries, Water and the Environment. On line at: http://www.dpiw.tas.gov.au/inter.nsf/ThemeNodes/ DREN-4VH86L?open (consulted: 27.10.2006).

Gray, Alan T. (ed.). 2004. *The Earth Garden Water Book*. Trentham, Vic.: Earth Garden Books.

Hay, Peter. 2002. *Main Currents in Western Environmental Thought*. Sydney: University of New South Wales Press.

Hodge, Bob. 1994. 'Poetry and Politics in Oodgeroo: Transcending the Difference' in Shoemaker, Adam (ed.) *Oodgeroo: A Tribute. Australian Literary Studies* 16(4): 63-76.

Hooper, R.H. 1973. *The King Island Story*. Sydney: Peko-Wallsend.

Ikin, Van. 1988. 'Dreams, Visions, Utopias' in Laurie Hergenhan (ed.) *The Penguin New Literary History of Australia*. Ringwood: Penguin: 253-66.

'Islands'. Australian Government Geoscience. On line at: http://www.ga.gov.au/ education/facts/landforms/largisle.htm (consulted: 11.10.2006).

Kempton, Helen. 2005. 'Animal Rights Group Targets Island Export' in *Examiner* (27 May 2005).

'The King Island Problem'. 2006. On line at: http://www.utas.edu.au/spatial/locations/ spaking.html (consulted: 25.10.2006).

Knudsen, Eva Rask. 1994. 'From Kath Walker to Oodgeroo Noonuccal? Ambiguity and Assurance in *My People*' in Shoemaker, Adam (ed.) *Oodgeroo: A Tribute. Australian Literary Studies* 16(4): 105-18.

Leaman, David. 2004. *Water: Facts, Issues and Problems*. Hobart: Leaman Geophysics.

Leopold, Aldo. 1989. *A Sand County Almanac: And Sketches Here and There*. Oxford: Oxford University Press.

Lines, William J. 2006. *Patriots: Defending Australia's Natural Heritage 1946-2004*. St Lucia, Qld.: University of Queensland Press.

Love, Glen A. 2003. *Practical Ecocriticism: Literature, Biology, and the Environment*. Virginia: University of Virginia Press.

Low, Tim. 2003. *The New Nature: Winners and Losers in Wild Australia*. Camberwell, Vic.: Penguin.

Marsh, Helene, et al. 2005. 'Historical Marine Population Estimates: Triggers or Targets for Conservation? The Dugong Case Study' in *Ecological Applications* 15(2): 481-92.

McCall, Grant. 1994. 'Nissology: A Proposal for Consideration' in *Journal of The Pacific Society* 17(2-3, 63-64): 1-14.

McCall, Grant., 1997. 'Nissology A Debate and Discourse from Below'. On line at: http://southpacific.arts.unsw.edu.au/resourcenissology.htm (consulted: 18.08. 2006).

Murray-Smith, Stephen and John Thompson (gen. eds). 1981. *Bass Strait bibliography: a guide to the literature on Bass Strait covering scientific and non-scientific material*. Melbourne: Victorian Institute of Marine Sciences.

Murray-Smith, Stephen (ed. and intro). 1979. *Mission to the islands: the missionary voyages in Bass Strait of Marcus Brownrigg, 1872-1885*. Facsimile. Brownrigg, Marcus. 1872. *The cruise of the Freak*. Hobart: Cat and Fiddle Press.

Norman, L. 1946. *Sea Wolves and Bandits: Sealing, Whaling, Smuggling and Piracy*. Hobart: J. Walch.

Robinson, Roland. 1966. *Aboriginal Myths and Legends*. Melbourne: Sun Books.

Smith, Angela. 1994. 'Long Memoried Women: Oodgeroo Noonuccal and Jamaican Poet, Louise Bennett' in Shoemaker, Adam (ed.) *Oodgeroo: A Tribute. Australian Literary Studies*. 16(4): 77-91.

Steele, John. 1994. 'Minjerriba, The Historical Evidence for a Place Name' in Carter, Paddy, Ellen Durbridge and Jenny Cooke-Bramley (eds) *Historic North Stradbroke Island*. Dunwich: North Stradbroke Island Historical Museum Association: 29-32.

'Tomato Mosaic Virus'. 1998. On line at: http://www.hort.uconn.edu/ipm/ (consulted 27.10.2006).

"A Place of Ideals in Conflict": Images of Antarctica in Australian Literature

Elizabeth Leane

Abstract: This chapter examines Australian literature (poetry, fiction, and plays) dealing with Antarctica, focussing on each text's engagement with the Antarctic environment and the debates surrounding it. Beginning with two late nineteenth-century Antarctic utopias, the survey moves through the work of well-known writers such as Douglas Stewart and Thomas Keneally in the mid-century to more recent writing by Dorothy Porter, Les Murray, Caroline Caddy, and others. Less familiar material, such as poetry by Antarctic expeditioners themselves, is also discussed. The essay traces a rough progression in Australian representation of the far southern environment, from an initial utopian approach to an emphasis on its stark, 'timeless' icescape as a minimalist backdrop for human dramas to an appreciation of its change-ability, complexity, and fragility.

1. Introduction[1]

For Australian novelist and essayist Helen Garner, on a writing assignment to describe a tourist cruise to the Antarctic Peninsula, the very task of representing Antarctica comes to seem like an act of despoliation:

> I fiercely wish I had no prior inkling of this place, that everything I'm looking at were completely new to me. I hate movies and TV and videos. People with cameras are busybodies, writers are control freaks, spoiling things for everyone else, colonising, taming, matching their egos against the unshowable, the unsayable. I long to have come down here in a state of infantile ignorance. (1998: 18)

Likewise, the idea that there should be a body of imaginative expression about Antarctica — an accretion of tropes, motifs, and narratives attempting to give human shape to the most shapeless of continents — is one that is often resisted and denied.[2] This is an environment so

pure that words themselves become a form of pollution. To identify
and analyse a 'literature of the Antarctic', then, is to threaten the sense
that this is one place on Earth that culture has not reached, where a
direct, unmediated encounter with nature can be achieved — to
threaten the vision of Antarctica as the 'last true wilderness'. Yet the
concept of wilderness, as William Cronon has argued, is itself a highly
problematic one for environmentalism: "Idealizing a distant wilderness too often means not idealizing the environment in which we
actually live" (Cronon 1996: 85). The pristine wilderness of Antarctica, compartmentalised and offered for consumption on tourist cruises
such as the one Garner undertook, risks becoming compensation for
environmental damage in the rest of the world: a "sop for our con-
sciences", as one critic writes (Prosser 1995: 120). By focussing on
Antarctica as a cultural landscape and examining the various narratives that writers inscribe messily upon its 'wide white page',[3] we
come closer to understanding it not as a place apart to be fetishised,
but rather as contiguous with the wider physical and cultural environment. With this aim in mind, this article offers an ecocritically inflected survey of imaginative literature (poetry, plays, and fiction)
about Antarctica published by Australian writers.[4] My aim is not to
give an exhaustive survey (there are more than ninety Antarctic-
related poems by Australian writers), but to examine a representative
variety of texts, addressing a series of questions: what function does
the Antarctic icescape take on in the text? What kind of relationship
between Australia and Antarctica does the text evoke? To what extent
is the natural environment a topic in its own right? And how does an
awareness of environmental issues relating to the continent inform the
text?

   Of all the critical tools available to analyse 'Antarctic literature',
ecocriticism is among the more obvious choices. Admittedly, there are
many genre novels — horrors; military, spy and nautical action-
thrillers; science-fiction utopias — that use Antarctica as a conven-
iently remote and glamorous backdrop, paying little attention to political, historical, or physical specifics. However, the continent has also
provoked a good deal of material that would fit some or all of Lawrence Buell's criteria for "environmentally oriented work" (Buell
1995: 7-8). This is especially true in the last few decades, during
which conservation of the Antarctic environment has come to the fore

in policy discussion and in the media; but one of the first examples of Antarctic literature in English, Samuel Taylor Coleridge's 'Rime of the Ancient Mariner', also puts forward (arguably) an environmental moral. Surprisingly, given Antarctica's importance as a test-case in developing new approaches to the environment (Prosser 1995: 116), in previous ecocritical collections (e.g. Kerridge and Sammells 1998; Tallmadge and Harrington 2000; Armbruster and Wallace 2001), it is difficult to locate any references to the continent. In one instance, a discussion of 'arctic literature' briefly references accounts by Robert Scott and Ernest Shackleton under that category, as if the South Polar region were merely an adjunct to the North (Horne 2001: 78).[5] Given this context, and the current paucity of humanities-based research into the continent and its communities, ecocritical analysis of writing about Antarctica (and of representations of the continent in all media) is overdue.

Less straightforward is the case for examining a particularly Australian Antarctic literature. Although a number of prominent Australian writers, including Douglas Stewart, Thomas Keneally, Les Murray, and Dorothy Porter, have imaginatively engaged with the continent, it might be asked whether there is anything to be gained from examining these and other Australian writers as a national group, rather than linking them with a wider international literature about the continent. Antarctica is, after all, held up as an example of international cooperation — the one continent that, for the duration of the current Antarctic Treaty at least, is owned by no nation, even though it has been claimed by many. Unsurprisingly, several Antarctic-based texts by Australians deal with events and places that have little obvious connection with Australia: Douglas Stewart's play *The Fire on the Snow* is a re-telling of British explorer Scott's ill-fated polar journey; David Burke's *Monday at McMurdo* takes place in and around the eponymous American station, located on territory claimed by New Zealand; Matthew Reilly's *Ice Station*, although set in Australian-claimed territory, narrates the hair-raising adventures of a US marine who finds himself at the centre of an international espionage plot involving French and British forces. In what ways, then, can one talk about 'Australian Antarctic literature'? More broadly, in what sense can Antarctica be claimed as an 'Australian context'?

The most obvious reply is Australia's sovereignty claim — not only its existence, but its sheer size. Australian Antarctic Territory (AAT) covers forty-two percent of Antarctica — nearly half the continent, a significantly larger fraction than that claimed by any other nation, and more than three-quarters of the size of the Australian landmass itself. This sovereignty claim, however, is not recognised by many nations. 'Frozen' indefinitely, like all sovereignty claims, by the 1959 Antarctic Treaty, it currently translates to custodianship. Australia maintains its presence in the region by running three year-round bases; a fourth is located on the sub-Antarctic Macquarie Island (a part of Tasmania rather than the AAT). Politically symbolic gestures, such as the continuing efforts to restore Mawson's huts,[6] or the recent (2006) voyage of the Melbourne Commonwealth Games baton to Casey station, also reinforce Australia's interest in the region.

In its emphasis on ownership and imperial expansion, the treatment of Antarctica as a potential or actual Australian 'annex' is problematic for an ecocritical approach. Antarctica is considered here as an 'Australian context' on the basis of relationship rather than ownership. The connections between the two continents — geological, geographical, historical, legal, and political — are strong, and are explored in much (although not all) literature about Antarctica written by Australians; sovereignty claims are just one component of this multi-faceted connection.

2. Early Australian Fiction Set in Antarctica

One could argue that, prior to Tasman's voyages of exploration, all imaginative accounts of Antarctica were also accounts of Australia, as only then was the separation between the latter from any possible polar continent clearly confirmed. Even then, the extent to which the proposed Antarctic continent extended towards Australia and New Zealand was unknown until Cook's voyages in the late eighteenth century proved that it must be confined to the regions around the South Pole. The 'great southern land' posited by European myth-makers and map-makers covered the regions now occupied by both Australia and Antarctica. Early utopias and fantastic voyages set in *Terra Australis Incognita* could thus be claimed equally as proto-Australian or proto-Antarctic. During the nineteenth century, as the now-separate continent of Australia became increasingly settled by Europeans, and thus decreasingly suitable as the 'blank space' required by the utopian writer, Antarctica became the new favoured location for fictions of an ideal land.

It is not surprising, then, that the earliest known examples of Australian fiction set in Antarctica are utopian tales: Christopher Spotswood's novella *Voyage of Will Rogers to the South Pole* (1888) and George McIver's better-known novel *Neuroomia: A New Continent* (1894). Neither writer is much interested in engaging with the Antarctic environment on its own terms: in both cases, the icy coast encountered by explorers is merely a barrier hiding a temperate, inhabitable, and peopled land. Both narratives, however, give an indication of Australian attitudes towards the Antarctic region at the time.

Australia's geographical proximity to Antarctica meant that its southern ports, especially Hobart, were staging posts for many Antarctic voyages. The nineteenth century saw a number of official voyages of geographical and scientific exploration, including expeditions by Britain, France, and the United States in the late 1830s and 1840s (all of which stopped off in Australia). However, most activity in the Antarctic regions during this period was dependent on the whaling and sealing industries. The devastation of seal populations on sub-Antarctic islands led to exploratory journeys further south in search of new grounds; the first sighting of and landing on the continent were (arguably) made by sealers (Joyner 1992: 4). Likewise, the "period of averted interest" in the continent from around 1840 to 1890 was due to the exhaustion of seal colonies and a global downturn in the whaling industry (Joyner 1992: 6; Anon. 1985: 126). When Australian interest in Antarctica revived in the mid-to-late 1880s, with public calls for an Australian expedition and the establishment of a committee to promote this aim, a key factor was still commercial exploitation of resources, particularly whaling (considered newly viable as Arctic seas were by this stage exhausted) (Swan 1961: 47-60). It was in the wake of this interest that Spotswood's and McIver's novels were published.

Spotswood sets his novel in the mid-nineteenth century and sends his eponymous British protagonist to the far southern regions on a whaling ship via Van Diemen's Land (the author himself lived in Tasmania). When a catch goes wrong, Rogers is dragged in a boat behind a whale through an opening in the Antarctic ice. Eventually he discovers the country of "Bencolo", home to a "model people" (Spotswood 1888: 22) and also, significantly, near-limitless natural resources: the animals are "pretty numerous", there are "plenty of birds", the fish are "good and abundant", the wood supply "wonderful" with "no limit to the quantity" (p. 23); there is also "plenty of silver and gold" (p. 30). The population is kept in check only by a mysterious illness that strikes older people, a phenomenon that Rogers associates loosely with "the climate" (p. 24). Armed with a supply of gold, Rogers returns to his homeland, now an independent man, thanks to his cargo. Historian Peter Beck has suggested that the novella's concluding sentiments — that "it would be a pity" if further European contact disturbed the "peaceable and innocent" Bencolians (Spotswood 1888: 40) — pre-empt late twentieth-century desires to "preserve Antarctica's wilderness values" (Beck 1991: 41). It is, however, the newly found human society — white, Christian, and "civilized" (Spotswood 1888: 17) — that is considered worth preserving in the novel; regarding the land and its resources, Spotswood's approach comes closer to cornucopianism than preservationism.

The narrator of McIver's *Neuroomia*, Captain Periwinkle, similarly travels south from Hobart on a whaling venture, having already "accumulated a small fortune" through "successfully whaling" in the area (1894: 1). McIver is primarily concerned with the social and political relations of the utopian civilisation that Periwinkle discovers within the ring of Antarctic ice, although his narrator does at various points raise environmental issues. Like Bencolo, Neuroomia is a lush region with abundant gold (pp. 135-36) and "large tracts of virgin soil and forest" (p. 120). Nonetheless, measures are in place to ensure sustainability: all cities are capped at one million inhabitants (p. 120), and the health of Neuroomia's long-lived people, as well as animals and plants, is sustained by regular migration, so that parts of the countryside are deliberately left vacant for hundreds of years (p. 50). However, when Periwinkle asks how the population increase threatening other parts of the Earth is avoided, he is told vaguely that "climatic conditions" prevent this (p. 121). So while McIver does not depict a cornucopian Antarctica, and does suggest alternative ways of inhabiting land, like Spotswood he provides only handwaving solutions to obvious environmental problems. The title of *Neuroomia* conveys the essential function of Antarctica for these two late nineteenth-century

Australian authors: in the face of the realities brought home by a hundred years of Australian colonisation, it offers new, ideal, resource-filled space to be imaginatively colonised.

When an actual Australasian expedition to Antarctica finally took place in 1911-14 (the Australasian Antarctic Expedition, or AAE), under the leadership of geologist Douglas Mawson, a British-born Australian, the various resources Antarctica might provide if annexed continued to play an important role in garnering public support. In his account of the expedition, *The Home of the Blizzard,* Mawson defends the 'usefulness' of the expedition and the continent itself in terms of both science and economics. Pointing to the history of profitable whaling and sealing ventures in Antarctic waters, he predicts that the outlook for further "economic development" will widen, citing as an analogy the development of the Australian colony itself (1996: xxix). Elsewhere he outlines more specifically the potential resources for "exploitation" in Antarctica, from the obvious (whaling, minerals) to the less expected (wind power, the breeding of Arctic foxes) to the disturbingly prescient ("summer pleasure cruises amongst the pack ice") (1935: 36, 37). At the same time, Mawson protested against the wholesale slaughter of penguins and elephant seals on the sub-Antarctic Macquarie Island (the location of one of the AAE bases), and campaigned publicly to ensure the protection of its animal life. Mawson was no deep ecologist — his arguments were based on "the economic and scientific value of perpetuating [...] the varied forms of life" on the island (1923: 92) rather than an acknowledgement of their intrinsic value — but his efforts show that environmental debate about conservation of Antarctic wildlife is not a recent development in Australia. Largely as a result of Mawson's outcries, Macquarie Island was declared a wildlife sanctuary in 1933 (Ayres 1999: 206).

Mawson claimed in "the name of the King and the British Empire" the area of Antarctica below Australia that the AAE explored (Laseron 1999: 41), but there was nonetheless an ongoing sense that Australia itself had a particular right and responsibility to explore the region by virtue of its proximity. The first sign of interest in an Australian Antarctic expedition came in 1885, in an article in the Melbourne *Leader* that declared that "Australians must bestir themselves. It is part of their destiny to explore these southern solitudes" (qtd. in Swan 1961: 46). Although these initial efforts came to nothing, the idea remained in public consciousness: the turn of the century saw the Antarctic take centre stage in "the greatest Australian pantomime of all" (Williams 1983: 191). Performed on Boxing Night 1900 and set a century later, *Australis, or the City of Zero* depicted a future in which Antarctica had become part of a federated Australian empire in the south (p. 192). The actual departure of the AAE just over a decade later certainly inspired patriotic sentiments in some quarters, as South Australian poet Ellie Wemyss's 'Australia for Antarctica!' illustrates:[7]

> Advance, Australia, into lands unknown!
> Antarctica shall be Australia's own!
> First to divine the south magnetic pole,
> Australia now aspires to win the whole.
>
> [...]
>
> 'Tis ours by right of Southern Sovereignty!
> Ours, too, shall prove an Empire of the Sea!

A decade later, Mawson was emphasising the importance not only of exploration but occupation of Antarctica's 'Australian Quadrant'; the Melbourne *Argus* reported his view that it is "an axiom accepted by the whole world that the uninhabited polar regions should be controlled by the nearest civilized nation". Ironically, given the continent's political and environmental future, he worried that an Antarctic "No Man's Land" would cause suffering for the animals which inhabited it, as no controls on hunting would be in place (qtd. in Ayres 1999: 150-51). Mawson led another expedition to the Antarctic between 1929-31, designed primarily to consolidate the British territorial claim in the 'Australian Quadrant'. In 1933, Britain handed this claim to Australia.

3. Re-writing the Heroic Era: Stewart and Keneally

It was, however, the efforts of the British explorer Scott, rather than those of Mawson, which inspired what is probably the most prominent Australian literary text set in Antarctica, Douglas Stewart's verse play for radio *The Fire on the Snow* (1944), first performed in 1941.[8] The 'Heroic Era' of Antarctic exploration — roughly the first two decades of the twentieth century, during which exploration was essentially on foot — has inspired numerous literary works. Stewart's play, a complex and thoughtful fictional re-telling of Scott's 1912-13 journey to the South Pole, is one of the earliest. In many of these texts, including Stewart's, the Antarctic continent tends to function as a catalyst for, antagonist in, and sometimes a metaphor for, human endeavour and drama, more than a subject in its own right. As all of the action of Stewart's play takes place in Antarctica's interior, it is the emptiness and deathliness of the continent, and its impact on the men trekking through it, which is emphasised:

> We have seen life stake its claim of tussocks and hold fast
> In uplands bleak enough; but this is abandoned ground;
> Lichens reject it; moss.
>   What monstrous crop will grow
> When five madmen, hauling the sledge behind them, grind
> Through thirteen frozen days, ploughing the wastes of snow? (Stewart 1944: 11)

Stewart's narrator (the 'Announcer') figures the land as inorganic, hard and metallic — "The surface breaking like glass. / The snow slowing the sledge / Like waves of white iron" (p. 11) — with its own brilliant, purifying beauty: the "fire on the snow". Simultaneously, and somewhat incongruously, he draws on the well-established equation between land and female body: "In kinder places of the world we have seen the wind comb / The green hair of the grass and the golden tresses of wheat, / But this is a dead woman" (p. 11). Early twentieth-century writers and artists often depicted Antarctica as a woman — not, as in images of the African continent, as a seductive, fertile female body — but as an aloof, virginal woman, a sleeping beauty to be awoken and 'won' through chivalrous deed.[9] Mawson himself, an unlikely but occasional poet, represents the continent this way in unpublished verses written around the time of the AAE expedition:

Antarctica, whose bosom, cold, knows but the throb of southern-lights,
Behold, the day has come when pulse of life shall rout thy night,
Wak'ning thee from pristine slumbers, unto motherhood of men
Who know thy worth, would win thee honour, and 'stablish thy fame![10]

In Stewart's play, the image of continent-as-female-body is morbidly transformed by foreknowledge of the explorers' fate: their anticipated deaths are projected onto the land itself. As the play continues, the border between human and landscape (or rather icescape) becomes increasingly blurred. The dying Scott proclaims,

If we had a shovel handy, Wilson, I'd ask you
To shovel away the snow that's inside my head,
That's where it is falling now. My brain's a snowdrift.
Somewhere deep down there's a fire. (p. 29)

The continent, figured as a female body when the expeditioners trudged over it, becomes a male brain when they are stationary and dying in it; in both cases, the environment is impossible to comprehend without the help of anthropomorphism. The play concludes with its central image of the "fire on the snow": both a literal description of Scott's memory of moonlight "pure and burning" as it reflected off ice (p. 41), and a metaphor for human struggle and endurance, "hard and heroic" (p. 40), which "remains like a fire" after death (p. 42).

Although Stewart chose to write about not Australia's seminal Antarctic expedition but rather Britain's, it is difficult not to draw parallels between Scott's journey into the interior of a desert continent and Australia's own history of European exploration. Certainly this is the argument made by Anthony Hassall, who observes that the image of the "difficult, challenging terrain" of Antarctica "recurs in Australian literature": "Like the unexplored heart of Australia, Antarctica inspired epic journeys of courage and endurance, not against heat and thirst, but cold and starvation, and it provided stories of heroic endurance and survival" (Hassall 1988: 393). Noting the centrality of "failure and disappointment" to Australian quest narratives (p. 391), Hassall argues that Scott's expedition "fitted the Australian myth of exploration [...] precisely" (p. 393) and that Stewart's portrayal of the journey as a voyage "into the void", a "psychic adventure", is "very Australian in its mythic pattern" (p. 394).

Similar readings have been applied to Thomas Keneally's two Antarctic-based novels, *The Survivor* (1969) and *Victim of the Aurora* (1977). Unlike Stewart, Keneally had personally travelled to Antarctica, as a guest of the US military in 1968. By this stage the Antarctic Treaty had been ratified: in addition to 'freezing' territorial claims, this document prohibits military activity, advocates international scientific cooperation, and bans nuclear explosions and nuclear waste disposal. A number of nations, including Australia and the US, had already established permanent scientific bases on the continent. Keneally visited McMurdo and Scott-Amundsen (South Pole) stations, both maintained by the US. But where some other novelists writing about Antarctica at this time, such as David Burke in *Monday at McMurdo* (of which Keneally was aware [Keneally, 1969: 12]), dealt with the contemporary Antarctic issues of mineral exploitation, nuclear energy and political machinations, Keneally, like Stewart, remained fascinated by the personalities and events of the Heroic Era, and more particularly with Scott. Although *The Survivor* recalls events of a fictional Australian expedition and *Victim of the Aurora* a fictional British one, the former expedition is partly, and the latter quite closely, based on Scott's actual last expedition of 1910-13 (see Ryan 1989; Keneally 1969: 11). Literary critic Peter Pierce, while recognising Scott's expedition as a source for both novels (Pierce 1995: 110), argues that Antarctica nonetheless functions as "a surrogate land for Australia" in the two texts. Drawing on Hassall, he suggests that Keneally transposes "[t]he search for the nature and identity of Australians [...] from Australia to Antarctica" (p. 111). In particular, Pearce argues that Keneally, in his second Antarctic novel, deals with the identity of the Australian writer: "In imagining the imperilled groups of Europeans marooned on an (icy) desert continent, Keneally offered his parable of the artist's fate in Australia, or at least, wrily guessed at his own" (p. 131).

While Pierce's reading is intriguing, his interpretation of Antarctica as a transposed Australia means that the differences between the two continents are downplayed, reduced here to a single parenthesised adjective. This is justifiable to the extent that Keneally, like Stewart, is more interested in the internal and interpersonal experiences of male explorers than the environment they explore. But it is important to acknowledge that what qualifies Antarctica as a setting in which to address these themes is not only its similarity to Australia but also its difference. In the early exploration of Australia, the masculine quest journey, with its hardship and endurance, was complicated both by the fact that the territory explored was already inhabited and by the violence and conflict that its invasion had entailed. This 'complication', along with many others (such as heterosexual relations), disappears when the setting is moved to Heroic-Era Antarctica. The physical environment is similarly simplified. In *The Survivor*, the icescape of Antarctica is starkly contrasted with the dust, heat, and mundanity of its northern neighbour. One of the narrative's debates centres on whether to return the body of the (fictional) expedition leader Stephen Leeming back from Antarctica to Australia. But just as the material artefacts of the expedition are transformed from "wreckage" of "a holy saga" to "a few silly mementoes" when transported to "the sardonic landscape of Australia" (1969: 75-76), so Leeming's body, buried in Antarctic ice, has a dignity that an Australian burial, with its "banalities" and "blowflies", would negate (p. 168). It was this dignity, Leeming's wife suggests, which first led her husband south: in Antarctica, "your body doesn't smell, May's shirt is still clean in August, your excreta down in the permafrost offends no one" (p. 211). The stark, simple backdrop of Antarctic ice (as presented by these mid-century writers) lends a mythic quality to the human drama presented. Leeming at one point make this explicit: "'Antarctica can't be humanized, except in little ways [...]. Antarctica is a sacrament of the absolute, the same as all deserts are. It's a place for prophets [....] Of course, Australia is a country in the prophetic mould too, but we have done such a stale old European job of humanizing'" (pp. 173-74).

4. Timeless Ice: Mid-century Australian Poetry About Antarctica

The lure of Antarctica as a place apart from the ordinariness of life, as a mythic, timeless landscape, is also strong in Australian poetic engagements with the region at this time. R.A. Swan's poem 'The Last Land', which was initially published in his collection *Argonauts Returned* (1946) and reappeared at the beginning of his history *Australia in the Antarctic* (1961), is a case in point:

We went back, back from the South,
Back to the dull hours and old futilities,
Back to the fungoid sprawl of Life
With all its murky dreams and shapes;
But ever we knew, asleep or waking
A dreadful yearning, a strange, cold calling
Drifting from the jewelled iciness of empty spaces
And the pale, clear glitter of immemorial snows. (Swan 1946: 39)

Organic, parasitic human life here is contrasted with the Antarctic ice, seen once again as timeless, inorganic and metallic, jewel-like, and glittering. It represents death, but death as longed-for escape: "Here there were no weary years, / No empty toil, no sadness or despair; / There was only ice and snow [...]" (Swan 1961: viii). Frank Debenham, an Australian geologist who was part of Scott's last expedition, gives a similar sense of the Antarctic as a dreamscape outside of human time in his 1956 poem 'The Quiet Land': "Men are not old here / Only the rocks are old, and the sheathing ice [...]" (Debenham 1992: 10). As with Keneally's explorer, the ice becomes a "sheath", a dignified resting-place. The concluding lines make explicit the equation of Antarctica with a timeless, eventless after-life in which the explorer's body and the continent become co-joined:

To sleep here is to wake, and the resurrection
Lies in the passiveness of being one with the land.

Into the quiet land, dear Lord, we are delivered.
For here is peace, here in the quiet land. (p. 10)

A better-known poet, Rosemary Dobson, also drew on this sense of Antarctic timelessness in the title poem of her collection *The Ship of Ice* (1948). Dobson's stated source is a report of a nineteenth-century schooner, the *Jenny*, which was frozen in Antarctic ice for thirty-seven years; when it was discovered by a whaling ship, the bodies of all those on board were found perfectly preserved.[11] The poem imagines the sensations of the inhabitants of this "ship caught in a bottle / [....] / Becalmed in Time and sealed with a cork of ice" (Dobson 1948: 35). This is an Antarctic purgatory, which ends only with discovery and death: "Dead now in a world that gives no other entombment / Than a winding sheet of ice and a drift of snow —" (p. 49).

Poems such as these shift the focus from Heroic-Era exploration to the strange physical qualities of the Antarctic environment itself. However, the tendency to see the continent as ancient and timeless means that its own complexities and natural processes are disregarded. Similarly, the sense of the continent as something hard and metallic renders it apparently impervious to human influence. Yet, far from being eternal and timeless, Antarctica is in some ways the most changeable of continents, doubling its size from summer to winter, covered with continually moving glaciers, constantly fissuring and, at its edges, calving off enormous icebergs. Science in recent decades has revealed the impact human activity can have on these changes and on other aspects of the Antarctic ecosystem.

5. Mounting Threats: Environmentalism Enters Antarctic Literature

The sense of Antarctica as a threatened — rather than merely a threatening — environment becomes detectable in Australian literary texts from the late 1960s. *Monday at McMurdo* (1967), by Australian journalist David Burke, delivers an action-packed narrative which in some senses anticipates the familiar form of the 'Antarctic eco-thriller' that would emerge in later decades. Taken from the author's "first-hand experience at McMurdo" and identified as "fiction based on fact" (Burke 1967: vi), Burke's novel centres on the potentially destructive results of a visit to Antarctica by an unscrupulous American politician, who plans to mine a secret supply of gold using nuclear power (p. 161). His foil is a veteran British explorer, Dr Armsworth, who sees the continent as "'something sacred, something beautiful'" (p. 191) and represents Heroic-Era codes of behaviour: in order to save his party he walks to his death, emulating the famously understated sacrifice of Scott's companion 'Titus' Oates ("I'm just going outside ..."). While the politician comes to a reassuringly gruesome end (eaten by killer whales), Armsworth himself acknowledges the inevitably of economic resource development in the continent: "'One day there will be gold mined in Antarctica, I suppose, when the world is hungry enough for it. A lot of other minerals we've found will be dug out too [...] They'll harvest plankton for food from the seas. Tourists will come [...]'" (pp. 190-91). Armsworth also mentions the possibility of "'a new age of doom — the retreat of the ice and a rise in the world's sea levels'", but notes that this is a natural process which "'won't happen for another hundred thousand years'" (p. 158). A vague but ominous sense of fragility in the relationship between the Antarctic and global environments is evident in a very different Australian text of the period, John Blight's short poem 'Antarctica' in his collection *Hart* (1975):

> The big white continent that is Antarctica,
> the piece of egg-shell which this world sits in;
> this shrivelling chicken of a planet. Such a
> precarious egg-cup its squeezed life fits in.
> Antarctica — forgotten as the shell from which the chicken steps;
> seeming, to life, now useless as the bleached white scraps
> which once wrapped all of the chicken, were the wraps
> that held the embryo; and when some poulterer dressed
> the cockerel, like scraps of paper tossed
> in the bottom of a bin, were wind-torn waste
> at the bottom of a world. Antarctica,
> not yet quite kicked away, demolished; a
> chicken still sits shivering in your shell.
> Your winter hems him round, a white walled hell. (p. 64)

Antarctica is both threatening and threatened in this poem, menacing yet delicate — a "white walled hell" imprisoning the shivering world, and a "precarious egg cup" protecting it. The sense of interdependency of the Antarctic and rest of the planet is clear, as well as the vulnerability of both. While the poem describes, rather than decries, a world that has "forgotten" what protects it, a latent environmentalist moral is evident, especially as the following poem in the collection, 'Leviathan', protests the wholesale slaughter of whales by "That fiercest monster, man" (p. 65).

6. "In sisterhood remembered": Gondwana in Australian Antarctic Literature

A different perspective on Antarctica's relationship with the world around it drew the particular attention of Australian poets in the 1980s and 90s: the theory that Australia and Antarctica were once joined as part of the same continent (Gondwana), and that they are closely linked, geologically and paleontologically, due to this ancient unity. First hypothesised early in the twentieth century, the theory of continental drift gathered strength in the mid-century and was "clinched" for many scientists by 1969 fossil discoveries in Antarctica (Elliot 1985: 42-43). The idea of Gondwana proved evocative for Australian writers and introduced into literary engagements with Antarctica a heightened awareness of details of the natural environment.

Dorothy Porter's 'Auroral Corona with Two Figures', published in her collection *The Night Parrot* (1984), weaves a complex pattern around this idea. As Rose Lucas has observed, the poem raises questions that "are couched in the language of place, situated at the cusp of literal and metaphoric geographies" (1997: 166). A glossary provided along with the poem explains the theory of continental drift and the existence of the "great southern super-continent of Gondwanaland", noting that "Antarctica and Australia were the last parts to separate" and that the latter "supported an extensive flora and fauna" (Porter 1984: 74). No longer an empty, inorganic expanse, the Antarctic takes on physical and symbolic layers in Porter's poem:

Underneath the miles of ice
   lies a rainforest
      trapped in rocks;
its ferns
   and its insects
      leave a crushed gallery
        of faint silhouettes
which you and I
   chip through in a cold dream
      of time passing — (p. 62)

Where in previous poems the continent with its preserving ice provided a metaphor for timelessness, here its depths stand as a physical record of passing ages. Meditations on Antarctica's history are entwined in the poem with the voices of Heroic-Era expeditioners. Porter, like Keneally, is clearly fascinated by Scott's last expedition; prior to 'Auroral Corona' she published an earlier poem on the subject, 'Wilson's Diary' (1982), and later added to it 'Oates' Diary' (1989). 'Auroral Corona' takes its title from that of a painting by the scientist and expedition artist, Edward Wilson, and draws on two of his sledging journeys: the famous 'winter' journey in search of an emperor penguin egg and the journey to the Pole during which he died alongside Scott. In the poem, the experiences of Scott's expeditioners blend with those of two modern-day lovers, and of the two southern continents themselves:

> can passion for a lover
>   be an impossible nostalgia
>   for Gondwanaland,
> the longing to glue
>   huge spaces together
> to encourage strange animals
>   to mate?

> if you and I
>   drift, separate
> what will I call myself?
> what new continent
>   shall I be?
> perhaps, like Antarctica,
>   I'll drift to a far pole
>   and cool
>   my wild life
>   to deep, deep
>   fossils. (Porter 1984: 74)

Antarctica functions here not as an emptied-out 'surrogate' for Australia, but as its Platonic other. As in Stewart's verse drama, Antarctica comes to stand for the human body and psyche, but in Porter's poem, the continent, as well as its human inhabitants, has its own embedded history. The poem thus approaches Antarctica in ways that for Buell characterise "environmentally oriented work" (1995: 7-8): it recognises the Antarctic environment as a process rather than a constant, it displays interest in more than just human concerns, and it implicates human history in natural history.

A briefer poetic engagement with a similar theme is Alan Alexander's single-stanza poem 'Antarctica' in his collection *Principia Gondwana* (1992):

> Glossopterid trunk, stem and leaf,
> ancient life form in repose
> stays Antarctica.
> Who can build her pain,
> touch these eggs, age by age?
> The fruit that lies unseen,
> intricacies slowly unroofing
> that, with a gravid pleasure,
> bother their form by and by
> are hair and toe of her.
> That, in sisterhood remembered,
> she had the page of another in her garden,
> Antarctica declares to Australia
> a thin flame runs under her skin. (Alexander 1992: 65)

Here, the ancient connection between Australia and Antarctica reveals something of interest to present-day nations: mineral resources. The discovery of *Glossopteris* fossil flora in the Gondwana Series of rocks in India as well as in southern lands was one of the factors that led to the hypothesising of the Gondwana super-continent and the theory of continental drift (White 1994: 19). But *Glossopteris* fossils are also associated with coal. The Gondwana theory suggested that Antarctica might, like the continents to which it was connected, have substantial mineral deposits; and indeed the existence of large deposits of coal was well established by the 1980s (Coates, Stricker and Landis 1990: 133). Thus Antarctica, by announcing its geological "sisterhood" with Australia, also announces its possible coal seams: the "thin flame" running "under her skin". Once more, Antarctica is figured as a body, but here it is a female body pregnant with an unseen "fruit" of mineral richness.

7. Antarctic Fiction Post-CRAMRA

Alexander's poem was published almost a decade after Porter's first appeared, a decade in which environmental issues had come to the forefront of Antarctic (and Australian) politics. The question of possible mineral exploitation in Antarctica became increasingly pressing in the 1970s and 1980s, spurred on by the 1972 oil crisis; at the same time, the preservation of the continent became an important symbol in environmental movements, with calls for it to become a World Park (Prosser 1995: 115-16). In 1988, the Convention on the Regulation of Antarctic Mineral Resources Activities (CRAMRA) was adopted by the Antarctic Treaty nations. This document "establishes principles, prescribes rules and procedures and creates institutions for the purpose of regulating Antarctic mineral activities should they be considered acceptable" (Elliott 1994: 135). Environmental NGOs campaigned against CRAMRA, and in 1989, France expressed concern about the agreement and Australia refused to ratify it, advocating instead a 'Wilderness Reserve' (Elliott 1994: 166). By 1991, a new compromise agreement had been drawn up: the Protocol on Environmental Protection to the Antarctic Treaty, or 'Madrid Protocol', which banned mining for fifty years. It also introduced provisions for environmental protection which were more "rigorous and extensive" than those that had been incorporated into the Antarctic Treaty system over the previous decades (Elliott 1994: 196).

Given Australia's significant role in rejecting CRAMRA, it is not surprising that Australian writers were eager to explore these environmental themes. Scientist and documentary-maker David Smith's *Freeze Frame* (1992) is an eco-thriller set in the wake of Australia's rejection of CRAMRA. It centres on an Australian film-maker, the aptly named Richard Southeby, who discovers a covert uranium mine operating under the guise of scientific investigation near a French Antarctic station and thereby becomes the target of an assassin. Other nations interested in mining attempt to discredit Greenpeace and unsettle plans for an Antarctic World Park by orchestrating apparent eco-terrorist attacks around the globe. Part of novel's political intrigue stems from the questionable motivation behind France's opposition to CRAMRA. While in reality critics suggested that both France and Australia were motivated by concerns other than preserving Antarctica's wilderness (see Elliott 1994: 166-72), in *Freeze Frame* Australia becomes an environmental hero, pushing for the World Park idea, and France is revealed a villain, publicly supporting Australia's campaign with one hand while secretly preparing for mineral exploitation with the other. By the novel's conclusion, world opinion appears to be moving towards the World Park concept, and the rogue mining station, with its nuclear reactor, has been swallowed up during a shift in the Antarctic ice.

Antarctic environmental politics and film-making play similarly important roles in Liane Shavian's *Surfing Antarctica* (1999). Billed on its cover as the "darkest, funniest eco-warrior novel since Ben Elton's *Stark*", *Surfing Antarctica* is more playful and knowing in its representation of environmental politics than *Freeze Frame*. Its title is not a reference to its setting, but rather a shorthand for global warming: "'the Antarctic ice sheet is bigger than the US and if it melts from the hole in the ozone and global warming [...] the sea level will rise sixty metres and we'll all be surfing the Antarctic'" (Shavian 1999: 30). Although the action takes place entirely in Australia, Antarctica enters the story as the subject of *Hot Ice*, a documentary filmed by the novel's eco-hero Darwin Brown (and love interest of Zan, the female protagonist). The premiere of the film as a Greenpeace fundraiser is described in detail:

> There is no soundtrack. No voiceover to tell you what the camera is saying and what your response is. Just a slowmoving flow of Antarctic icons. Striking. Straight-forward. Without artifice. There is nothing of man in his film. No man-made constructions. No tools. No footprints. No human voices. No brave men in dogsleds on brave expeditions. Just deepfrozen silence. A boundless white landscape [...]. (p. 19)

While this approach impresses Zan, it is hardly radical; numerous documentaries emphasise Antarctica's pristine beauty, packaging the continent for human consumption while de-coupling it from human activity, including that of the film-makers and their own "man-made constructions". Karla Armbruster has criticised documentaries that represent nature as "a place without room for human beings, ultimately distancing humans from the non-human nature with which they are biologically and perceptually interconnected, and reinforcing the dominant cultural ideologies responsible for environmental degradation" (1998: 221). A similar point is in fact raised by a young woman watching the film, who asks in an "aggressively 'intellectual' manner" whether the invisibility of humans in the film is "'a lie'" which ignores "'the cusp between humans and nature in the deep ecological sense'" (Shavian 1999: 23). Darwin, with first-hand experience of "the aggressive indifference of that inhuman landscape", refutes such "armchair" speculations (p. 24). The fast-moving narrative does not delve deeply into these concerns, but this glancing reference to the environmental politics not only of Antarctica but also its representation indicate the currency of these issues in the 1990s.

Not all late twentieth-century Australian Antarctic novels, however, are directly concerned with contemporary environmental debates; Australian writers put Antarctica to diverse purposes in fiction at this time. Adrian Caesar revived the tradition established by Stewart and Keneally, writing a semi-fictional account of the last days of Scott and Mawson, *The White* (1999). For Matthew Reilly, author of *Ice Station* (1998), the continent provided the same remoteness and exoticness that the Peruvian jungle did in his following novel. Nikki Gemmell, who travelled to Antarctica as an official writer-in-residence with Australian National Antarctic Research Expeditions (ANARE), presented the journey south as a personal journey for her fictional female protagonist (a familiar theme in recent international 'Antarctic fiction' by women[12]). Gemmell's novel *Shiver* (1997) canvasses environmental controversies current at the time of her journey — such as the ethics of an intrusive crabeater seal monitoring program — but her interest is primarily in the masculinist culture of Antarctic communities rather than the natural environment. Nonetheless, the conceit of Antarctica as surrogate Australia is strong again here: on returning to Australia, Gemmell's heroine heads into the red centre: "*I'm here because Antarctica has given me a taste for deserts*" (Gemmell 1997: 1; italics in original). Tess Williams's *Map of Power* (1996) creates a similar parallel. This science-fiction dystopia takes place in a future devastated by global warming and nuclear war, and is set in three equally isolated, hostile locations: Western Australia, where Perth lies in ruins; a warmer Antarctica, where a nomadic people eke out a harsh living; and a satellite orbiting the Earth. Williams's dystopia, while ultimately hopeful, gives a sobering perspective on twentieth-century debates about Antarctic sovereignty and mineral resources, by showing their redundancy in the face of massive environmental devastation.

After this rush of Antarctic-related fiction in the 1990s, Australian novelists' interest in the continent appears to have died away. At the same time Macquarie Island and its specific environmental problems have been brought into the foreground by novelist Danielle Wood, who travelled there with ANARE in 1998. Situated above the Antarctic convergence, 1500 km southeast of Tasmania, Macquarie Island is physically very different from the Antarctic continent. Its bleak but ice-free landscape can support mammals such as rabbits, cats, rats, and mice, all of which were introduced by sealers in the nineteenth century, wreaking predicable havoc on the local fauna and flora. Mawson in 1923 observed that the "introduction [...] of the domestic cat" had caused "irreparable losses" (Mawson 1923: 97); in the late 1990s, the Australian Government made a concerted effort to minimise these losses by funding a systematic eradication of feral cats on the island. Hunters were employed by Tasmania Parks and Wildlife to wander the island, shooting, trapping, or gassing the cats. Wood's Vogel-award-winning novel, *The Alphabet of Light and Dark* (2003), focuses partly on a Tasmanian Aboriginal man, Pete Shelverton, who has recently returned from one such spell as a Macquarie Island cat-eradicator. Pete must deal not only with the genocidal history of his own ancestors, but also with the myth that this genocide was complete; there is a poetic irony, then, in his task of removing non-native species from another Tasmanian island. His attraction to Macquarie Island lies in its very lack of obvious signs of human history: "No treading in the footsteps of ancestors, no imagining what's happened to some poor bastard on that square of earth" (Wood 2003: 47). Eradicating feral cats for Pete comes to symbolise other erasures — of his personal history, and the history of Tasmanian colonisation. Wood's second, forthcoming novel will deal more closely with Macquarie Island, focussing on a related effect of human activity: the depletion of its albatross populations due to fishery. Listed since 1997 as a World Heritage Area, and currently the subject of media debate due to reports that Australian Antarctic Division may soon abandon its activities there (Neales 2006: 7), Macquarie Island is likely to remain an important site in future Australian ecofiction.

8. Recent Antarctic Poetry

Australian poets writing about Antarctica in recent years have, like novelists, dealt with a diverse range of topics: Chris Wheat's poem 'Antarctica' (1996), for example, unexpectedly draws on the continent, "as silent as starched sheets" (Wheat 1996: 132), in order to understand a friend's death from HIV/AIDS. However, environmental concerns, particularly the increasing impact of tourism, remained in the foreground. Les Murray's 'Antarctica', published in his collection *Dog Fox Field* (1990), recounts the continent's various identities through history, the penultimate stanza hinting at its growing role as a tourist attraction:

> Sterility Park, ringed by sheathed animals.
> Singing spiritoso their tongueless keens
> musselled carollers fly under the world.
> Deeper out, our star's gale folds and greens. (Murray 1990: 83)

The lyrical beauty of the continent's surrounds — the Antarctic marine life, the aurora australis — is starkly contrasted with the interior, "Sterility Park", in a phrase which itself evokes both the World Park advocated by environmental groups and the theme park which Antarctica threatens to become. Caroline Caddy's poem 'Glasnost', which describes an encounter between a tourist ship "disgorging [...] black smoke" (the Russian icebreaker *Kapitan Khlebnikov*) and the Australian expedition vessel on which she is travelling, deals more explicitly with the contradictions of a packaged wilderness:

> Set free on the ice
> American and Japanese eco-tourists
>   snap penguins
> and us
> thrilled to be experiencing
>   two wildernesses
>   for the price of one —
> Antarctica and Australia. (Caddy 1996: 66)

The ironies here are clear: "eco-tourists" in their polluting ship, happily treating Australian expeditioners and Antarctic animals as equally exotic, unknown and therefore camera-worthy. The encounter would have been very different, one imagines, if Caddy's ship had been another tourist cruiser, rather than a scientific expedition vessel:[13] tourist ships tend to hide from each other in the Antarctic, as to maintain the 'wilderness encounter' tourists must temporarily repress the impact of their own presence. As this poem indicates, Caddy travelled to Antarctica with ANARE, as a writer-in-residence. The collection of poems she produced, entitled *Antarctica*, gives a complex, multi-faceted view of the continent and Australia's activities there. In the title poem, Caddy emphasises the contradictions and tensions inherent in human involvement in far south:

> the people who think
> no one should go there
> go there.
> It is a place of ideals in conflict
> with our four limbs
> ten fingers two eyes
> and homeothermy
> that makes every land green land
> and anyway we have a job to do —
> the naming of the animals —
> whether they like it
> or not. (p. 55)

As Caddy makes clear, even the apparently neutral activity of science is in a sense an attempt to master and control the land, to impose human categories upon the non-human, regardless of the impact this may have on the latter.

The same might be said of 'Antarctic literature' — that to write about the continent is to attempt to bring it under control, to humanise Antarctica whether it likes it or not. But the solution is not to abandon such attempts; or to disguise them by emptying Antarctica out, in the manner of Shavian's film-maker with his shots of unending ice; or to wish them away, as Garner does (with a touch of self-irony) in the excerpt with which this discussion began. Antarctica is not a 'wide white page' endlessly waiting to be inscribed, nor is literature a cultural pollutant blocking access to its pristine wilderness. Even to speak about Antarctica is to assume a human relationship with it; imaginative writing about Antarctica is one way in which humans can gain insight into this relationship, as well as its possible alternatives.

Notes

[1] I would like to thank the Australian Antarctic Division for awarding me an Antarctic Arts Fellowship that allowed me to travel to Antarctica in early 2004. This journey has informed and influenced all of my subsequent Antarctic-related research. Thanks also to Stephanie Pfennigwerth and Danielle Wood for their comments on parts of this essay in its draft form.

[2] Stephen Pyne spends a significant part of his book *The Ice* describing Antarctic literature and art, but nonetheless insists that "the Antarctic has largely been a waste-land for imaginative literature" (1988: 154). Thomas Keneally, himself the author of two Antarctic-based novels, claims that Antarctica has produced "no native tongue, no rites, no art, no jingoism" (2003: 20). In response, one could point to the work of the many artists who have journeyed to Antarctica, as expedition artists or on one of a number of national writers and artists programmes; the century-old rituals of Antarctic bases, such as mid-winter dinners; and the vocabularies that have developed in response to the Antarctic environment, as recorded in Bernadette Hince's dictionary of 'Antarctic English' (2000).

[3] *The Wide White Page* is the title of Bill Manhire's recent anthology of Antarctic literature, which is in turn borrowed from a "very bad" 1936 novel set in Antarctica (2004: 19). Manhire notes travellers' tendency to see Antarctica as "a bare canvas, a clean slate, a *tabula rasa* awaiting inscription and impression" (p. 20).

[4] This category is employed here to include writers who have spent substantial time in Australia, not only those born there. I have excluded from this discussion the large category of Australian non-fiction about Antarctica, and all Antarctic-based literature for children and young adults, such as Katherine Scholes's *Blue Chameleon* (1989) and Hazel Edwards's *Antarctica's Frozen Chosen* (2003).

[5] See Leane (2004) for an argument that cultural and literary analyses need to resist conflating the Antarctic and Arctic regions.

[6] See Collis for an analysis of how the huts enable Antarctica to be "produced as a space for perpetual aggressive imaginal occupation" (1999: 29).

[7] The undated clipping from the Adelaide *Register* containing Wemyss's poem is located in a book of newspapers clippings dealing with the AAE's departure and return, held in the Mawson Collection at the South Australian Museum (and marked 92 M462.m).

[8] The play existed before this time, however; an extract was published in *The Bulletin* in 1939. Stewart later published a poem about Shackleton's *Endurance* expedition, 'Worsley Enchanted', initially in *The Bulletin* (1948) and in expanded form in his collection *Sun Orchids* (1952).

[9] See Jones (2003: 239-41) for a discussion of the use of chivalrous imagery to describe Scott's last expedition.

[10] This poem, written under the pseudonym 'Aboriginae', can be found in the Mawson Collection (South Australian Museum); see items 184AAE/6 [26 and 30.6]. The poem is listed in item 184AAE/6 [27] under Mawson's name, with a note "must be improved".

[11] See 'The Drift of the *Jenny*, 1823-40' (Anon. 1965) for a reprint and discussion of the original (and unsubstantiated) 1862 report. Dobson adds twenty years onto the time the ship was reported to have been trapped in ice.
[12] See US author Elizabeth Arthur's *Antarctic Navigation* (1995); British writer Rosie Thomas's *Sun at Midnight* (2004); and French writer Marie Darrieussecq's *White* (2005).
[13] Thomas Keneally, who recently travelled south on the *Khlebnikov*, describes one such uncomfortable encounter between tourist vessels in his account of the voyage: "It revealed us to be tourists, just like those others over there" (2003: 24).

Bibliography

Primary Sources

Alexander, Alan. 1992. 'Antarctica' in *Principia Gondwana*. South Fremantle, WA: Fremantle Arts Centre Press: 65.

Anon. 1985. *Antarctica: Great Stories from the Frozen Continent*. Sydney: Reader's Digest.

Anon. 1965. 'The Drift of the *Jenny*, 1823-40' in *Polar Record* 12(79): 411-12.

Arthur, Elizabeth. 1995. *Antarctic Navigation*. New York: Alfred A. Knopf.

Blight, John. 1975. *Hart*. Melbourne: Thomas Nelson.

Burke, David. 1967. *Monday at McMurdo*. Wellington, Auckland and Sydney: A. H. and A. W. Reed.

Caddy, Caroline. 1996. *Antarctica*. South Fremantle, WA: Fremantle Arts Centre Press.

Caesar, Adrian. 1999. *The White*. Sydney: Picador-Pan Macmillan.

Darrieussecq, Marie. 2005. *White*. (tr. Ian Monk). London: Faber.

Debenham, Frank. 1992. 'The Quiet Land' in Backs, June Debenham (ed.) *The Quiet Land: The Antarctic Diaries of Frank Debenham*. Bluntisham, Huntingdon: Bluntisham Books; and Harleston, Norfolk: Erskine Press: 10.

Dobson, Rosemary. 1948. 'The Ship of Ice' in *The Ship of Ice with Other Poems*. Sydney and London: Angus and Robertson: 34-49.

Garner, Helen. 1998. 'Adrift in the Floating World' in *Good Weekend* (30 May 1998).

Gemmell, Nikki. 1997. *Shiver*. Sydney: Vintage-Random House.

Keneally, Thomas. 1969. *The Survivor*. Sydney: Angus and Robertson.

——. 1977. *Victim of the Aurora*. London: William Collins and Sons.

Mawson, Douglas. 1996. *Home of the Blizzard: The Story of the Australasian Antarctic Expedition, 1911-1914*. Kent Town, SA: Wakefield Press.

——. 1923. 'Macquarie Island and its Future' in *The Australian Zoologist* 3(3): 92-102.

——. 1935. 'The Unveiling of Antarctica' in *Australian and New Zealand Association for the Advancement of Science: Report of Meeting* 22 (Melbourne): 1-37.

McIver, G. 1894. *Neuroomia: A New Continent. A Manuscript Delivered by the Deep.* London and Melbourne: George Robinson.

Murray, Les. 1990. 'Antarctica' in *Dog Fox Field.* North Ryde, NSW: Collins/Angus and Robertson: 83.

Porter, Dorothy. 1984. 'Auroral Corona with Two Figures' in *The Night Parrot.* Wentworth Falls, NSW: Black Lightning Press: 60-79.

——. 1989. 'Oates's Diary' in *Driving Too Fast.* St Lucia, Qld.: University of Queensland Press: 14.

——. 1982. 'Wilson's Diary' in *Overland* (88): 29.

Scholes, Katherine. 1989. *The Blue Chameleon.* Melbourne: Hill of Content Publishing.

Shavian, Liane. 1999. *Surfing Antarctica.* North Fremantle, WA: Fremantle Arts Centre Press.

Smith, David. 1992. *Freeze Frame.* Ringwood, Victoria: Penguin Books.

Spotswood, Christopher. 1888. *Voyage of Will Rogers to the South Pole.* Launceston, Tas.: Offices of the *Examiner* and the *Tasmanian.*

Stewart, Douglas. 1944. *The Fire on the Snow and The Golden Lover: Two Plays for Radio.* Sydney and London: Angus and Robertson.

——. 1952. 'Worsley Enchanted' in *Sun Orchids.* Sydney and London: Angus and Robertson: 43-61.

Swan, R. A. 1961. *Australia in the Antarctic.* Parkville, Vic.: Melbourne University Press.

——. 1946. 'The Last Land' in *Argonauts Returned and Other Poems.* Melbourne: Bread and Cheese Club: 38-39.

Thomas, Rosie. 2004. *Sun at Midnight.* London: HarperCollins.

Wemyss, Ellie. n.d. 'Australia for Antarctica!' in *Adelaide Register.*

Wheat, Chris. 1996. 'Antarctica' in *Meanjin* 55(1): 132-37.

Wood, Danielle. 2003. *The Alphabet of Light and Dark.* Crow's Nest, NSW: Allen and Unwin.

Secondary Sources

Armbruster, Karla. 1998. 'Creating the World We Must Save: The Paradox of Television Nature Documentaries' in Kerridge and Sammells (1998): 218-238.

——, and Kathleen R. Wallace. 2001. *Beyond Nature Writing: Expanding the Boundaries of Ecocriticism.* Charlottesville and London: University Press of Virginia.

Ayres, Philip. 1999. *Mawson: A Life.* Carlton, Vic.: Melbourne University Press.

Beck, Peter. 1991. *Why Study Antarctica?* Kingston Upon Thames, Surrey: APEX Centre, Kingston Polytechnic.

Buell, Lawrence. 1995. *The Environmental Imagination: Thoreau, Nature Writing, and the Formation of American Culture.* Cambridge, MA, and London: Belknap-Harvard University Press.

Coates, D.A., G.D. Stricker and E. R. Landis. 1990. 'Coal Geology, Coal Quality, and Coal Resources in Permian Rocks of the Beacon Supergroup, Transantarctic

Mountains, Antarctica' in Splettstoesser, John F., and Gisela A. M. Dreschhoff (eds) *Mineral Resources Potential of Antarctica* (Antarctic Research Series 51). Washington, D.C.: American Geophysical Union.

Collis, Christy. 1999. 'Mawson's Hut: Emptying Post-Colonial Antarctica' in *Journal of Australian Studies* 63: 22-29.

Cronon, William. 1996. 'The Trouble with Wilderness; or, Getting Back to the Wrong Nature' in Cronon, William (ed.) *Uncommon Ground: Rethinking the Human Place in Nature*. New York and London: W. W. Norton: 69-90.

Edwards, Hazel. 2003. *Antarctica's Frozen Chosen*. South Melbourne, Vic.: Lothian Books.

Elliot, D.H. 1985. 'Physical Geography — Geological Evolution' in Bonner, W. N., and D W. N. Wilson (eds) *Antarctica*. Oxford: Pergamon: 39-61.

Elliott, Lorraine M. 1994. *International Environmental Politics: Protecting the Antarctic*. New York: St Martin's Press.

Hassall, Anthony J. 1988. 'Quests' in *Australian Literary Studies* 13(4): 390-408.

Hince, Bernadette. 2000. *The Antarctic Dictionary: A Complete Guide to Antarctic English*. Collingwood, Vic.: CSIRO Publishing and Museum of Victoria.

Horne, William C. 2001. 'Samuel Johnson Discovers the Arctic: A Reading of a "Greenland Tale" as Arctic Literature' in Armbruster and Wallace (2001): 75-90.

Jones, Max. 2003. *The Last Great Quest: Captain Scott's Antarctic Sacrifice*. Oxford: Oxford University Press.

Joyner, Christopher C. 1992. *Antarctica and the Law of the Sea* (Publications on Ocean Development 18). Dordrecht, Boston and London: Martinus Nijhoff.

Keneally, Thomas. 1969. 'Origin of a Novel' in *Hemisphere* 13(10): 9-13.

——. 2003. 'Taking the Biscuit' in *Good Weekend* (10 May 2003).

Kerridge, Richard, and Neil Sammells. 1998. *Writing The Environment: Ecocriticism and Literature*. London and New York: Zed Books.

Laseron, Charles. 1999. *South with Mawson* in *Antarctic Eyewitness: Charles F. Laseron's* South with Mawson *and Frank Hurley's* Shackleton's Argonauts. Sydney: Angus and Robertston-HarperCollins: 1-168.

Leane, Elizabeth. 2004. 'Romancing the Pole: A Survey of Nineteenth-Century Antarctic Utopias.' *ACH: The Journal of the History of Culture in Australia* (23): 161-84.

Lucas, Rose. 1997. 'Ancient Continents: A Poetics of Place in Dorothy Porter's "Auroral Corona with Two Figures"' in *Southern Review* 30(2): 159-69.

Manhire, Bill. 2004. 'Introduction' in *The Wide White Page: Writers Imagine Antarctica*. Wellington: Victoria University Press: 9-28.

Neales, Sue. 2006. 'Goodbye to Macquarie' in *The Mercury* (11 Jan 2006).

Pierce, Peter. 1995. *Australian Melodramas: Thomas Keneally's Fiction*. St Lucia, Qld.: University of Queensland Press.

Prosser, Robert. 1995. 'Power, Control and Intrusion, with Particular Reference to Antarctica' in Cooper, David, and Joy A. Palmer (eds) *Just Environments: Intergenerational, International and Interspecies Issues*. London and New York: Routledge: 108-20.

Pyne, Stephen. 1988. *The Ice: A Journey to Antarctica*. New York: Ballantine Books.

Reilly, Matthew. 1998. *Ice Station.* Sydney: Pan-Macmillan.
Ryan, J.S. 1989. *Antarctic* Hoosh: *The Genesis of a Keneally Novel.* Unpublished thesis. Scott Polar Research Institute. University of Cambridge.
Tallmadge, John, and Henry Harrington. 2000. *Reading Under the Sign of Nature: New Essays in Ecocriticism.* Salt Lake City: University of Utah Press.
White, Mary E. 1994. *After the Greening: The Browning of Australia.* Kenthurst, NSW: Kangaroo Press.
Williams, Margaret. 1983. *Australia on the Popular Stage: 1829-1929.* Melbourne: Oxford University Press.
Williams, Tess. 1996. *Map of Power.* Sydney: Random House.

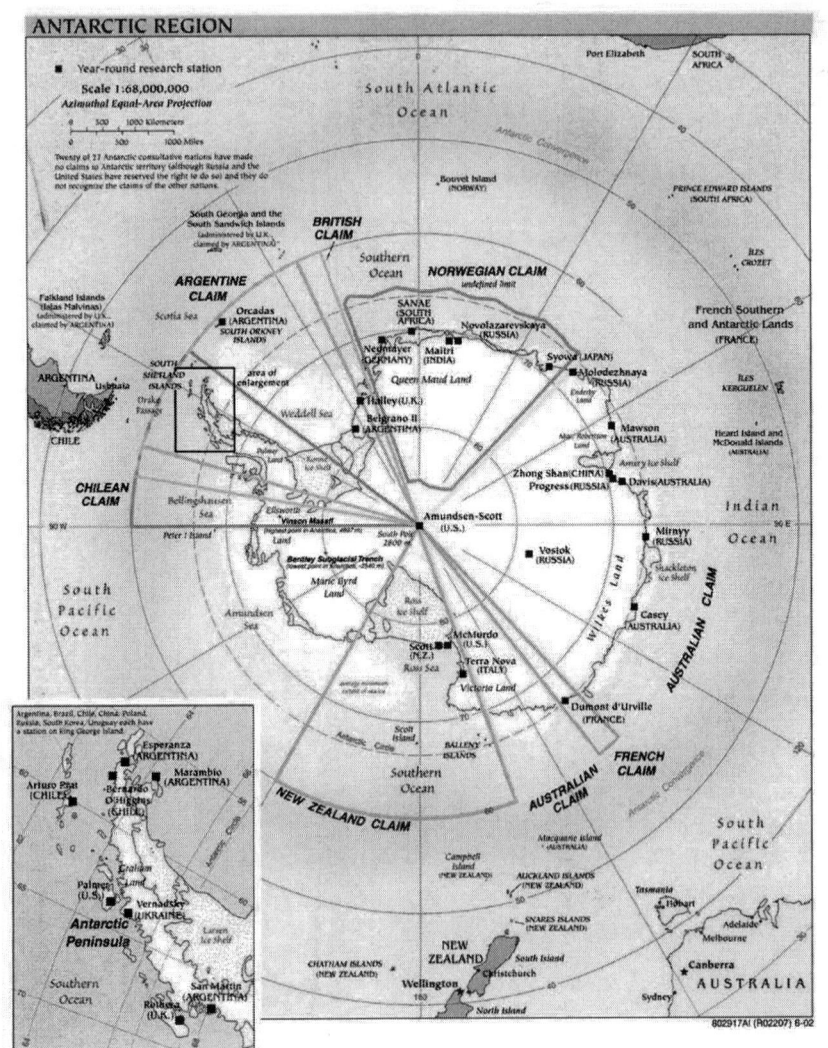

Figure 11

Notes on Contributors

Bruce Bennett is Emeritus Professor at the University of New South Wales at the Australian Defence Force Academy in Canberra. He holds Adjunct Professorships at the Australian National University and the University of Queensland. He is a member of the Australia-India Council and in 2003 was made an Officer of the Order of Australia (AO) for service to Australian literature and education. In 2005-06, he was Group of Eight Professor of Australian Studies at Georgetown University, Washington DC. Since *An Australian Compass* (1991), his work has given close attention to place, region and community. His books include *Spirit in Exile* (1991), *The Oxford Literary History of Australia* (1998) with Jennifer Strauss, *Australian Short Fiction: A History* (2002) and *Homing In: Essays on Australian Literature and Selfhood* (2006).

Ruth Blair is an Honorary Research Fellow in the School of English, Media Studies and Art History at the University of Queensland where, as previously at the University of Tasmania, she taught American literature and environmental literature, a field she helped to establish in Australia. Her Ph.D at Cornell University in Comparative Literature was on Herman Melville; she has published essays on his Pacific writings and edited his first Pacific novel *Typee* for Oxford World's Classics (1996). She has also a strong interest in Australian literature and has published on Henry Handel Richardson and Jessica Anderson. She contributed to a collaborative essay, 'Myth Management, Image-making and Whaling', for the conference 'Situating the Environment' (2001) and was co-convenor of an international conference 'Environment, Culture and Community' (2003), both held at the University of Queensland. Currently she is investigating conjunctions between environmental and narrative theories and French ecological writing and continues to explore environmental aspects of current Australian writing.

Veronica Brady is an Honorary Senior Research Fellow in the Department of English, Communications and Cultural Studies at the University of Western Australia. Her research interests are in the area of Australian culture, in particular in issues to do with Aboriginal

Australia and the environment. A political activist, critic, writer and member of the Loreto Order, she has held a Rockefeller Foundation grant to work at the Rockefeller Centre at Bellagio in Italy, and received another grant from the Rockefeller Foundation to work on environmental issues at the University of Oregon at Eugene. She has published widely in national and international journals. Her work includes *Polyphonies of the Self: Essays by Veronica Brady* (1993), *Caught in the Draught: On Contemporary Australian Culture and Society* (1994), *Can These Bones Live?* (1996), and *South of My Days: a Biography of Judith Wright* (1998).

CA. Cranston lectures in Australian, US, and British literature at the University of Tasmania, where she runs an online American Nature Writing course. She has lectured in ecocriticism at the Alps-Adriatic University (Klagenfurt, Austria) and by invitation at Appalachian State University. Her interest is in the disruption between theory and praxis in ecocritical discourse. Publications include a place-based anthology titled *Along These Lines* (2000); 'Tasmanian Nature Writing and Ecocriticism' in *Australian Literary Studies in the 21st Century* (2001); as contributor, World Wildlife Fund publication *Tarkine* (2004); and nature writing, 'Narrative Streams', *Island #101* (2005). Formative geographies include Egypt, Ceylon (Sri Lanka),and Hong Kong, fourteen years in the American Southwest; and twenty years on a temperate island in the Southern Ocean.

Tony Hughes-d'Aeth is a Lecturer in English and Cultural Studies at the University of Western Australia. His book *Paper Nation: The Story of the Picturesque Atlas of Australasia, 1886-1888* (2001) won the Ernest Scott and Keith Hancock prizes for history. He is currently writing a literary history of the Western Australian wheatbelt. Recent publications include 'Thematising the Global: Recent Australian Film', with co-author Tanya Dalziell, *PostScript* 24.2 (2005); 'Old Walls and New: The Australian Poet in the Asia-Pacific', in *Complicities* (2003); 'History by Instalment: Australian Centenary and Picturesque Atlas of Australasia, 1886-1888', in *Divided Selves: The British Press and Imperial Co-Histories* (2002); 'Australian Writing, Deep Ecology and Julia Leigh's The Hunter', in *Journal of the Association for Studies in Australian Literature* 1 (2002); 'Which Rabbit Proof

Fence? Empathy, Assimilation, Hollywood', *Australian Humanities Review* (2002).

Elizabeth (Elle) Leane is a Lecturer in the School of English, Journalism and European Languages at the University of Tasmania. She holds undergraduate degrees in both Physics and English Literature, and a doctorate in English Literature from the University of Oxford. Her research interests include the relationship between literature and science and representations of Antarctica. In 2004, she was awarded an Antarctic Arts Fellowship by the Australian Antarctic Division, which enabled her to travel to Antarctica and Macquarie Island on the expedition ship *Aurora Australis*. Her first book, *Reading Popular Physics: Disciplinary Skirmishes and Textual Strategies,* is forthcoming (2007). She is currently working on a second book, provisionally entitled *Fictions of the Far South: Imagining Antarctica.* She has published articles in a diverse range of journals including *Review of English Studies, Ariel, Polar Record, Essays in Arts and Sciences, Theatre Notebook* and *Science Fiction Studies.* She lectures in the University of Tasmania's new Bachelor of Antarctic Studies as well as in the English programme.

Tom Lynch is an Assistant Professor at the University of Nebraska, Lincoln, where he teaches ecocriticism, place-conscious literature and theory, and American literature. His book *Xerophilia: Ecocritical Explorations in Southwestern Literature* is forthcoming. In 2001 he was a visiting fellow at the Centre for Cross-Cultural Research at the Australian National University in Canberra, where he researched the literature of the Australian deserts. He is currently at work on a book titled *Outback/Out West*, an ecocritical comparative study of the literature of the Australian Outback and the American West as seen through the lenses of postcolonial and bioregional theory.

Kate Rigby, Fellow of the Australian Academy of the Humanities (FAHA) and Fellow of the Alexander von Humboldt Foundation, is Associate Professor in Comparative Literature and Director of the Centre for Comparative Literature and Cultural Studies at Monash University in Melbourne, where she has worked since 1991. She is a co-editor of *PAN (Place Activism Nature)*, and publishes widely in the areas of ecocriticism, ecophilosophy, and ecology and religion, as well as in German Studies. The author of *Topographies of the Sacred. The Poetics of Place in European Romanticism* (2004), she is a co-founder and President of the Australia-New Zealand Association for the Study of Literature and Environment (http://www.asle-anz.asn.au) and a member of the national working party on the Ecological Humanities. She also serves on the editorial advisory board of the journal *Interdisciplinary Studies in Literature and Environment* (*ISLE*) and the Rodopi book series *Nature Culture and Literature.* She is currently working on an ecocultural history of the Canberra region, while also co-editing with Axel Goodbody a volume of essays on ecocritical theory and European thought.

Mitchell Rolls is Senior Lecturer in Aboriginal Studies, University of Tasmania, where he is Co-Director (Academic) of Riawunna, the Aboriginal Studies Centre, and Deputy Director, Centre for Colonialism and Its Aftermath. He holds a degree from the University of South Australia and a Masters and PhD from Monash University. His current research interests include cultural identity, race and representation, cultural appropriation, and place-making in settler societies, the latter including how environments are understood. He has published in *Australian Studies, Australian Cultural History*, and *Australian Humanities Review,* and he has a chapter in *Reconciliations* (2005, Agnes Toth and Bernard Hickey, eds).

Mark Tredinnick is a poet, essayist, critic, and writing teacher. His books, published in Australia and the United States, include *A Place on Earth* (2003; an anthology of Australian and US nature writing), *The Little Red Writing Book* (2006), *The Land's Wild Music* (2005), and the forthcoming landscape memoir *The Blue Plateau.* He has co-edited two collections of Australian literature, *Watermarks* (with Nicolette Stasko, a landscape oriented issue of *Southerly*, 2005) and *Where Rivers Meet* (with Larissa Behrendt and Barry Lopez, an Australian issue of the US literary journal *Manoa,* 2007); and with Kate Rigby he edited an issue of the Australian online journal *PAN*, dedicated to the literature and scholarship of place (*PAN* 4, 2007). He has won or been shortlisted for a number of awards, including the Wildcare Nature Writing Prize, *The Australian Book Review*, Broadway;

Gwen Harwood, and Newcastle Poetry Prizes. He runs writing programs at the University of Sydney and in 2002, was a visiting writer at
The Island Institute in Sitka, Alaska. In 2004, he was one of six US,
Australian and Hawaiian writers who took part in the 'Language of
the Land' program of the Pacific Writers Connection in Hawaii. He
lived for seven years at Katoomba in the sandstone plateau west of
Sydney; after a brief return to the city, he now lives with his family
outside Bowral, in the Southern Highlands of New South Wales.

Robert Zeller is Professor of English at Southeast Missouri State
University, where he teaches courses in Australian Culture, Australian
Literature, and Writing and the Environment. His research interests
include the study of place in Australian literature generally and North
Queensland in particular. He has travelled widely in Australia and
taught in Britain and the Netherlands. His articles have appeared in
such publications as *Antipodes, College Composition and Communication, ISLE, Queensland Review*, and *World Literature Written in
English*.

List of Illustrations

Index